EDUCATION POLICY AND CONTEMPORARY THEORY

This book aims to posit theory as a central component to the study of education and education policy. Providing clear, introductory entries into contemporary critical theories and their take up in education policy studies, the book offers a generative invitation to further reading, thought and exploration. Instead of prescribing how theory should be used, the contributors elaborate on a set of possibilities for researching and critiquing education policy.

Education Policy and Contemporary Theory explores examples of how theoretical approaches generate a variety of questions for policy analysis, demonstrating the importance of theory as a necessary and inevitable resource for exploring and contesting various policy realms and dominant discourses. Each chapter provides a short overview of key aspects of a particular theory or perspective, followed by suggestions of methodological implications and recommended readings to extend the outlined ideas. Organized around two parts, the first section focuses on theorists while the second section looks at specific theories and concepts, with the intention that each part makes explicit the connection between theory and methodology in relation to education policy research.

Each contribution is carefully written by experts in the field to introduce new scholars to theoretical concepts and policy questions, and to inspire, extend or challenge established policy researchers who may be considering working in new areas.

Kalervo N. Gulson is Associate Professor in the Faculty of Arts and Social Sciences at the University of New South Wales, Australia.

Matthew Clarke is Professor of Education at York St John University, UK.

Eva Bendix Petersen is Professor of Higher Education at Roskilde University, Denmark.

EDUCATION POLICY AND CONTEMPORARY THEORY

Implications for research

Edited by Kalervo N. Gulson, Matthew Clarke and Eva Bendix Petersen

LONDON AND NEW YORK

First published 2015
by Routledge
2 Park Square, Milton Park, Abingdon, Oxon OX14 4RN

and by Routledge
711 Third Avenue, New York, NY 10017

Routledge is an imprint of the Taylor & Francis Group, an informa business

British Library Cataloguing in Publication Data
A catalogue record for this book is available from the British Library

Library of Congress Cataloging in Publication Data
Education policy and contemporary theory : implications for
research / edited by Kalervo N. Gulson, Matthew Clarke and Eva
Bendix Petersen.
pages cm
Includes bibliographical references and index.
1. Education and state—Philosophy. 2. Educational change—
Philosophy. 3. Education—Research. I. Gulson Kalervo N., editor
of compilation. II. Clarke, Matthew, 1964- editor of compilation.
III. Bendix Petersen, Eva, editor of compilation.
LC71.E327 2015
379.01—dc23
2014048890

ISBN: 978-0-415-73655-8 (hbk)
ISBN: 978-0-415-73656-5 (pbk)
ISBN: 978-1-315-81842-9 (ebk)

Typeset in Bembo
by Swales & Willis Ltd, Exeter, Devon, UK

CONTENTS

Notes on contributors   viii
Acknowledgements   xii

Introduction: theory, policy, methodology   1
Kalervo N. Gulson, Matthew Clarke and Eva Bendix Petersen

PART I
Theorists   **13**

1 Bourdieu and doing policy sociology in education   15
    Shaun Rawolle and Bob Lingard

2 Michel de Certeau, everyday life and cultural policy
    studies in education   27
    Sue Saltmarsh

3 Repeating Deleuze and Guattari: towards a politics of
    method in education policy studies   39
    Sam Sellar

4 Derrida: the 'impossibility' of deconstructing educational
    policy enactment   51
    Greg Vass

5 Education policies as discursive formations: a Foucauldian optic   63
    Eva Bendix Petersen

6 Lacanian perspectives on education policy analysis 73
Matthew Clarke

PART II
Concepts and theories **85**

7 Situated, relational and practice-oriented: the actor-network theory approach 87
Radhika Gorur

8 Thinking educational policy and management through (frictional) concepts of affects 99
Dorthe Staunæs and Justine Grønbæk Pors

9 Assemblage theory and education policy sociology 110
Deborah Youdell

10 Counterpublics, crisis and critique: a feminist socio-historical approach to researching policy 122
Jessica Gerrard

11 Embodying policy studies: feminist genealogy as methodology 134
Wanda S. Pillow

12 Governmentality: Foucault's concept for our modern political reasoning 147
Kaspar Villadsen

13 Taking a 'material turn' in education policy research? 160
Stephen Heimans

14 Mobilities paradigm and policy research in education 171
Fazal Rizvi

15 A narrative approach to policy analysis 183
Peter Bansel

16 Queer theory, policy and education 195
Mary Lou Rasmussen and Christina Gowlett

17 Thinking rhizomatically: using Deleuze in education
    policy contexts 208
    Eileen Honan

18 Relational space and education policy analysis 219
    Kalervo N. Gulson

Index 230

CONTRIBUTORS

Peter Bansel is a Research Fellow with the Sexualities and Gender Research Network in the School of Social Sciences and Psychology at the University of Western Sydney, Australia. His interest in governmentality, narrative, subjectivity and experience informs interdisciplinary research in the areas of: education, labour markets and work; sex, gender and sexuality; and technology, young people and wellbeing.

Matthew Clarke is Professor of Education at York St John University, UK. His research interests include the insights of psychoanalytic theory for critical analysis of educational policy and politics.

Jessica Gerrard is a McKenzie Postdoctoral Research Fellow at the University of Melbourne, Australia. Her research centres on the relationship between education and social change, social inequality and identity. She works across the disciplines of history, sociology and critical theory. Her recent monograph – *Radical childhoods: schooling and the struggle for social change* (Manchester University Press, 2014) – examines the history of radical working-class and black community education in Britain.

Radhika Gorur is a Senior Research Fellow in the Victoria Institute at Victoria University, Australia. Her current research is in four distinct areas: the sociology of knowledge, contemporary education policy, collaborative knowledge production, and youth policies. She uses assemblage and other concepts from science and technology studies as the main analytical and methodological approach.

Christina Gowlett has recently moved from the University of Melbourne, Australia, where she held a McKenzie Postdoctoral Research Fellowship to the

University of Queensland where she is now a lecturer in Curriculum Studies. Her research entails the use of post-constructionist research methodologies, especially the use of Judith Butler. Her current project explores the structure of senior schooling curriculum and the way secondary schools 'guide' students with their post-schooling aspirations.

Kalervo N. Gulson is Associate Professor in the Faculty of Arts and Social Sciences at the University of New South Wales, Australia. His scholarship covers educational policy, race and social and cultural geography.

Stephen Heimans is a lecturer in the School of Education, University of New England, Australia. He researches education policy and is particularly interested in participatory research methodologies that focus on identifying and resolving problems of inequity and disadvantage.

Eileen Honan is a senior lecturer in the School of Education at the University of Queensland, Australia. Her research interests include the interactions between teachers, students and digital texts; the relationships of teachers and policy texts and the use of rhizomatic methodologies and the implications for doctoral research and writing.

Bob Lingard is Professorial Research Fellow in the School of Education at the University of Queensland, Australia. He researches in the sociology of education and focuses on policy. His most recent book is *Politics, policies and pedagogies in education* (Routledge, 2014). He is also a co-editor of the journal *Discourse: Studies in the Cultural Politics of Education* and is a Fellow of the Academy of Social Sciences in Australia.

Eva Bendix Petersen is Professor of Higher Education at the Roskilde University, Denmark. She is interested in academic work and subjectivities, and how they are traversed by neoliberal discourse.

Wanda S. Pillow is Associate Professor jointly appointed in Gender Studies and the Department of Education, Culture and Society at the University of Utah, USA. She is author of *Unfit subjects: Educational policy and the teen mother*; co-editor of *Working the ruins*; and additional publications focusing on research methodology, education policy, and analyses of gender, race and sexuality.

Justine Grønbæk Pors is an assistant professor at the Department of Management, Politics and Philosophy at Copenhagen Business School, Denmark. Her research focusses on intersections of different reform agendas in public policy within areas of education and ageing. She strives to develop new theoretical and methodological frameworks by combining deconstructive thinking with the philosophy of Michel Serres, and the systems theory of Niklas Luhmann.

Mary Lou Rasmussen is Associate Professor in the Faculty of Education, Monash University, Australia. Her principal research areas are sexualities, gender and education. She has authored *Becoming subjects: Sexualities and secondary schooling* (Routledge, 2006), and co-edited (with Allen and Quinlivan) *The politics of pleasure in sexuality education: Pleasure bound* (Routledge, 2014). She also has a forthcoming monograph with Routledge entitled *Progressive sexuality education: The conceits of secularism.* She is on the editorial board of the journal *Sex Education* (Routledge), and on the book series *Cultural studies and transdisciplinarity in education* (Springer) and *Critical studies in gender and sexuality in education* (Routledge).

Shaun Rawolle is a senior lecturer in the School of Education, Deakin University, Australia. His research is concerned with education policy, and he has published widely on issues related to media impact on education, global forces on education and the use of contracts in education.

Fazal Rizvi is currently a professor in Global Studies in Education at the University of Melbourne, Australia, and an emeritus professor at the University of Illinois at Urbana-Champaign, USA. Educated in India, Australia and the UK, he is also a fellow of the Academy of the Social Sciences in Australia. He has published extensively on issues of identity and culture in transnational contexts, theories of globalization and education policy and internationalization of higher education. His recent books include: *Globalizing education policy* (Routledge, 2010) (co-authored with Bob Lingard) and *Encountering education in the global: Selected works of Fazal Rizvi* (Routledge, 2014).

Sue Saltmarsh is Associate Professor of Educational Studies at the Australian Catholic University, Australia. She has undertaken a range of ethnographic, social semiotic and discourse analytic studies across early childhood, primary, secondary and tertiary educational settings, focusing primarily on the connections between economic discourse, cultural practices and subjectivities. Her research is informed by cultural and poststructural theories of consumption, subjectivity and everyday life. She serves on a number of national and international research committees, and is founding editor of the journal *Global Studies of Childhood*.

Sam Sellar is a Postdoctoral Research Fellow in the School of Education at the University of Queensland, Australia. His research interests are in education policy, education theory and pedagogy. His current projects focus on data infrastructure in education and pedagogies of emergent futures. He is an associate editor of *Critical Studies in Education* and *Discourse: Studies in the Cultural Politics of Education*.

Dorthe Staunæs is Professor and Director of the research programme on Organisation and Learning at the Department of Education, Aarhus University, Denmark. Her fields of study are the processes and effects on subjectivities and diversity due to new forms of psy-management/leadership in education. She has specifically worked with the development of post-psychological and post-constructionist approaches; affective-semiotic-material concepts, methodologies and reconfiguring 'thinking technologies'.

Greg Vass is a lecturer at the University of New South Wales, Australia. Building on his experiences as a high school teacher, his work is concerned with learner identities and schooling practices that contribute to sustaining disparities in the experiences and achievements of students. His research interests are focused on investigating relationships between policy enactment, pedagogy/curriculum and educational inequities. The theoretical and methodological framing of his approach is informed by the ideas and work of poststructural, feminist and Critical Race Theory scholars.

Kaspar Villadsen holds a PhD in sociology from the University of Copenhagen, Denmark. He is currently Associate Professor at the Department of Management, Politics and Philosophy, Copenhagen Business School, Denmark. His current research is on the concept of the state and state phobia in Michel Foucault and his successors' work. He has a forthcoming book on this subject (with Mitchell Dean). He has published extensively on the application of concepts from Foucault and other post-structural theories on studies of social policies and welfare organizations. His work has been published in journals such as *New Political Science, Constellations, Public Management Review* and *Social Theory and Health*.

Deborah Youdell is Professor of Sociology of Education and Director of the Public Service Academy at the University of Birmingham, UK. Her work is concerned with the interplay of institutional and everyday practices, subjectivities, policy, politics and inequalities. She is author of *Rationing education* (with David Gillborn), *Impossible bodies, impossible selves* and *School trouble*.

ACKNOWLEDGEMENTS

This book is the outcome of many conversations about theory and education policy analysis, and about how to encourage and inspire others to look anew at theory and policy.

Some of these conversations were informal, taking place in cafes, bars and airport lounges, between the editors and the contributors in different configurations. Some came to pass in formal settings, and here we thank the School of Education, University of New South Wales, Australia, for funding a workshop in 2011 on 'The role of theory in education policy analysis'. Many of the contributors in this book attended that workshop and provided the impetus to put the collection together.

We made exacting demands on the authors, asking them to be particularly pedagogical in their writing, and we were quite ruthless with word counts. We thank them all for their willingness to work with us, and for entering into the spirit of the book.

We would like to thank our editor at Routledge, Anna Clarkson, for her support and suggestions about how to put this collection together.

Finally, thanks to Kim, Finn, Kobi and Aila, Liz and Ella, and Paul, Oscar and Eric.

INTRODUCTION

Theory, policy, methodology

Kalervo N. Gulson, Matthew Clarke and
Eva Bendix Petersen

The book is written for researchers and students with an interest in the critical and creative potential of social theory in education policy analysis. It sets out to achieve (at least) three aims in relation to education policy research and theory: it argues for the utility and necessity of theory; it celebrates the pleasures and rewards of theory; and, it offers models of, and advice on, the use of theory in education policy research. This book, as such, complements a body of existing work arguing for the value of theory in educational research (Anyon, 2009; Ball, 1995; Dimitriadis and Kamberelis, 2006; Dressman, 2008; Sikes, 2006).

Although we seek to entice you as the reader with notions of utility and necessity, pleasures and rewards, models and advice, we would also add that theory is inevitable. In other words, theory is not a something we can decide to bypass or ignore – theory is not a choice we can decline. When we begin researching education policy, each of us, whether a professor, an early career researcher or a doctoral candidate, brings a set of assumptions to our research – assumptions about the social world and the way it works, its characteristics, categories and dynamics. Our position is that good, responsible and interesting scholarship makes a concerted effort to scrutinise these assumptions and their implications and that we engage with more formalised sets of assumptions – *theory* – as part of this process. In other words, we read theory and engage with theory in order to challenge, elaborate, alter and affirm already held beliefs about how the world works.

There are many wonderful books around that serve as good introductions to contemporary social and cultural theory (Gane, 2004; Seidman, 2013), including some that are specifically focused on education (Dimitriadis and Kamberelis, 2006; Murphy and Allan, 2013). What we have found, however, as researchers, doctoral supervisors and teachers in education policy studies courses, is that few of these help novice researchers with the methodological implications of theoretical frameworks, particularly in relation to policy research. That is:

- What does it mean to carry out policy research if one takes up particular theories, involving particular sets of assumptions?
- What kind of research questions do particular theories provoke and what kind of analytical strategies might follow as a result?

With these questions in mind, we were looking for something with a different emphasis than found in other collections and something that was pedagogical in intent. Our aim for this book is to make explicit the connection between theory and methodology in relation to education policy research. To meet this aim we have invited policy researchers with a passion for theory to write succinct chapters focussing on this link.

The aspiration that our book be pedagogical does not, however, mean that we were aiming to produce a 'manual' for the use of theory in policy analysis. Rather, we see this as a book offering suggestions, inspirations, possibilities and provocations that supports you as a reader and scholar in efforts to produce theoretically sophisticated and informed methodologies for your own substantive studies. The book is an invitation and opening to consider or reconsider education and education policy, and how to study them. In this sense the book embodies a valorisation of theory that runs counter to some recent assaults on the place of theory in education (e.g. Kitching, 2008) and in cultural studies more widely (e.g. Eagleton, 2004). But whilst advocating an affirmative view of theory, we do not wish to prescribe how theory could or should be used in the development, analysis and critique of education policy. There are many possible ways theory can be engaged with, many possible forms of entanglement, even with the same theorist, theory or concept. Theories are tools to think with, to (make) sense with, but that can mean many different things, and this book provides illustrations of exactly that. For example, the reader will see how different authors engage with the work of Gilles Deleuze and Felix Guattari. Such illustrations serve to show that there is no one way of getting theoretical engagement right and that the onus lies on each of us to develop considered take-ups.

A further ambition for this book is to showcase a range of contemporary perspectives and to demonstrate different ways of working with theory in policy research. In terms of the former, from the outset this book could never be complete; it could never hold all possible contemporary perspectives, partly because of the material limitations of a book, partly because the category of 'contemporary' is impossible to seize in an absolute sense, and partly because circumstances meant that certain perspectives went missing and others were added in the process of assembling the book. Yet the result, we believe, is a book that meets the ambition of showcasing an interesting range of theorists and theories and enabling readers to ask methodological questions of theoretical perspectives presented elsewhere. In terms of the latter ambition, to illustrate ways of working with theory, the chapters in the book identify the two most common and productive ways of beginning to 'do' theory, namely one which proceeds via engagement with a particular theorist, perhaps with a starting point of being curious about a particular oft-cited name in the field, and one which enters via a particular concept, starting perhaps from a similar place of curiosity. To reflect these approaches we have organised the book in two parts, with the first part dedicated to introducing a well-known theorist's thinking technologies and showing some of the ways in which their perspective can be applied, and with the second part dedicated to introducing a key concept and showcasing its methodological potential. One of the strengths of this approach is that it enables not only a fairly quick overview of some of the contemporary possibilities but also allows for comparison and cross-referencing, which may be helpful for the reader in the process of identifying where her or his own passions and interests may lie. Neither we nor the other authors in this book would ever suggest that any of the chapters do full justice to either a theorist's entire *oeuvre* or to a concept's full range of take-ups – after all each author was asked to write only 5,000 words.

In engaging with the challenges and possibilities for theoretically informed encounters with education policy, this book provides a range of detailed examples of the use of social theories in analyses of education policy. The theories covered range from continental philosophy, feminist theory, political theory, psychoanalytic theory, queer theory and social and cultural geography. Key thinkers engaged include: Pierre Bourdieu, Judith Butler, Michel de Certeau, Gilles Deleuze, Jacques Derrida, Michel Foucault, Nancy Fraser and Jacques Lacan, among others. We note that this medley of thinkers appear different from those who inspired another generation of policy scholars – who may have drawn on Louis Althusser, Theodore Adorno, Jürgen Habermas or Iris Marion Young. This suggests that social and cultural theory in a certain sense has a time and space (e.g. post-1968 and French) and is of a time and space; although theoretical preoccupations and insights developed at one timespace may continue into other timespaces, while others fall by the wayside. Therefore we recognise the partiality and temporality of the selection, although it is also important to recognise that the perspectives presented in this book do not agree ontologically, epistemologically and methodologically; rather, the book celebrates a multiplicity of contemporary theorisations and the openings this generates for fruitful juxtapositions and generative contrasts and contestations.

What is theory?

While it is outside the scope of this introduction to provide a survey of the ways in which theory has and could be conceptualised, we do want to summarise where we, as editors, stand.

We have already suggested that we see theory as a set of assumptions about how the world works. This breaks with the tradition in education of understanding theory as little more than a hypothesis, implying, therefore, that theories are something to be tested (does this factor cause that effect?). We also stated that in a sense, theory is 'always-already'. As Judith Butler (2004: 205) notes, 'we are all . . . lay philosophers, presupposing a vision of the world, of what is right, of what is just, of what is abhorrent, of what human action is and can be, of what constitutes the necessary and sufficient conditions of life'. The task of scholarship is to begin to get a sense of one's own presuppositions, one's values and one's habituated ways of explaining things and of making sense, and importantly, to get a sense of other possible presuppositions and so on. One way of gaining this perspective is to begin to name traditions of sense making (e.g. –isms and –ologies) and to begin to compare and juxtapose them; test them to see how far they agree and when they break ways, and so on. In the process one may well change not only one's presuppositions and values but certainly also one's habituated ways of making sense. This is why the three of us read theory and why we insist that the students we work with do the same. It is a reflective and perspectivising exercise, with the aim of becoming more knowledgeable, more capable of arguing for one's position, and better equipped to understand the perspectives of others. We do not propose that scholars read theory just for the sake of it, to develop a fancy vocabulary for instance, but because it carries potential for transformation and for appreciation of the wealth of possible perspectives. Further, we need theory for its capacity to, not just inspire or provoke, but 'to offend and interrupt: We need theory to block the reproduction of the bleeding obvious, and thereby, hopefully, open new possibilities for thinking and doing' (MacLure, 2010: 277). In other words,

> theory provides the possibility of a different language which is not caught up with the assumptions and inscriptions of policy-makers or the immediacy of practice (or embedded in tradition, prejudice, dogma and ideology . . .). It offers a potential location outside the prevailing discourses of policy and a way of struggling against 'incorporation'.
>
> *(Ball, 1997: 269)*

Moreover, theory has the capacity to generate wonder (MacLure, 2010) and enchantment (Bennett, 2001) in social and scholarly life, as well as serving as a source of critical, albeit contingent and tentative, explanations of the operations of power and policy in education.

From this it is clear that we reject the theory-practice, theory-methodology divides, whereby theory is seen as an optional extra or, even worse, as an indulgent luxury. Or the idea that theory distorts or gets in the way of seeing and addressing policy problems. What is implicit in this book is there is no such thing as theory-free research (Dressman, 2008), just as there is no such thing as theory-free data (Brinkmann, 2014) or theory-free facts (Geertz, 1995; Poovey, 1998). Indeed, there is no such thing as a theory-free policy problem (Bacchi, 2000). This is not about reifying theory but about acknowledging its inevitable enabling and constraining effects on problem-seeing, problem-making and research practice. Theory frames perspectives on social reality, and hence some lines of inquiry into those realities, as legitimate and intelligible and others as illegitimate and unintelligible; theory is therefore always a form of epistemic 'violence' (Ball, 2006; Spivak, 1988). It cannot be any other way. What we hope to encourage with this book is not only that realisation, and the incitement to study that it carries, but also to share the joy and excitement theory brings.

What is education policy studies?

Following on from the above it is obvious why we cannot in this introduction provide an overarching definition of what policy 'is'. What emerges as a policy during an analysis depends on the specific thinking technologies brought to bear. Is it a text, a narrative, a technique of subjectification, a defensive strategy of disavowal, a fold, a spatial and spatialising orchestration? Part of the point of the book taken in its entirety is to disrupt taken-for-granted agreements about 'what is policy?'. Within narrow functionalist definitions a policy may be seen as a program of action or considered in terms of 'a cycle', including 'agenda-setting', 'implementation' and 'evaluation'. Yet what this book shows is that such metaphors are already loaded with assumptions and that there are many other possible conceptualisations. Consequently we cannot either provide a neat definition of what education policy research is. Again the book shows that it can be many things and even that it may need to be something entirely different to what we are used to thinking that it is or ought to be. As some chapters argue, perhaps policy analysis ought to decentre the traditional central placement of policy texts? (See also, Rizvi and Lingard, 2010; Simons, Olssen and Peters, 2009.)

Even so, we want to wager that despite the differences and incommensurabilities of the perspectives and despite the possibility that some of the contributing authors would not adhere to the description of themselves or their work, the book leans up against and contributes to critical policy studies. While subject to much debate about its approaches and purposes as a field, critical policy studies aims for both critique and change in the world. Simons, Olssen and Peters (2009: vii) propose that 'critical' denotes a particular attitude or ethos:

> [C]ritical does not refer to how the researcher of education policy relates to her research (methodology, data, results, peers . . .). Indeed, in that sense, all research is expected to be critical. Neither is the term used here to charac- terise the kind of analytical framework that informs the research usually thought of as critical social or political theory. In our vernacular critical first of all indicates a particular engagement with, or relation to, the domain that is being studied. What we have in mind is a critical attitude or ethos, and thus a way of relating to the present . . . there is more at stake for scholars than the theoretical or analytical framework that [scholars] adopt. Their work seems to articulate a form of public concern.

In tandem with this point, Wendy Brown (2005: 1–16) notes that the role of the critical scholar is manifold; it involves being ready to call into 'crisis', to make problematic, the seemingly given and the seemingly 'technical'. This means, for example, to recognise that what might at first glance look like procedural or prac- tical questions, such as how best to implement a particular policy, how to identify best practices, or how to design evaluations, are always already epistemic and political questions. One will recognise also that all 'answers' are non-innocent in that they in turn ask us to know in a certain way and act in a certain way (Bacchi, 2000). Critique, as Butler argues, in contrast to criticism, is not, in the first instance, about fault-finding or judgement; for 'judgements operate . . . as ways to subsume a particular under an already constituted category, whereas critique asks after the occlusive constitution of the field of categories themselves' (Butler, 2002: 213). In other words, critique is about asking questions, good questions – about the definitions and categories we might otherwise take for granted, even in relation to the activity of critique itself.

Just as we note above in relation to theory, the aims of critical policy studies are also always in need of being renewed, reinvented and rejuvenated; and indeed, what we see in this book are examples of theory being used to reinvigorate enduring problems of education policy studies. Remaining alert to these possibilities can prevent both theory and policy from becoming ossified, oversimplified and reproductive. For example, in the desire to sit at the 'policy-table' and to contribute to the improvement of existing systems and policies policy scholars can become implicated in furthering the intent and methodologies of the policy-makers (St Pierre, 2011; Webb and Gulson, 2014), which may not always be the best way of making a contribution. Moreover, critical policy studies might aim to improve equity and processes of education without recognising the possibility that education policy itself (or education discourses more widely) is part of the problem as well as the potential solution. We need new theories and theorisations then, in order to remain alert to new ways of conceiving of and conducting policy research. Indeed, what the authors in this book provide are problematisations (Bacchi, 2012; Webb, 2014) of the claims of policy *through* theory, by seeing policy as something to be problematised rather than accepted on face-value as part of governmental and everyday life. As Webb (2014: 365) asks:

> To what extent does policy benefit from espousing 'problems' and 'solutions'? Who benefits? Who does not? Should researchers participate in practices that even suggest solutions? Should researchers assist others in 'solving problems' by tapping into 'participatory' and 'community' sentiments? What alternative roles might policy researchers assume within a framework of problematization?

Critical policy studies entail the refusal to cease thinking about how things could always be otherwise. As part of its problematisation of policy, this book focuses on policy in a range of ways that trouble simple models or metaphors – policy as texts and processes, as intentions and actions, and as phenomena that are created and enacted, or implemented, across temporal series and geographical scales, from the local to the global. Or as Ball (1994: 10) puts it, in an oft-cited formulation, 'Policy is both text and action, words and deeds, it is what is enacted as well as what is intended'. This sense of alertness to 'what *is* policy?' is important in thinking about how to research policy – deciding what is to be the *object* of study is critical as part of the process of considering possible alternatives.

Evident in the chapters is the importance of removing policy from its pedestal, as the realm of sovereign government (Ozga, 2000; Vidovich, 2007), instead recognising it as an arena of contestation, struggle and negotiation between actors who may operate outside of the formal governmental structures (e.g. parents, teachers, community activists, etc.). What the chapters identify is that theories and policies work on the basis of provoking action, even when the policy direction is not fully formed or when people are not fully cognisant of what the policy content entails (e.g. see Ball, Maguire and Braun, 2012). This suggests the necessity of critique – not in the sense of assuming that all policy is a problem, but in the sense of recognising that all policies aim to steer actions (whether they are successful or not is another matter). In other words, policy is an inherently future-oriented exercise, an intervention and promise of change.

The issue of how to do policy research raises the question of what we understand by 'methodology'. Here we agree with Brinkmann (2012: 48–49) regarding the need to avoid 'methodolatry' – the valorisation of technique as something to be scrupulously followed and uncritically adhered to for its own sake – and the importance of recognising the ever-present need for human subjective judgement in addressing (contingently) and answering (tentatively) the questions and issues with which we are grappling. 'The concepts and vocabularies of significant theories can assist us in doing just that' (Brinkmann, 2012: 49). Above all, the claim is here that the theories you take up as your own make a difference – in this sense, theory is a provocation in education policy studies, engendering new ways of conceiving and doing policy. Hence we can extend the question, 'what do people do in the name of policy?' (Wedel, Shore, Feldman and Lathrop, 2005: 35), to ask, what do people do – what will *you* do? – in the name of being and becoming policy *analyst*?

The chapters

Deciding how to organise an edited collection on theory and policy is a complicated task. In some ways, it has affinities with the task of deciding which theory is appropriate for a study, for a topic, or with the challenges flowing from the recognition that theory has a different kind of relationship to 'data', depending on whether you are taking an inductive, deductive or abductive approach to your research (see Brinkmann, 2014). We could have organised this collection alphabetically, by authors' names; in fact, we originally did do this, but then decided it did not provide enough signposting for a reader. We thought about organising the chapters according to a chronology of theory, or by age and/or mortal status of author, or by geographical region. But in the end we decided upon a structure that we think, as noted above, reflects and constitutes how people tend to come to theory – through the name of the theorist or the concept or theory itself. As such, the chapters are organised in this manner.

For each chapter, we asked the author(s) to give the reader a sense of the where this theorist or concept might take the novice researcher concerned with critical education policy research. We also asked authors to include in their reference list, sources that readers could follow up on should they want to pursue in more detail the illustrations, exemplifications and suggestions offered here. In other words, for this book we chose to offer 'glimpses' and 'potentials'; yet we were also adamant that each 'glimpse' be developed by a passionate expert, with a trained eye and an alert ear for the possibilities, potentials and provocations of the theorist or concept comprising the focus of each chapter.

The first section of the book, as noted above, is organised around 'theorists'.

Bob Lingard and Shaun Rawolle argue for the usefulness of *Pierre Bourdieu's* social theory to doing policy analysis in education within a policy sociology frame, despite Bourdieu having written nothing explicitly about education policy. The chapter draws on Bourdieu's 'thinking tools', including the concepts of habitus, capitals, fields and practice, and applies them to an approach for doing education policy analysis. The chapter considers the education policy field, logics of practice of different fields in relation to the policy cycle, policy habitus and the emergent global education policy field.

Sue Saltmarsh considers the work of *Michel de Certeau* in relation to cultural approaches to policy studies. The chapter explores concepts of culture as everyday practice, and policy as cultural practice, and argues that policy and culture are reciprocal and co-constitutive. Saltmarsh examines the importance of understanding the everyday activities and meaning-making practices of policy makers and stakeholders, as well as (meta)methodology and the ethical and political implications of Certeau's work for approaches to policy research.

Sam Sellar explores how the work of *Gilles Deleuze* and *Felix Guattari*, specifically their theory of philosophy and science, might inform education policy studies. Deleuze and Guattari's concepts can help us to pose questions about our intellectual obligations as education policy scholars, our methodologies and our relations to the practices of others. The chapter addresses the relationship between social theory and social data in contexts of policy production and analysis. Some thoughts are offered towards a politics of method for strengthening engagement from the side of theory with scientific practices of measurement and commensuration.

Greg Vass writes his chapter as an open letter to work with ideas associated with *Jacques Derrida's* 'happening', known as deconstruction. While Derrida himself distanced deconstruction from research methodology and analysis, recent contributions have shown that deconstruction can open up interesting and insightful questions and ways of thinking about the 'impossibility' of education policy enactment. This letter invites readers to consider the potential of related concepts such as logocentrism, the absent presence, under erasure and aporias to help with reconsidering both the 'doing' of education policy analysis, and the ethical responsibilities asked of education researchers undertaking this work.

Eva Bendix Petersen presents a brief introduction to *Michel Foucault's* concept of discourse and his overall historicising and 'destabilising' perspective. It then goes on to discuss what a policy is when it is conceptualised as a discursive formation, which is distinguished from a 'dispositif' and a 'regime of truth'. The argument is made that the enactment of radical historicisation, including the regimes of truth that holds the analyst, is central to Foucauldian work. Lastly the chapter summarises the kinds of questions that drive various discourse analytic approaches, namely studies that focus on policy formulation, policy as document and policy enactments.

Matthew Clarke explores key concepts from *Jacques Lacan's* psychoanalytic theory, including a view of knowledge as indelibly marked by ignorance and of subjects as irremediably split between conscious and unconscious modes. The chapter goes on to examine the consequences of this theoretical framing for education policy analysis, highlighting policy's reliance on fantasy as part of an attempt to recapture a purportedly lost fullness, to mask and compensate for a troubling absence of harmony in the social body, and to scapegoat those perceived as threatening this complete and coherent – yet fantasmatic – view of social reality.

The second section of the book focuses on 'theories' and 'concepts'.

Radhika Gorur outlines the ways *actor-network theory* (ANT) is a material-semiotic approach that offers theoretical and methodological resources that direct attention to the practices that create, mobilise, sustain or challenge relations between actors in any social phenomenon. Using empirical case studies, ANT researchers describe the mundane and everyday practices through which, eventually, ideas are stabilised, systems are established and actors become powerful. Researchers of policy who are as interested in policy processes, doings and enactments, and who seek to explore the messiness and uncertainty that attends the lives and careers of policies, would be drawn to ANT.

Dorthe Staunæs and Justine Grønbæk Pors explore *a methodology of reading through concepts of affects* in empirical research of education policy. They present a tentative analytical framework for studying the production and reconfiguration of affect in education policy. The chapter presents Deleuzian/Massumian concepts of indeterminate affectivity and potentiality and concepts of more determinate and linguistically captured affects and registers, specifically the concept of shame developed by queer-theorists Eve Sedgwick, Sara Ahmed and Elspeth Probyn. In order to unfold the methodology and 'thinking with (different and frictional) concepts of affect', the authors engage with a specific Organisation for Economic Co-operation and Development (OECD)-report entitled Teaching and Learning International Survey (TALIS) and its reception.

Deborah Youdell explores the contribution that *assemblage theory* can make to the study of education policy. It outlines Deleuze and Guattari's notion of assemblage and allied concepts, and shows a variety of uses of assemblage theory in education and other fields and the insights into moving and complex social formations that thinking with assemblage allows. The chapter concludes that shifting from 'policy sociology' that places 'policy' at the centre of analysis, to 'assemblage ethnography' where the assemblage is the object of study offers new analytic potential by situating policy processes in wider forces of assemblage and disassembly.

Jessica Gerrard outlines a *feminist socio-historical* approach to researching policy in the context of economic and social crises under capitalism. Following feminist critical theorist Nancy Fraser's critique of the public sphere and her analysis of neoliberalism, this approach seeks to understand the wider struggles over education in arenas seemingly outside the legitimated policy field – what Fraser terms subaltern counterpublics. It also aims to develop insight into the messy convergences of ideas that become realised in policy, and the broader dynamics of critique and crisis in capitalism that create the conditions for what policies are deemed possible, or not.

Wanda Pillow engages three conceptual terms of feminist poststructuralism – 'feminism', 'embodiment', 'genealogy' – and explores the usefulness of these terms as educational policy studies methodology, specifically *feminist genealogy*. She utilises the topic of educational opportunity of pregnant/parenting students under Title IX, the preeminent 1972 United States federal civil rights law prohibiting sex discrimination in education, as a working exemplar to identify how teen pregnancy is being defined and not defined as an educational policy issue. The chapter concludes with a discussion of how utilisation of feminist genealogy can assist in regulation and litigation efforts to enforce Title IX.

Kaspar Villadsen argues that Foucault's concept *governmentality* has had considerable impact across the social sciences and humanities. This chapter explains Foucault's decentred, anti-institutional approach to political power and institutions. Governmentality marked a fundamental transformation in political reasoning in the eighteenth century, from sovereign rule over a territory to concerns with securing a living population. The chapter breaks down the key components of governmentality – pastoral power, security, self-governance – and suggests some links to education policy.

Stephen Heimans examines the new *material turn* in theory and education policy research. In this turn the focus is on the 'more than human only', and entanglements of words and matter – of how bodies (of all kinds) materialise and have effects. There is a shift away from revealing the conditions of human actors, to an interest in post-human–human material practices and relations, what emerges in these, and with what effects. The chapter highlights some of the key features of a new material turn and then discusses, with examples, how this turn might be taken up in education policy research.

Fazal Rizvi identifies some of the challenges John Urry's arguments about *global mobility* pose for policy research in education. Urry calls for a 'new mobilities paradigm' in which a concern with flows and movements of people, money, objects and information moves to the centre stage of social research. The chapter posits that while some of Urry's arguments are a little exaggerated, the attention he draws to diverse mobilities that characterise contemporary social formations cannot be so easily dismissed. While his call for a 'sociology beyond societies' appears somewhat extravagant, it is hard to deny that global processes have reconstituted the nature and scope of social institutions, making them subject to a whole range of new forces.

Peter Bansel examines how the *narrative* approach to policy and its analysis is animated by an ontological politics that foregrounds relations between the real, the conditions of possibility we live with and the political. The chapter articulates some of the theoretical and methodological possibilities for working with narrative as an approach to policy and its analysis, and applies these to an analysis of Higher

Education Policy in Australia. The analysis, as both critique and practice, signals the possibilities and politics of generating alternative policy narratives.

Mary Lou Rasmussen and Christina Gowlett provide a brief history of the term *queer theory* and introduce two of the key theorists often associated with queer theorising in education – Judith Butler and Michel Foucault. The chapter sketches of how notions like performativity, discourse and disciplinary power might inform policy analysis. In thinking about connections between education policy and queer theory, the authors contend that ideas associated with queer theory can be utilised in analysis of education policies that shape our educational aspirations. The authors argue that how we become intelligible as different sorts of educational subjects is surely a key question for policy makers in education – queer theory provides resources and a rationale for the continued examination of the politics of intelligibility, within and outside schooling.

Eileen Honan draws on the *rhizomatic ontology* developed by Deleuze and Guattari and applies it to analytic methods. In particular, the analytic methods associated with 'rhizo-textual analysis' are explicated. These methods are used to develop an understanding of texts themselves, and the readings of those texts, as rhizomatic. These understandings can help develop analyses of policy texts that disrupt common assumptions about the relations between teachers and policy.

Kalervo Gulson examines how the concept of *relational space* helps us to understand the where of policy. It draws predominantly on the work of two geographers Doreen Massey, especially her later work, and Jonathan Murdoch. The chapter outlines three interlinked features of relational space – interrelations, multiplicity and openness. The chapter concludes by identifying the ways relational space might inform ontological and methodological examinations of education policy.

References

Anyon, J. (2009). *Theory and educational research: Toward critical social explanation*. New York: Routledge.

Bacchi, C. (2000). Policy as discourse: What does it mean? Where does it get us? *Discourse: Studies in the Cultural Politics of Education, 21*(1), 45–57.

Bacchi, C. (2012). Why study problematizations? Making politics visible. *Open Journal of Political Science, 2*, 1–8. doi: 10.4236/ojps.2012.21001.

Ball, S. J. (1994). *Education reform: A critical and post-structural approach*. Philadelphia, PA: Open University Press.

Ball, S. J. (1995). Intellectuals or technicians? The urgent role of theory in educational studies. *British Journal of Educational Studies, 43*(3), 255–271.

Ball, S. J. (1997). Policy sociology and critical social research: A personal review of recent education policy and policy research. *British Educational Research Journal, 23*(3), 257–274.

Ball, S. J. (2006). *Education policy and social class: The selected works of Stephen J. Ball*. London: Routledge.

Ball, S. J., Maguire, M. and Braun, A. (2012). *How schools do policy: Policy enactments in secondary schools*. London: Routledge.

Bennett, J. (2001). *The enchantment of modern life: Attachments, crossings, and ethics*. Princeton, NJ: Princeton University Press.

Brinkmann, S. (2012). *Qualitative inquiry in everyday life: Working with everyday life materials*. London: Sage.

Brinkmann, S. (2014). Doing without data. *Qualitative Inquiry, OnlineFirst*, 1–6. doi: 1077800414530254.

Brown, W. (2005). *Edgework: Critical essays in knowledge and politics*. Princeton, NJ: Princeton University Press.

Butler, J. (2002). What is critique? An essay on Foucault's virtue. In D. Ingram (Ed.), *The political: Readings in continental philosophy* (pp. 212–226). London: Blackwell.

Butler, J. (2004). *Undoing gender*. New York: Routledge.

Dimitriadis, G. and Kamberelis, G. (2006). *Theory for education*. New York: Routledge.

Dressman, M. (2008). *Using social theory in educational research: A practical guide*. New York and London: Routledge.

Eagleton, T. (2004). *After theory*. New York: Basic Books.

Gane, N. (2004). *The future of social theory*. London: Continuum.

Geertz, C. (1995). *After the fact*. Cambridge, MA: Harvard University Press.

Kitching, G. N. (2008). *The trouble with theory: The educational costs of postmodernism*. Philadelphia, PA: Penn State Press.

MacLure, M. (2010). The offence of theory. *Journal of Education Policy, 25*(2), 277–286.

Murphy, M. and Allan, J. (Eds.) (2013). *Social theory and education research: Understanding Foucault, Habermas, Bourdieu and Derrida*. London: Routledge.

Ozga, J. (2000). *Policy research in educational settings: Contested terrain*. Buckingham, UK: Open University Press.

Poovey, M. (1998). *A history of the modern fact*. Chicago, IL: University of Chicago Press.

Rizvi, F. and Lingard, B. (2010). *Globalizing education policy*. London: Routledge.

Seidman, S. (2013). *Contested knowledge: Social theory today*. Chichester, UK: John Wiley & Sons.

Sikes, P. (2006). Towards useful and dangerous theories: Commentary on symposium: Educational research and the necessity of theory. *Discourse: Studies in the Cultural Politics of Education, 27*(1), 43–51.

Simons, M., Olssen, M. and Peters, M. A. (2009). Re-reading education policies: Part 1: The critical policy orientation. In M. Simons, M. Olssen and M. A. Peters (Eds.), *Re-reading education policies: A handbook studying the policy agenda of the 21st century* (pp. 1–35). Rotterdam, Netherlands: Sense Publishers.

Spivak, G. C. (1988). Can the subaltern speak? In C. Nelson and L. Grossberg (Eds.), *Marxist interpretations of culture* (pp. 271–313). Basingstoke, UK: MacMillan.

St Pierre, E. A. (2011). Post qualitative research: The critique and the coming after. In N. K. Denzin and Y. S. Lincoln (Eds.), *The SAGE handbook of qualitative research* (4th edn) (pp. 611–625). Thousand Oaks, CA: SAGE.

Vidovich, L. (2007). Removing policy from its pedestal: Some theoretical framings and practical possibilities. *Educational Review, 59*(3), 285–298. doi: 10.1080/0013191070 1427231.

Webb, T. (2014). Policy problematization. *International Journal of Qualitative Studies in Education, 27*(3), 364–376.

Webb, T. and Gulson, K. N. (2014). Policy scientificity 3.0: Theory and policy analysis in-and-for this world and other-worlds. *Critical Studies in Education*, 1–14. doi: 10.1080/17508487.2014.949812.

Wedel, J. R., Shore, C., Feldman, G. and Lathrop, S. (2005). Toward an anthropology of public policy. *The ANNALS of the American Academy of Political and Social Science, 600*(1), 30–51.

1

BOURDIEU AND DOING POLICY SOCIOLOGY IN EDUCATION

Shaun Rawolle and Bob Lingard

Introduction

In this chapter we draw on the social theories of practice and fields of Pierre Bourdieu (1990a; 1993), which were major contributions of his writing. However, and given Bourdieu's approach to research, we discuss these theories in relation to the methodology and research approach adopted in his work. While Bourdieu drew on a variety of traditions of intellectual thought to inform his theories, they were also open to engagement and change in relation to different social phenomena. This is the reflexive theory/empirical data relationship we will touch on later in the chapter, which was generative in his work and also for those in education research.

Our overarching claim is that Bourdieu's work provides a specific form and application of the sociological imagination, which carries within it a generative *way of worldmaking* (Goodman, 1978). This is a world populated and made meaningful through concepts like agents and habitus, practices and fields, but also capitals, logics and strategies. For our work, one of the key strengths has been Bourdieu's conceptual and theoretical flexibility – he rejects 'theoreticism', where formal theories are developed in absence of empirical encounters. In doing so, Bourdieu developed a wide range of resources for research, as well as a language base for representing problems in education policy. He also rejects an atheoretical empiricism, in which the categories and language of everyday life are taken for granted and accepted without interrogation and then used as the basis for statistical, descriptive, explanatory or representational analyses.

This engagement with Bourdieuian theory and methodology aims to explore its utility for education policy analysis and policy sociology in education. The initial premise of this account is that the adaptation of Bourdieuian theory and concepts to education policy, though not impossible, does raise some initial problems that require resolution. As will be discussed later, much of this can be attributed to the historical unfolding of Bourdieu's research and theoretical developments, and the incompleteness of his overarching theory of social fields (Bourdieu, 1993). Though challenging, these problems are not insurmountable and have proven quite productive for some researchers. Indeed, Bourdieu has been the source of inspiration for a variety of researchers in education, of which many have drawn directly on aspects of his work to understand and research problems either explicitly or implicitly related to education policy (Albright and Luke, 2008; Kenway and Koh, 2013; Ladwig, 2014; Reay and Ball, 1997; Thomson, 2005).

In outlining this account of Bourdieu's theory, we start with two premises. The first premise is that Bourdieu's concepts and theories are adaptable as a methodological base for research on education policy and useful to describe and understand the connections between the field of education policy and other education fields and sub-fields, such as schooling, university, VET, early childhood and so on. This implies that Bourdieu's concepts and theories can be extended and applied to new objects of research, with the caution that further refinement and additional theorisation may be required to develop coherent accounts of practices in each field or sub-field, which may equally loop back and cast light on Bourdieu's own theories and concepts. The second premise is that Bourdieu concepts are useful to understand broad processes of social change, which apply also to fields and sub-fields, particularly those related to mediatisation, globalisation and continuous education policy change.

This second premise is in opposition with some prominent critiques of Bourdieu's theory (e.g. Connell, 1983: 151), but we would point to our own and other researchers' work drawing on Bourdieu to explain broad processes of change like globalisation and mediatisation (Lingard and Rawolle, 2004, 2011). Here we agree with Wacquant's (2014: 5) critique of this criticism that Bourdieu is only about social reproduction rather than change and emergence, when he makes the important point that habitus never necessarily results in a specific practice, rather,

> it takes the *conjunction of disposition and position*, subjective capacity and objective possibility, habitus and social space (or field) to produce a given conduct or expression. And this meeting between skilled agent and pregnant world spawns the gamut from felicitous to strained, smooth to rough, fertile to futile.

This dis- or con- junction between disposition and position, between habitus and field, is a source of either change or reproduction. In order to elaborate on this account, we will draw primarily on and emphasise developments in Bourdieu's own writing, in particular his theoretical, conceptual and methodological approaches. As an illustration of the felicity of Bourdieu's work, we also provide brief accounts of the use of Bourdieu's concepts by researchers in education that relate to education policy.

Although Bourdieu never directly offered an approach to education policy analysis in relation to schools or universities (van Zanten, 2005), he did offer one example and approach to policy analysis drawn from his work. In an account of the development and effects of a housing policy in France, described in *The social structures of the economy* (Bourdieu, 2005), Bourdieu provided something of an approach to policy analysis in respect of housing. This work, linked to research on the preconditions, introduction and effect of the French housing policy of 1977 during a time of restructuring of housing policies and markets in France, was revisited in a latter account of the role of the state and the abdication of the neo-liberal, managerialist state from its obligations, in *The weight of the world* (Bourdieu et al., 1999). Bourdieu's account of housing policies in France involved a close analysis of state decision-making in the *creation of* market conditions and demand for housing (Bourdieu, 2005: 89–122).

It is thus our contention that Bourdieu's theoretical ensemble, his 'thinking tools', including the concepts of habitus, capitals, field and practice, which sit in synergistic relationship to each other, can assist research on education policy, especially important is their relationality. Bourdieu's work on language and symbolic power, including the classificatory capacities of the state, policy and schools, is also useful for policy analysis. As Swartz (2013: 39) notes, 'Symbolic power creates a form of violence that finds an expression in everyday classifications, labels, meanings, and categorisations that subtly implement a social as well as symbolic logic of inclusion and exclusion'. Policy can be seen to function in this way and is linked to Bourdieu's extension of Weber, who saw the state having the capacity and monopoly for expressions of legitimate violence (e.g. through the work of armies, the police, etc.), which Bourdieu extended to include the legitimate right to symbolic violence. Bourdieu's work on language also draws our attention to the significance of the language of policy texts and their role in symbolic violence, especially when connected to the state's claim for the universal application of policy.

Our use of Bourdieu in policy sociology of education moves beyond a straightforward application of his thinking tools to understanding the policy cycle and the inevitable refractions in policy implementation or enactment across competing logics of practice. In Bourdieu's (1998: 57) terms, the state holds a monopoly on the constitution and application of the 'universal', while we know classroom practices are contingent and specific. Herein resides the basis of a Bourdieuian approach to understanding implementation infidelities: policy production and enactment sit within different fields with different logics of practice. Here we might see policy in these terms as simplifying and seeking to be applied universally across a schooling system to all schools. In contrast, the logics of practice of schools and classrooms, including pedagogies are more complex and much more contingent and specific – each school has its 'thisness' (Thomson, 2002), as does each classroom. Herein we see in Bourdieu's terms an argument about gaps between policy texts and policy enactment. We note the usefulness of Bourdieu's thinking tools – his concepts and theories – in policy sociology in education and also some necessary additions derived from his approach. The fruitfulness of Bourdieu's thinking tools, however, is intricately linked with his methodology.

Bourdieu's methodology

Bourdieu's concepts of rejecting epistemological innocence, being reflexive, and 'objectivating' one's self as researcher demand that the policy sociology researcher deal with their 'positionality' within the field of policy sociology and within putative national education policy fields (Hardy, 2009). Positionality here refers to the researcher's position in relation to the object of study and in relation to the relevant or cognate academic field. In Bourdieu's terms, we might define researcher positionality as position within various fields, encompassing the field of the object of research and the academic field/s in which the research is positioned. Rizvi and Lingard (2010: 47–48) suggest that such positionality demands reflexivity and consideration of the researcher's position in relation to the field and object of research, actual location in respect of analysis, theoretical/methodological stance, spatial location, temporal location and so on. In a sense, this is the reflexive application of Bourdieu's concept of 'socioanalysis' to the positionality of the policy sociology researcher. Socioanalysis for Bourdieu is a way of understanding how individuals are social products and that people's dispositions and engagements with practices relates to their social history, which is embodied in their habitus. Socioanalysis involves providing a context for examining the relationships between a researcher's own arguments about social objects and their social history; this context involves a recount of the significant social events and social trajectory through different fields that are relevant to the research. In this way, socioanalysis represents a rethinking of a researcher's declaration of interest, and of the impossibility of disinterested research. Bourdieu's argument here is that acknowledgement of this produces better social science research.

In field terms, we also see policy developed within an international organisation such as the OECD and its implementation within nations meaning there are often times slippages between text and enactment, given the competing logics of practice of the field of policy text production and policy practice and particularly when spread spatially across the globe. In his later work, Bourdieu (2003) also noted that the amount of national capital possessed by a given nation mediated to varying extents global impacts. Think here of the contrast between World Bank policy impact on developing nations and OECD impact say on the USA.

An education policy field

The first and most direct account treating education policy as a field was outlined by James Ladwig (Ladwig, 1994). The key innovation that Ladwig (1994) provided was an account of education policy as a field through an examination of its emergence in the USA during the 1990s. We would note that Ladwig equated the policy field in the USA with federal policy making in education, a shortcoming in our view, given the weakness of the federal presence in education policy at the time. There were two ways in which Ladwig's argument was important for education policy sociology. The first is that it took a coherent and broad scale account of Bourdieu's work and applied it systematically. From this, a number of methodological applications of the field concept can be discerned. Secondly, Ladwig's use of the term policy field and in particular of the idea of policy effects highlighted the limitations of a Bourdieuian account of policy, if not supplemented with additional concepts. In particular, Ladwig argued that policy effects should be used to designate effects of policy and policy practice on policy makers within the field of education policy. That is, that the development and maturation of an education policy field meant that its effects did not travel beyond the field and that debates were largely academic and located within a field of political discourse, rather than classroom practice. Ladwig's intent here in using Bourdieu was to highlight this disconnect and to suggest that educators should look elsewhere beyond policy to make changes in classrooms.

However this usage of policy effects seems counter intuitive, particularly in education policy sociology and policy studies more broadly. We would also suggest that in the 20 years since Ladwig wrote his paper that the (federal) education policy field in the US now has more effects in states and schools: think here of Bush's *No child left behind* and associated accountability regime and Obama's *Race to the top*, both of which have had real impact on schools, teacher practices and classrooms, particularly through testing and more recently the Common Core State Standards Initiative for Mathematics and English Language Arts. In current times we also see the emergence of a global education policy field above the nation with effects within the nation. Think here, for example, of Obama's concern at Shanghai 'coming top' in the 2009 Programme for International Student Assessment (PISA) (Sellar and Lingard, 2013).

In Bourdieu's work then, 'fields' replace 'institutions' and the social world is seen as consisting of multiple social fields, overlain by a field of power and field of gender relations. It is also within the concept of field that Bourdieu's emphasis on relationality comes to the fore. With this argument, Bourdieu appears to be working across and together Weber, Durkheim and Marx by suggesting the relative autonomy of each field (stretched on a continuum from highly autonomous to heteronomous) with its own logics of practice, so as to reject a deterministic account, whereby in the last instance all is determined by the economic field, as with classical Marxism. Rather, Bourdieu postulates an overarching field of power on which struggles for the principles for determining the capitals most highly valued within societies are defined, that is, these are not necessarily determined as economic capital or cultural capital or social capital, but are a contingent mixture at particular points in time. A field of gender also cuts across other fields. We also need to recognise that in Bourdieu's work all capitals have the potential for 'tran-substantiation' into economic capital. Significant in Bourdieu's work as well is the acceptance that all relations are affected by and involve power, while this reality is most often misrecognised in everyday life. Herein for Bourdieu lie naturalisation and misrecognition.

In Bourdieu's work:

- instead of policy, he would talk of the policy field;
- instead of politics, 'the field of politics';
- instead of the media, 'the journalistic field'; overarched by fields of power and gender.

His following observation on the circulation of policy texts also provides insights into both the policy field and the policy cycle (Ball, 1994), and also the gaps in policy enactment:

> The fact that texts circulate without their context, that – to use my terms – they don't bring with them the field of production of which they are a product, and the fact that recipients, who are themselves in a different field of production, re-interpret the texts in accordance with the structure of the field of reception, are facts that generate some formidable misunderstandings and that can have good or bad consequences.
>
> *(Bourdieu, 1999: 221)*

This observation about the re-interpretations and re-contextualisations involved in policy enactment has particular pertinence to the translation involved in national enactment of global education policy texts (e.g. the OECD's PISA). Some other points to note about conceptualising a policy field include:

- competing logics of practice across the policy cycle (Cf. Ladwig, 1994) to understand the policy/implementation or enactment 'gap';
- logics of practice of the 'bureaucratic field: claims to the universal, gives the state the legitimate right to exercise symbolic violence (Bourdieu, 1998);
- left hand (high spending, social state) and right hand (treasury and finance, fiscal austerity) of the state sitting in tension; 'distinctions' within the field of schooling; the 'magisterial discourse' of some policy texts – unidirectional and often authoritative in character and 'performative usage' of globalisation in policy talk, where globalisation is taken as neo-liberal globalisation, bracketing out more pertinent social science definitions (Bourdieu, 2003).

In concluding this section on the notion of a policy field, we would note that researching a field involves creating a rupture with everyday language by representing key problems in consistent and considered ways, identifying practices attached to the field, the logics of practice, locating key positions in the field (drawing on descriptive and statistical forms of analysis), identifying dominant and dominated agents within the field and measuring different forms of capital possessed by agents (cultural, social, symbolic), which are the focus of struggles within the field.

We should also say something, albeit briefly here, about the place of the state in Bourdieu's theorising. We have noted that Bourdieu would speak of the field of education policy, rather than simply education policy, the field of the state bureaucracy, rather than the bureaucracy or the state. Like Foucault, Bourdieu initially ignored the state in his theorising and came to it late in his career. For Bourdieu (1998: 41):

> The state is the *culmination of a process of concentration of different species of capital*: capital of physical force or instruments of coercion (army, police), economic capital, cultural or (better) informational capital, and symbolic capital.

He saw the state as holding a monopoly over symbolic power and violence, effected through policy and the classificatory powers of the state with schools seen to be central here. Herein lies the 'invisibility' of educational policy for Bourdieu (van Zanten, 2005). Bourdieu saw the state as holding a form of 'statist capital' that allows it to exercise power over other kinds of fields that constitute the society. As Swartz (2013: 131) observes, 'Statist capital represents an emergent metacapital, a regulatory power over the field of power and the broader society. It is state authority'. In his later political writing, it is the abdication of some of this authority associated with neo-liberalism that Bourdieu critiqued. We can see this abdication in new forms of policy governance and networking in education such as contractualism (Rawolle, 2013) and in the marketisation and privatisation agendas (Ball and Junemann, 2012).

Policy implementation/enactment and competing logics of practice

In considering the focus of policy sociology as the field of education policy or the policy field, we have alluded to the way in which this Bourdieuian approach allows another take on policy/implementation 'gaps', 'deficits', 'differences'. In Ball's (1994) 'policy cycle' approach this is the gap between the context of policy text production (the text itself) and the context of policy practice or implementation. Ball, of course, uses the context of policy practice rather than implementation to align with his rejection of a straightforward linear policy/implementation relationship. Bourdieu's approach – thinking of a policy field – works with a similar rejection of straightforward linear relationship as well. Some more recent education policy work talks of policy enactment, which gets closer to a Bourdieuian account (Ball and Junemann, 2012). We see here the gap between the simplifying tendencies of the universal claims of state policy as opposed to the complexities and messiness of school and classroom practices.

To reiterate, Bourdieu would see the context of policy text production occurring within the policy field with its specific logics of practice; itself located within the bureaucratic state field. Idiosyncratic to the bureaucratic state field, according to Bourdieu (1998), is its claim to the universal. Thus policy produced within this field claims universal undifferentiated application across all sites of policy practice or implementation. Yet we know the school field, particularly classrooms, have different logics of practice and are also located within other fields. The logic of the classroom is one of contingency and specificity, so that we have another fruitful explanation of implementation issues in terms of disjuncture between competing logics of practice, including competing and disjunctive temporalities. Here we also see another explanation for policy/practice de-coupling. Contemporary top-down, test-based accountability is an attempt to more tightly couple policy and practice across different fields and competing logics of practice, and in the process often challenging the broader goals of schooling in a mode of goal displacement or means/ends decoupling.

Policy habitus

We will first deal with the concept of habitus generally, which has its roots in philosophy from Aristotle. For Bourdieu, habitus is used to theorise practice without identifying either rational mental states as the sole origin of action, and without appealing to the mind's ability to generate and act on representations of actions (Burkitt, 2002). Habitus provides the connection between agents and practices through 'systems of dispositions', which are bodily incorporations of social history and dispositions associated with previous practices, which are transposable to different contexts. Like practice, habitus is an open concept that, in its most general applications, indicates the socially developed capacity to act appropriately.

Dispositional accounts of practice do not of themselves explain the expression of that predisposition in the actual production of a practice. For example, holding critical or sceptical dispositions towards education policy does not, on its own, explain why agents (e.g. policy makers or teachers) will selectively oppose some policies, while engaging others. Given that the relationship between habitus and practice is socio-genetic, it could be that resolutions offered in genetic theory fit this problem. To explain: genes provide a predisposition to the expression of different characteristics in living things, such as particular genes associated with different cancers. Yet the expression of these genes does not always follow in people who have these genes. Rather, it is in the interaction between genes and environment that the predisposition may be expressed. The environment provides the stimulus for the expression of predispositions, with the concept of field providing the stimulus in Bourdieu's theory. Wacquant (2011, 2014) has written similarly about the contingent relationships between dispositions of agents (habitus) and position in ever volatile and pregnant fields. Here we see habitus as a dispositional theory of action or practice (Wacquant, 2011). There is, however, something of an ontological complicity between habitus and field, especially when agents have a 'feel for the game'.

In his use of habitus Bourdieu refers to the overall 'system of dispositions' that are both attached to a person and some of which are collectively shared by others who have similar trajectories through fields. But Bourdieu also developed ways of talking about stages of development of a habitus, distinguishing between primary and secondary habitus, the former the product of child rearing in the home, the latter the product of more structured pedagogies of education. With the latter, we get a sense of the potential malleability of habitus (Wacquant, 2011: 86). But

Bourdieu also uses habitus to talk about divisions of habitus, such as scientific habitus and journalistic habitus. This second use refers to specific sets of dispositions that are developed and related to practice within a specific social field. Hence, as with other applications of Bourdieu, we could talk about a 'policy habitus', a concept which we have discussed elsewhere (Rawolle and Lingard, 2008), and initially proposed by Stensli (2006).

The concept of policy habitus raises interesting questions about how one researches habitus. Some current work (Lingard, Sellar and Baroutsis, forthcoming) is considering this in respect of the emergent global education policy field and how a particular policy habitus appears to be significant in the emergence of such a field with similar dispositions expressed by policy makers within international organisations such as the OECD and national policy leaders. Such an approach to understanding the effects of globalisation in education policy, works with Bourdieu's (1990b: 122) depiction of his theoretical framing as being both 'constructivist structuralism' and 'structuralist constructivism', giving emphasis to both structures and agents, helping us see the actual processes of globalisation of education policy. International and national policy makers both have a similar 'feel for the game', operating within the same epistemic community, which sees and constitutes the globe as a commensurative space of measurement. Against Dianne Reay's (2004) argument that habitus has been a (too) heavily used concept in educational research, we would argue that this is not the case in policy sociology and indeed call for more research into 'policy habitus'. There is some useful recent work in terms of thinking about the policy habitus of senior policy makers in respect of the emergent global education policy field and its effects into national education policy fields (see above). We might think of globalisation actually being the capacity to imagine the globe as a commensurative space of measurement, implying that a crucial part of a global education policy habitus might be the disposition to imagine practice and possibilities in this space and to do the required commensurative work. This is a capacity today of both national policy makers and those in international organisations. We would argue that the constitution of the global education policy field results at one level from this alignment between the habitus of policy makers in international organisations and those of national policy makers.

Globalisation and an emergent global education policy field

We developed the concept of a global education policy field from Bourdieu (2003) and his concept of a global economic field (Lingard, Rawolle and Taylor, 2005; Rawolle and Lingard, 2008), as well as his inchoate work on 'national capital', and used research conducted by one of us with others on the OECD (Henry et al., 2001; Sellar and Lingard, 2013) as an empirical basis. This research included the OECD's Indicators Project and PISA (Henry et al., 2001) and related work on policy as numbers (Grek et al., 2009; Ozga and Lingard, 2007). We have drawn on this research to empirically confirm the salience conceptually of a 'global education policy field' and in terms of policy effects.

While Bourdieu's concept of social fields had a primarily national focus, there is no logical reason why the concept could not be applied to social structures beyond the nation state. Indeed, the concept of field is more a social and spatial one than a geographical one. As noted above, Bourdieu was aware of the shortcomings of 'methodological nationalism', which unthinkingly equates space and social categories, processes and effects with national society. Processes associated with globalisation carry methodological implications for research, for which Bourdieu's theorising is useful. First and foremost, Bourdieu's concept of social field is a physical metaphor that can be applied to global relations. Indeed, in the empirical research that underpins our discussion, such methodological and conceptual developments are required in order to situate and understand how global comparisons between nations and the emergence of a commensurative global space of educational measurement have come to have such influence over national education policy fields.

Drawing on the work of historians of the development of national statistical systems (Desroiseres, 1998; Hacking, 1990; Porter, 1995; Rose, 1999) and on sociological work on policy as numbers (Lingard, 2011; Rose, 1999), we have argued that the creation of national comparative data on school performance, as with the OECD's PISA and the International Association for the Evaluation of Educational Achievement's (IEA) Trends in International Mathematics and Science Study (TIMSS) and Progress in International Reading Literacy Study (PIRLS), has helped constitute an emergent global education policy field, just as the emergence of national statistical systems constituted the nation as a commensurative space of measurement, helping to constitute the nation. This is associated with the 'governance turn' and comparison as a central mode of governance (Novoa and Yariv-Mashal, 2003). We have argued that comparative education policy analysis now must move beyond just nation-to-nation comparisons to take account of this emergent global field. The concept of 'reference societies' important in comparative education also needs to be rethought in this context (Lingard and Rawolle, 2011; Sellar and Lingard, 2013). Furthermore, the concept of cross-field effects can now be developed to consider global/national relations in policy development, and also global/provincial relations (Lingard and Rawolle, 2004) as globalisation reconstitutes global/national and global/local relations (Sassen, 2007). Here, as already suggested, we could also think of the policy habitus of both policy makers in national policy making positions and those within international organisations and their roles in the emergent global policy field and travelling globalised education policy discourses. However, we would stress the need for empirical research in relation to these matters.

Conclusion

We have argued that Bourdieu's 'thinking tools' (habitus, capitals, fields, practice), his argument concerning the necessity of the imbrications of the theoretical and the empirical and support for a researcher disposition of reflexivity, offer both a theory and a methodology for conducting policy sociology in education. Some such research and theorising have been done and referenced throughout, but we stress the necessity of the empirical – the pressing need for more empirical research – to develop the usefulness of Bourdieu's sociology for policy sociology in education and for understanding rapid developments in the face of neo-liberal globalisation of education policy today as the spaces and places of education policy continue to change.

References

Albright, J. and Luke, A. (Eds.) (2008). *Pierre Bourdieu and literacy education.* New York: Routledge.

Ball, S. J. (1994). *Education reform: A critical and post-structural approach.* Buckingham, UK: Open University Press.

Ball, S. J. and Junemann, C. (2012). *Networks, new governance and education.* Bristol, UK: The Policy Press.

Bourdieu, P. (1990a). *The logic of practice.* Stanford, CA: Stanford University Press.

Bourdieu, P. (1990b). *In other words.* Stanford, CA: Stanford University Press.

Bourdieu, P. (1993). *Sociology in question.* London: SAGE.

Bourdieu, P. (1998). *Practical reason.* Cambridge, UK: Polity Press.

Bourdieu, P. (1999). The social conditions of the international circulation of ideas. In R. Shusterman (Ed.), *Bourdieu: A critical reader* (pp. 220–228). Oxford, UK: Blackwell.

Bourdieu, P. (2003). *Firing back: Against the tyranny of the market.* London: Verso.

Bourdieu, P. (2005). *The social structures of the economy.* Cambridge, UK: Polity Press.

Bourdieu, P., Accardo, A., Balazs, G., Beaud, S., Bonvin, F., Bourdieu, L., Borgois, P., Broccolichi, S., Champagne, P., Christin, R., Faguer, J.-P., Garcia, S., Lenoir, R., Oevrard, F., Pialoux, M., Pinto, L., Podalydes, D., Sayad, A., Soulie, C. and Wacquant, L. J. D. (1999). *The weight of the world: Social suffering in contemporary society.* Cambridge, UK: Polity Press.

Burkitt, I. (2002). Technologies of the self: Habitus and capacities. *Journal for the Theory of Social Behaviour,* 32, 219–237.

Connell, R. W. (1983). *Which way is up? Essays on sex, class and culture.* Sydney: Allen & Unwin.

Desroiseres, A. (1998). *The politics of large numbers.* Harvard, MA: Harvard University Press.

Goodman, N. (1978). *Ways of worldmaking.* Indianapolis, IN: Hackett.

Grek, S., Lawn, M., Lingard, B., Ozga, J., Rinne, R., Segerholm, C. and Simola, H. (2009). National policy brokering and the construction of the European Education Space in England, Sweden, Finland and Scotland. *Comparative Education, 45*(1), 5–21.

Hacking, I. (1990). *The taming of chance.* Cambridge, UK: Cambridge University Press.

Hardy, I. (2009). The politics of educational studies: A preliminary analysis of leading educational policy journals. *Critical Studies in Education, 50*(2), 173–185.

Henry, M., Lingard, B., Rizvi, F. and Taylor, S. (2001). *The OECD, globalisation and education policy.* Oxford, UK: Pergamon Press.

Kenway, J. and Koh, A. (2013). The elite school as 'cognitive machine' and 'social paradise': Developing transnational capitals for the national 'field of power'. *Journal of Sociology, 49*(2–3), 272–290.

Ladwig, J. (1994). For whom this reform? Outlining educational policy as a social field. *British Journal of Sociology of Education, 15*(3), 341–363.

Ladwig, J. (2014). Theoretical notes on the sociological analyses of school reform networks. *British Journal of Sociology of Education, 35*(3), 371–388.

Lingard, B. (2011). Policy as numbers: Ac/counting for educational research. *The Australian Educational Researcher, 38*(4), 355–382.

Lingard, B. and Rawolle, S. (2004). Mediatizing educational policy: The journalistic field, science policy, and cross-field effects. *Journal of Education Policy, 19*(3), 361–380.

Lingard, B. and Rawolle, S. (2011). New scalar politics: Implications for education policy. *Comparative Education, 47*(4), 489–502.

Lingard, B., Rawolle, S. and Taylor, S. (2005). Globalizing education policy sociology: Working with Bourdieu. *Journal of Education Policy, 20*(6), 759–777.

Lingard, B., Sellar, S. and Baroutsis, A. (forthcoming). Researching the habitus of global policy actors in education. *Cambridge Journal of Education.*

Novoa, A. and Yariv-Mashal, T. (2003). Comparative research in education: A mode of governance or a historical journey? *Comparative Education, 39*(4), 423–438.

Ozga, J. and Lingard, B. (2007). Globalization, education policy and politics. In B. Lingard and J. Ozga (Eds.), *The RoutledgeFalmer reader in education policy and politics* (pp. 65–82). London: Routledge.

Porter, T. (1995). *Trust in numbers: The pursuit of objectivity in science and public life.* Princeton, NJ: Princeton University Press.

Rawolle, S. (2013). Understanding equity as an asset to national interest: Developing a social contract analysis of policy. *Discourse: Studies in the Cultural Politics of Education, 34*(2), 231–244.

Rawolle, S. and Lingard, B. (2008). The sociology of Pierre Bourdieu and researching education policy. *Journal of Education Policy, 23*(6), 729–740.

Reay, D. (2004). 'It's all becoming a habitus': Beyond the habitual use of habitus in educational research. *British Journal of Sociology of Education, 25*(4), 431–444.

Reay, D. and Ball, S. J. (1997). 'Spoilt for Choice': The working classes and educational markets. *Oxford Review of Education, 23*(1), 89–101.

Rizvi, F. and Lingard, B. (2010). *Globalizing education policy.* London: Routledge.

Rose, N. (1999). *Powers of freedom: Reframing political thought.* Cambridge, UK: Cambridge University Press.

Sassen, S. (2007). *Sociology of globalization.* New York: W.W. Norton.

Sellar, S. and Lingard, B. (2013). 'Looking East': Shanghai, PISA and the reconstitution of reference societies in the global education policy field. *Comparative Education, 49*(4), 464–485.

Stensli, H. O. (2006). Oceans apart: Ideologies of extraterritorial foreign policy in Northern Europe and the USA. Unpublished PhD dissertation, University of Bergen, Norway.

Swartz, D. (2013). *Symbolic power, politics, and intellectuals, the political sociology of Pierre Bourdieu.* Chicago, IL: The University of Chicago Press.

Thomson, P. (2002). *Schooling the rust-belt kids.* Sydney: Allen & Unwin.

Thomson, P. (2005). Bringing Bourdieu to policy sociology: Codification, misrecognition and exchange value in the UK context. *Journal of Education Policy, 20*(6), 741–758.

van Zanten, A. (2005). Bourdieu as education policy analyst and expert: A rich but ambiguous legacy. *Journal of Education Policy, 20*(6), 671–686.

Wacquant, L. (2011). Habitus as topic and tool: Reflections on becoming a prizefighter. *Qualitative Research in Psychology, 8,* 81–92.

Wacquant, L. (2014). *Homines in Extremis:* What fighting scholars tell us about habitus. *Body & Society, 20*(2), 3–17.

PART I

Theorists

2

MICHEL DE CERTEAU, EVERYDAY LIFE AND CULTURAL POLICY STUDIES IN EDUCATION

Sue Saltmarsh

This chapter considers cultural approaches to policy studies, informed by cultural theorist Michel de Certeau. It considers how theories and methodologies concerned with the everyday can illuminate the dynamics of 'policy cultures' (Stein, 2004). Conceptual tools examined here include culture as everyday practice, and policy as cultural practice. This recognises the dynamic and productive nature of the everyday, and constitutes policy within a proliferation of cultural practices that can be subverted, resisted and reconfigured (Certeau, 1984). The chapter argues that cultural approaches to policy analysis need to be grounded in a thorough under-standing of the everyday activities and meaning-making practices of those who are the makers, analysts, targets, beneficiaries, implementers and end-users of policy. For each of these, education policy produces meanings, enactments and effects that need to be considered in dialogue with extant and emergent cultural practices. The first part of the chapter discusses conceptual tools of culture, practice and policy, and the second turns to questions of (meta)methodology and the ethical and political implications of Certeau's work for approaches to policy research.

Conceptual tools: culture, practice and policy

As a cultural theorist, Michel de Certeau's work is profoundly concerned with the heterogeneous practices of everyday life. These he takes as a focus in historio-graphical, psychoanalytic, anthropological, religious and political writings, and as the ground for the 'methodological imagination' (Highmore, 2006: 2) from which his analytic work proceeds. Certeau is particularly interested in the reciprocal relations between everyday practices, logics and social orders, each working on the other to constitute dynamic and continually evolving cultures. In much of his work, he envisages and elaborates culture and practice beyond sites of scholarly description and analysis, in order to:

provide an ethical provocation for thinking about how we might dispense an obligation to the ordinary. This ethical provocation is accompanied by an invitation to 'listen otherwise' to the ordinary and to the texts it might hide in.

(Highmore, 2001: 254–255)

This section of the chapter explores these concepts in relation to the reciprocal relationships of education, policy and cultural practices and production; the significance of heterogeneity in cultural approaches to policy analysis, and ethical demands that accompany cultural approaches to policy analysis.

A central premise of this chapter, which is woven throughout Certeau's work, is an understanding of ordinary, everyday practices – described by Certeau as '"ways of operating" or doing things' (Certeau, 1984: xi) – as something of theoretical and methodological significance to all domains of social activity. It is the plurality of everyday practices and their 'systems of operational combination', he argues, 'which compose a "culture"' (Certeau, 1984: xi). This interest in the everyday draws upon, yet differs somewhat from, analytic traditions that posit 'an elementary unit – the individual – on the basis of which groups are supposed to be formed and to which they are supposed to be always reducible' (1984: xi). This is not to imply that the individual is discounted in Certeau's work, but rather to suggest that the irreducibility of the individual requires analysis to proceed from the cultural.

Certeau takes the multiplicity and heterogeneity of the everyday and its vocabularies, logics and relations of practice as primary sites of analysis. The practice of everyday life, for Certeau, is not merely a matter of cultural reproduction or the embodiment of a habitus acquired through social interactions and cultural norms. Rather, he sees everyday practices as productive of cultures that are in a continual process of being re-worked and re-made by ordinary, creative and often unanticipated activities, appropriations and resistances. Thus his interest is in showing how the often unmarked practices of everyday life both produce and open up spaces for change within cultural logics, relational networks and institutions and operational systems. This has implications for the way that Certeau and scholars of his work perceive policy not merely as a strategy of institutional power *but also* as a form of cultural practice in which the everyday is imbricated.

The policies, institutions, texts and practices of education are important sites in the production of culture, and several decades of socially critical educational research have highlighted the importance of understanding how education policy, schooling and educational experiences can function in shaping subjectivities and social relations (see Ball, Maguire and Braun, 2012; Gillborn and Youdell, 2000; Youdell, 2011). As Noel Preston and Colin Symes once observed, 'education has become one of the core cultural experiences of modern life' (1992: 4), and as such needs to be understood as enmeshed within, rather than as separate to, cultural life. This view is consistent with Jeremy Ahearn's contention that education policies and practices work on everyday culture, '[instituting] forms or aspects of popular culture when they bring into their embrace all of a nation's people and become a routine part of popular experience' (Ahearne, 2011: 422). This work on culture via education is of course profoundly political, and is a primary means by which governments endeavour to act upon the values, beliefs, dispositions, goals and activities of populations. It is also a significant mechanism through which individuals, families and communities are positioned in relation to each other, institutions, the state and society more broadly. Thus as a 'political strategy that looks to work on the culture of the territory over which it presides' (Ahearne, 2009: 143), education can be considered in terms of what Ahearne refers to as an 'implicit cultural policy'. Education policy seeks to have an 'effective impact on the nation's culture of its action as a whole' (Ahearne, 2009: 144), and therefore functions as 'the basic foundation of a nation's cultural policy' (Ahearne, 2006: 9).

Educational and policy research have also been shown to have a cultural role in contributing new lenses for understanding, 'not only in that we can see things differently but also in that we may be able to see problems where we did not see them before' (Biesta, 2007: 297). This is not to suggest that educational policy research alters or determines practices in a simple transfer of knowledge and ideas or a leveraging of changes to educational practice. Rather, such research provides provocations to reflect and think anew, and invitations to reconfigure ways of being, knowing and doing that are part of a dialogue in which cultures of professional practice, educational institutions, and educational experience are formulated. Within these broader landscapes of educational policy, practice and experience, policy cultures emerge with their own language, behaviours, rituals and norms. However, as Ian Burkitt has observed:

> most social theory and philosophy overlooks this necessary relation between the official and the unofficial realms of everyday life. Instead, the focus is drawn towards either the official codification and normalization of practices and the institutional apparatuses of the state or to the emergent properties of daily life, as if these are two uncoupled realms.
>
> *(2004: 15)*

Cultural approaches to policy analysis are concerned with precisely these reciprocal relations between policy domains and everyday life, which are understood as co-extensive and co-implicated, rather than as separate domains. It is important to avoid thinking of policy cultures in terms of local responses to policies that have emanated from elsewhere (Stein, 2004). Rather, policy cultures are understood in terms of a recursive relationship that 'allows for consideration of the influence of local practice on congressional discourse as well as resistance to and adaptation of policy problem and solution definitions at various moments of the policy process' (Stein, 2004: xii). Scholars of Certeau's work similarly see policy and culture as operating reciprocally. Burkitt, for example, argues that 'There are aspects of everyday relations and practices more open to government, institutionalization, and official codification, while others are more resistant and provide the basis for opposition and social movements' (2004: 211). This is not to suggest that everyday life is distinct or separate from 'official' practices in institutional and policy domains, but rather 'as the single plane of immanence in which these two forms of practice and articulation interrelate and affect one another' (2004: 211). While forms of practice may differ, they are nonetheless permeable to one another. The 'everyday' in this sense refers both to codified and normalised practices such as those associated with institutions and the state *as well as* informal 'practices and articulations of experience' (2004: 211). These, Burkitt insists, 'should not be uncoupled in social analysis, as they are necessarily interrelated in processes of social and political change' (2004: 211).

A cultural approach to policy analysis, then, is concerned with more than policy formation, implementation, outcomes and effects, and moves beyond policy enactments as they are interpreted and translated by actors in educational contexts (Maguire and Ball, 1994; Maguire, Ball and Braun, 2010). Instead, it directs analytical attention to both the everyday practices that influence policy discourse, as well as attending to 'the multiple meanings that policies engender, through the myriad interpretations of policy makers, policy implementers, policy target populations and policy analysts' (Stein, 2004: 6). Cultural policy analysis is thus interested in how policy shapes culture, how culture shapes policy, and how in so doing, both are reinvented in multiple ways.

Certeau's contribution to cultural policy analysis lies in part in attending to the everyday in order to make 'explicit the systems of operational combination . . . which also compose a "culture"' (1984: xi). While a good deal of Certeau's work is concerned with ways of doing, using, making, appropriating, resisting and 'making do', his project is not, as Ian Buchanan suggests, concerned so much with 'the study of the everyday in its particulars' (2000: 98), nor is it located at the site of the individual per se. Instead, Certeau considers how culture is spoken, written and practised through embodied, individual subjects in 'an analysis of culture from the mute perspectives of the body, the cry, and the murmur, none of which needs to be identified with a specific, knowable individual, in order to be apprehended' (Buchanan, 2000: 97–98). The analysis of everyday practices thus becomes a means by which the nuance, complexity and heterogeneity of policy cultures can be considered as mutually constitutive.

With respect to education, the reciprocity between policy, analysis and culture may be apprehended through a whole range of everyday practices that are readily recognisable within a particular policy milieu. In one sense, education policy might be seen as being simultaneously imposed and enacted, resisted and subverted, and reconfigured in everyday practice by principals, teachers, students, parents or community members in ways not necessarily anticipated or intended by those who produced and authorised it. Certeau refers to these kinds of relations or 'ways of operating' (1984: xiv) in terms of 'strategies' and 'tactics' (1984: xvii–xx). For Certeau, the function of institutional strategies – be they policy pronouncements, procedural requirements or hierarchical relations – is to structure, conceal and maintain operations of power, in order to keep those without a 'proper place' within the institution at a distance. Tactics, on the other hand, are the operations of the weak against the strong – fleeting incursions and 'guileful ruses' (Certeau,

1984: 37) that accomplish temporary moments of agency and resistance, but that are unlikely to significantly alter the operations of power concealed and maintained by institutional strategies.

This conceptualisation is one of Certeau's better-known contributions to cultural analysis, and has not been without its critics. However, critiques such as Frow's (1991), tend toward reading strategies and tactics as dichotomous and oppositional. There are clearly distinctions in Certeau's work between the operational logics of institutions and the spatial territories and hierarchies of power they demarcate, and the more fragmentary, disruptive tactics of the everyday. However, the interplay between them allows for the emergence of new and unanticipated possibilities. According to Colebrook, 'A tactic works metaphorically: rather than returning the logic to some ground, it thinks the logic from a different point of view' (Colebrook, 2001: 546–547). Indeed, Certeau insists on the productive potential for the interplay of strategies and tactics to formulate cultures and inaugurate institutions anew. He sees this interplay as key to what policy is and accomplishes in cultural terms, observing that 'A policy is characterized by linking a tactic to a strategy' (Certeau, 1997: 79). The operational logics of strategies, however static they may appear, and the logics of everyday practices, however resistant or subversive, are both reciprocal and permeable and therefore able to be remade in symbolic and material ways. The interplay of strategies and tactics is not simply a struggle between the weak and the strong, but rather plays an important part in refiguring everyday cultural beliefs and practices over time.

While policy may form new links in the interplay of strategies and tactics, these links operate in dialogue with what has gone before. For de Certeau, the management of society in its multiple forms, including the introduction of new policy agendas leaves behind cultural 'remainders' (1997) – residual beliefs, expressions, meanings and practices. These are simultaneously reinvented and reworked, and in the process inaugurate new cultural formations that may not be immediately recognised as such.

> A reciprocity thus replaces 'transmission' or the 'integration' of the past. A new organization is inaugurated. But it is not yet recognized for what it is. It is folded into older structures as if it were a vice, whereas in reality it invents a new structure, that is, different relations among categories that have changed.
>
> *(Certeau, 1997: 89)*

This theoretical framework and its emphasis on everyday practice as cultural formation enables us to retheorise both extant and emergent configurations of everyday policy cultures, and leads to considerations of education policy as culture producing. Such a framework has methodological implications for policy researchers, drawing attention to both 'the historical moment in which a policy develops and the structural realities of institutions responsible for its implementation' (Stein, 2004: 6). Yet simultaneously, cultural policy analysis informed by Certeau takes account of 'the tragic frailty of policy' (2000: 29), and recognises the inadequacy of any policy vision or initiative in the absence of an accounting for the everyday and its relationship to policy and cultural production.

Another significant contribution made by Certeau to policy studies and taken up extensively by scholars of Certeau's work (Ahearne, 2001, 2004, 2009, 2011; Highmore, 2001, 2006) is his commitment to heterogeneity and the recognition of complicity in cultural production. This insistence in Certeau's work is informed by his interest in the 'marginality of a majority' (1984: xvi), and attends to heterogeneity, multiplicity and *un*manageability, insisting on an ethics of recognition and a commitment to everyday culture and its proliferation of practice as that which is 'already taking place' (Highmore, 2006: 157). For Certeau, the cartographic impulse that would map and articulate practices in order to render them knowable and bring them within grids of intelligibility and the gaze of regulatory frameworks, misses the point that 'we do not yet know what to make of other, equally infinitesimal procedures that have remained unprivileged by history yet which continue to flourish in the interstices of the institutional technologies' (1986: 189).

Certeau's contribution to policy studies is therefore predicated on his insistence that policy itself must be grounded in a recognition of that which cannot be captured or assimilated – everyday practices and tactical manoeuvres in relation to the social order:

> A practice of the order constructed by others redistributes its space; it creates at least a certain play in that order, a space for manoeuvres of unequal forces and utopian points of reference. That is where the opacity of a 'popular' culture could be said to manifest itself – a dark rock that resists all assimilation.
> *(1984: 18)*

While policy may attempt to establish orders that create parameters and shape social spaces within which people must operate, here Certeau underscores the impossibility of any established order apprehending cultural practices that exceed all such attempts. The proliferation of heterogeneous practices calls instead for a conception of cultural policy that creates space for others to operate and flourish. It also calls for new ways of attending in methodological terms to policy work that 'is dedicated to fashioning spaces more hospitable to the voices of others; and . . . completely committed to siding with the unmanageability of the ordinary and the radical heterogeneity of the multitude' (Highmore, 2006: 153).

This is a recurring interest in Certeau's theoretical and policy work, which maintains an insistence on the incommensurability of cultural practices despite policy attempts to define and shape them. For Ahearne, 'Certeau's analyses tend to decentre the ambition of strategic decision-makers to mould the social body in the image of their policy programmes' (Ahearne, 2004: 78). This is not to imply that unity or coherence can be attained simply by attending to the everyday, but rather to insist that the creativity, heterogeneity and 'often unpredictable re-employments to which users subject the cultural resources at their disposal (Ahearne, 2004: 12) merit legitimate spaces in which to operate. Rather than looking for threads that bind the social fabric, Certeau insists instead on looking for openings within it. The 'obligation to the ordinary' (Highmore, 2001) is not just concerned with describing and documenting. Rather, in looking for 'interruptions and fissures which put in question strategies of control and reproduction' (Ahearne, 1995: 191), he shows not just the operations, but also the limits of political, administrative and disciplinary procedures and mechanisms. This concern is theoretical as well as methodological, and for Certeau, leads to a '*polemological* analysis of culture' (1984: xvii) in which theory is forced 'to recognize its own limits' (Highmore, 2001: 257).

Certeau also maintains an insistence on uncovering how 'instances of "implicit" alterity involve interpreters in forms of "complicity"' (Ahearne, 1995: 131) in efforts to bring heterogeneous populations into conformity and compliance with political agendas. According to Cravetto, Certeau's body of work shows how

> the pretence of being objective and scientific – distort the question addressed to the object of the research. Only the assumption by the researcher of his lived experience and his history allows him to free himself from the constraints typical of knowledge techniques and technical knowledge.
>
> *(Cravetto, 2003: 122)*

This recognition, referred to by Ahearne as 'interpretive complicity' (1995: 128) brings policy analysis into focus as itself a subjective process. While Certeau was cautious of turning 'the human subject into the prime object of policy' as such (Ahearne, 2001: 456), his interest in opening up of space for a plurality of relations and practices 'sets up the space of human subjectivity, for agency and room to manoeuvre' (Ahearne, 2001: 457).

Yet the interpreter/analyst is no innocent bystander in this subjective space. Positioned in multiple ways, the analyst/interpreter's complicity in the regulatory and homogenizing endeavours of political programmes, the production of policy and expert knowledges, their conditions of possibility and the cultures in which they are implicated cannot be overlooked or treated as an irrelevant indulgence. The 'expert' and scientific practices that establish disciplinary and discursive authority are implicated in a conceptual cleavage that separates everyday life from the domain of knowledge production, thereby constituting 'the *whole* as its remainder; this remainder has become what we call culture' (Certeau, 1984: 6). Thus theoretical questioning, Certeau insists, '*does not forget,* cannot forget that in addition to the relationship of these scientific discourses to one another, there is also their common relation with what they have taken care to exclude from their field in order to constitute it' (1984: 61). Those closely involved in processes of policy formation and implementation can simultaneously be among its target populations, recipients of its effects and unintended consequences, and everyday makers of its cultures. For the cultural analyst of policy, there are imperatives to interrogate the privilege and practices of one's own particular 'body of analytical techniques' through which a 'science is mobilized' – in order to show 'how it introduces itself into our techniques . . . and how it can reorganize the place from which discourse is produced' (Certeau, 1984: 5).

(Meta)methodology: writing and practising cultures

Certeau's work spans a remarkable range of disciplinary fields, philosophical influences, scholarly and political concerns, thorough discussion of which is not possible here. While he defined himself primarily as a historian (Ahearne, 2001), his contribution to thought is largely considered a metamethodological one (Highmore, 2007). Scholars of his work argue that his methodological imagination is one that 'seeks to alter the very meeting ground for attending to culture' (Highmore, 2006: 2). This approach is not readily tethered to methodology as a tool-kit for acquiring, describing and analysing objects or data. Rather, it uses 'method and methodology to name the characteristics of our scholarly and intellectual contact with the world' (Highmore, 2006: 2). Methodology, for de Certeau, is a way of being in, and communicating with and about the world – a contact zone for the writing of culture, rather than the analysing of culture per se. Thus Certeau's methodological practice constitutes a form of attention to logics of practice and ways of operating whose own practices are simultaneously co-implicated and subject to scrutiny.

These concerns persist throughout his work, and underpin his approach to, for example, history, which he envisages as 'a practice (a discipline), its results (a discourse), and the relation between them' (Certeau, 1988: 102). The writing of history, for Certeau, cannot be separated from the work of the historian. It is a process that takes place within institutional and discursive conditions that shape history-writing as a particular form of labour, and that create history as a text or product with absences, silences and exclusions. Insisting on history-writing as a social practice, his approach is characterised by:

> scrutinising that which has been selectively filtered out, veiled, or reversed in the writing process. He argues that what historians do in the practice of history – collecting, arranging and analysing documents – is frequently the opposite of what they do in writing it.
>
> *(Reekie, 1995: 52)*

Such concerns are reflected in the ethical demand of Certeau's work across fields as diverse as religion, psychoanalysis, cultural policy and ethnology, and history is located in this concern with 'the business of writing human culture, a writing of culture in which the ordinary, the everyday is simultaneously both inscribed and excised' (Highmore, 2001: 255). It is a critical interrogation that looks not only to the everyday of others as observable domains, but that asks after the complicity within which that everyday is produced as a knowable artefact of scholarly practice.

Certeau's interest in complicity perhaps most famously finds methodological articulation in his insistence on the limits of theory and scholarship – whether historical, ethnological or political – that confine culture and analyst to separate domains without accounting for their relations of co-implication. Thus he observes:

> The Bororos of Brazil sink slowly into their collective death, and Lévi–Strauss takes his seat in the French Academy. Even if this injustice disturbs him, the facts remain unchanged. This story is ours as much as his. In this one respect (which is an index of others that are more important), the intellectuals are still borne on the backs of the common people.
>
> *(Certeau, 1984: 25)*

This provocation speaks to a significant theoretical and methodological concern across Certeau's extensive body of work, which 'centre[s] on a critical epistemology and an ethical demand to respond to epistemological skepticism' (Highmore, 2007: 16). For Certeau, it is not enough to describe, document, analyse and theorise culture, precisely because the analyst is always already imbricated in it in multiple and problematic ways. Scholarship as a form of cultural writing, therefore, 'can be read as a metamethodological argument that insists on our obligation to connect to the real in the face of epistemological scepticism' (Highmore, 2007: 14). This very skepticism underpins 'scholarly experimentation, one where permission is granted, not because "anything goes", but because there is an obligation to find better ways of telling "the cultural"' (Highmore, 2007: 16).

For education researchers interested in cultural policy analysis, methodological approaches informed by Certeau do not attend to questions of researcher reflexivity as a kind of self-indulgent or self-referential gesture toward political correctness, nor as an admission of what is commonly referred to as the 'limitations' of research studies. Rather, the critical and ethical attention to the processes of analytic work is a central premise from which any scholarly inquiry proceeds. This is because such an approach interrogates its own limits while insisting on the heterogenous every-day as always already exceeding the capacity of scholarship to apprehend.

> The imaginary landscape of an inquiry is not without value, even if it is without rigor. It restores what was earlier called 'popular culture,' but it does so in order to transform what was represented as a matrix-force of history into a mobile infinity of tactics. It thus keeps before our eyes the structure of a social imagination in which the problem constantly takes different forms and begins anew.
>
> *(Certeau, 1984: 41)*

Tactics and the practices of the everyday function here not merely as objects of inquiry. Instead they are central to an ethics and politics of practice within 'a metamethodology which is dedicated to encouraging heterogeneity and allowing alterity to proliferate' (Highmore, 2007: 16).

Certeau's interest in heterogeneity and that which disrupts structures and logics of practice does not imply a particular method or set of methodological tools. Rather it presumes a commitment to social scenes of proliferation and incommen-surability, requiring analysis to proceed from fragmentary moments and unanticipated events. It insists on 'the encounter between the plurality of everyday practice, its irreducibility and un-intelligibility, and the narratives of and at the margins' (Napolitano and Pratten, 2007: 10). This polemological approach, as Highmore (2001: 257) explains, places

> 'theory' and 'method' . . . into crisis as they encounter the everyday world. Such an approach can't be measured in terms of descriptive realism but should be judged in terms of its ability to generate new possibilities in an encounter with the ordinary.

Certeau's own cultural policy research in the 1970s–1980s provides examples of his approach to policy analysis and participation in policy processes. Through his involvement with the research unit of the French Ministry of Culture, the Council for Cultural Development, and the National Plan (Ahearne, 2004: 12), Certeau undertook several projects that would contribute to French cultural policy debates and exert influence in policy development circles. An extended discussion of his cultural policy work during this period is not possible here, however, Ahearne's detailed analyses (2001, 2004) highlight Certeau's recognition of the co-implication of academics in the constitution of policy cultures, and his relentless commitment to the heterogeneity of everyday life. For Certeau, engaging in policy research and consultative projects was a pragmatic intervention in which he endeavoured 'to overturn the frames of reference then dictating national cultural policy' (Ahearne, 2001: 448). His interest was not in supplanting one overarching framework with another, but rather in marking 'a space for alterity in reflection on cultural process' (Ahearne, 2001: 458). As Ahearne notes, 'The intervention [Certeau] posits is designed less to model society than to enable the individuals and groups that compose that society to intervene more forcefully in the shaping of their own social world' (Ahearne, 2001: 456). The practice of research and policy analysis is guided by:

> respect for the ability of individuals and groups to intervene creatively in society, recognition of the social subject's need for a plurality of interpretative systems, and commitment to assuring a meaningful two-way interaction between such interpretative systems (or cultural models) and effective social structures.
>
> *(Ahearne, 2001: 458)*

Certeau's meta-methodological approach, guided by an understanding of policy and culture as co-constitutive, opens up spaces for understanding analytic practice as part of policy cultures conceived in the broadest sense. The practice of policy analysis, in other words, is understood as a practice of culture – whether in the form of research, government consultation, scholarly critique, political activism or programmatic development and experimentation. For Certeau, such practices are resolutely committed to heterogeneity, such that the guiding objective of policy interventions irrespective of their form is 'to support and build up those cultures already to be found among the population' (Ahearne, 2004: 14).

Conclusion

Attending to the co-implication of culture, everyday practice and policy involves more than employing a set of methodological procedures in order to render a particular policy and its effects on groups or practices visible. Instead it involves a response to

> an ethical provocation for thinking about how we might dispense an obligation to the ordinary. This ethical provocation is accompanied by an invitation to 'listen otherwise' to the ordinary and to the texts it might hide in.
>
> *(Highmore, 2001: 254–255)*

Responding to this provocation that is central to Certeau's work most certainly involves, in a methodological sense, attending to the heterogeneity and alterity of everyday cultural practice as the starting point. Importantly, however, it requires a response to the political and ethical insistence that policy researchers attend to the ordinary and the 'otherwise' through which the cultures of their own fields of practice are formed and remade, and through which the broader everyday is constituted.

Suggested readings of education policy studies

Ahearne, J. (2009). Cultural policy explicit and implicit: A distinction and some uses. *International Journal of Cultural Policy, 15*(2), 141–153.

Ahearne, J. (2011). Designs on the popular: Framings of general, universal and common culture in French educational policy. *International Journal of Cultural Policy, 17*(4), 421–437.

Further reading on theories/tools

Ahearne, J. (1995). *Michel de Certeau: Interpretation and its other.* Stanford, CA: Stanford University Press.

Buchanan, I. (2000). *Michel de Certeau: Cultural theorist.* London: Sage.

Certeau, M. d. (1984). *The practice of everyday life* (Translated by S. Rendall). Berkeley, CA: University of California Press.

Certeau, M. d. (1997). *Culture in the plural* (Translated by Tom Conley, Edited by Luce Giard). London and Minneapolis, MN: University of Minnesota Press.

Highmore, B. (2006). *Michel de Certeau: Analysing culture.* London and New York: Continuum.

References

Ahearne, J. (1995). *Michel de Certeau: Interpretation and its other.* Stanford, CA: Stanford University Press.

Ahearne, J. (2001). Questions of cultural policy in the thought of Michel de Certeau (1968–1972). *The South Atlantic Quarterly, 100*(2), 447–463.

Ahearne, J. (2004). *Between cultural theory and policy: The cultural policy thinking of Pierre Bourdieu, Michel de Certeau and Régis Debray.* Centre for Cultural Policy Studies,

University of Warwick Research Papers, No. 7 (pp. 1–148). Coventry, UK: Centre for Cultural Policy Studies, University of Warwick Research Papers.

Ahearne, J. (2006). Notes from a French perspective. *International Journal of Cultural Policy, 12*(1), 1–15.

Ahearne, J. (2009). Cultural policy explicit and implicit: A distinction and some uses. *International Journal of Cultural Policy, 15*(2), 141–153.

Ahearne, J. (2011). Designs on the popular: Framings of general, universal and common culture in French educational policy. *International Journal of Cultural Policy. 17*(4), 421–437.

Ball, S., Maguire, M. and Braun, A. (2012). *How schools do policy.* London: Routledge.

Biesta, G. (2007). Bridging the gap between educational research and educational practice: The need for critical distance. *Educational Research and Evaluation: An International Journal on Theory and Practice, 13*(3), 295–301.

Buchanan, I. (2000). *Michel de Certeau: Cultural theorist.* London: Sage.

Burkitt, I. (2004). The time and space of everyday life. *Cultural Studies, 18*(2), 211–227.

Certeau, M. d. (1984). *The practice of everyday life* (Translated by S. Rendall). Berkeley, CA: University of California Press.

Certeau, M. d. (1988). *The writing of history* (Translated by T. Conley). New York: Columbia University Press.

Certeau, M. d. (1997). *Culture in the plural* (Translated by Tom Conley, Edited by Luce Giard). London and Minneapolis, MN: University of Minnesota Press.

Colebrook, C. (2001). Certeau and Foucault: Tactics and strategic essentialism. *South Atlantic Quarterly, 100*(2), 543–574.

Frow, J. (1991). Michel de Certeau and the practice of representation. *Cultural Studies, 5*(1), 52–60.

Gillborn, D. and Youdell, D. (2000). *Rationing education: Policy, practice, reform and equity.* Buckingham, UK: Open University Press.

Highmore, B. (2001). Obligation to the ordinary: Michel de Certeau, ethnography and ethics. *Strategies, 14*(2), 253–263.

Highmore, B. (2006). *Michel de Certeau: Analysing culture.* London and New York: Continuum.

Highmore, B. (2007). An epistemological awakening: Michel de Certeau and the writing of culture. *Social Anthropology/Anthropologie Sociale, 15*(1), 13–26.

Maguire, M., and Ball, S. J. (1994). Researching politics and the politics of research: Recent qualitative studies in the UK. *International Journal of Qualitative Studies in Education, 7*(3), 269–285.

Maguire, M., Ball, S. J. and Braun, A. (2010). Behaviour, classroom management and student 'control': Enacting policy in the English secondary school. *International Studies in Sociology of Education, 20*(2), 153–170.

Napolitano, V. and Pratten, D. (2007). Michel de Certeau: Ethnography and the challenge of plurality. *Social Anthropology, 15*(1), 1–12.

Stein, S. (2004). *The culture of education policy.* New York: Teachers College Press.

Youdell, D. (2011). *School trouble: Identity, power and politics in education.* Abingdon, UK: Routledge.

3

REPEATING DELEUZE AND GUATTARI

Towards a politics of method in education policy studies

Sam Sellar

This chapter engages with the work of Gilles Deleuze and Felix Guattari, specifically their last co-authored book, *What is philosophy?* (hereafter *WIP*) (1994). The aim of the chapter is to explore how Deleuze and Guattari's characterisation of philosophy as the creation of concepts might inform theoretical work in education policy studies. Policy is understood here as a process that is 'contested, interpreted and enacted in a variety of *arenas of practice*' (Ball, 2008: 7, emphasis added), both within government as formal public policy and in a range of other sites. The chapter addresses relationships between practices of policy analysis in which social theory is foregrounded and practices through which social data are produced and used for policy purposes. These data are generated through processes of commensuration, which involve 'the expression or measurement of characteristics normally represented by different units according to a common metric' (Espeland and Stevens, 1998: 315). Commensuration is a central practice in 'policy as numbers' (Lingard, 2011): policies that mobilise numerical data to justify prescribed values and actions. As Rose (1991: 675) has observed, 'numbers are intrinsic to the forms of justification that give legitimacy to political power in democracies'.

The focus of the chapter is situated against the rise of what Thrift (2005) calls 'knowing capitalism': a set of relations in which capitalism has made a business out of thinking the social, often through numerical data captured at various points in our everyday lives. Capitalism has become knowledgeable and this is altering the function both of academia, which has traditionally seen the production of knowledge about the social as its preserve, and of education, which assumes a new centrality in knowledge economies. We live in what Deleuze (1995) called societies of control, in which power operates through the modulation of behaviour within data-driven feedback loops: 'One is always in continuous training, perpetual assessment, continual incitement to buy, to improve oneself, constant monitoring of health and never-ending risk management' (Rose, 1999: 234). Information infrastructures, comprising technologies for quantifying, storing, accessing and representing data (Bowker et al., 2010), are embedded within control societies, including within contexts of policy influence, policy production and policy enactment (Verran, 2012).

Savage and Burrows (2007) argue that the routine collection and analysis of social data by governments, corporations and other organisations is leading to a potential crisis for empirical sociology. This shift of agency in relation to data is evident in contexts of education policy, where new actors, including corporations, philanthropies and international organisations, are using numbers to influence policy agendas and sell education services (Ball, 2012; Ball and Junemann, 2012). One response to these developments by education policy scholars has been to critique the limits of commensuration as a practice for producing useful knowledge about education, thereby preserving a distinctive role for the critical function of social theory. However, these critiques often mobilise social theories and ideologies to dismiss, debunk or delimit commensurative work and, in the process, establish a problematic opposition between what can be known through (an often homogenous characterisation of) measurement and commensuration, on the one hand, and what is properly the domain of theoretical knowledge, on the other.

Critiques of this kind risk disengaging the critic from new and influential ways in which data shapes the social, with potentially dire consequences for the survival of academic social science as a distinctive practice. With this risk in mind, Savage and Burrows (2007: 895) call for a 'politics of method' that involves 'greater reflection on how sociologists can best relate to the proliferation of social data gathered by others, which we currently largely ignore. We do not think it is a satisfactory critical response to shrug these issues off through invoking our sophistication in relation to social theory'. The chapter responds to this call for a politics of method, which can be understood as a concern for relationships between different knowledge traditions or ways of knowing. As Verran (2008: 25) argues, basic facility with philosophical concepts, such as ontology and epistemology, is 'necessary for discussing the workings of knowledge traditions, including science' and allows 'us to see how these realities might be connected and where they should be kept separate'. It is in this respect that the theory of thought Deleuze and Guattari outline in *WIP* might inform education policy studies that take an interest in the different methodologies employed in arenas of policy production and analysis.

The philosophy of Deleuze and Guattari has been taken up in education policy studies recently (e.g. Thompson and Cook, 2012a, 2012b; Webb and Gulson, 2012, 2013) and, perhaps even to greater extent, in other areas of education research. However, unlike the work of other French theorists, such as Michel Foucault or Pierre Bourdieu, whose writings have influenced education policy studies over recent decades, there are no orthodoxies regarding the application of Deleuze and Guattari's concepts to empirical studies in education. While this is due in part to the more recent take up of their work, it also reflects an inherent character of their conceptual systems, which resist stabilisation as theoretical or methodological frameworks that can be mastered, communicated and applied. 'Unabashedly systematic, Deleuze and Guattari's philosophy is not by that token doctrinal, in the sense that it would allow itself to be reduced or represented by a set of conveniently enumerable theses' (Toscano, 2004: xiv). Deleuze and Guattari's concepts lend themselves to creation and reactivation in new fields rather than stable documentation and application. For Deleuze and Guattari, the vocation of philosophical thought is to participate in the immanent becoming of the world rather than to provide stable representations of the world from a transcendent point of survey.

For Deleuze, philosophy involves the creation of concepts that can be taken up again and again as tools for thought in relation to specific problematics: '[A] concept's power comes from the way it is repeated' (Deleuze, 1995: 147). This approach suggests that 'we should be interested in tools for thinking, not an exegesis of ideas' (Stengers, 2005: 151). This is not to suggest that a systematic account of Deleuze and Guattari's conceptual system cannot be elaborated, but rather that such elaboration, if it is to remain within the spirit of their thought, must aim at creative repetition of these concepts, intensifying their force by reactivating and reconnecting them in relation to new problems. Deleuze's philosophical methodology, particularly in his early monographs, involved the inhabitation of others' concepts to make them his own by creatively repeating them and, in doing so, producing conceptual 'shifting, slipping, dislocations and hidden emissions' (Deleuze, 1995: 6).

There will be no happy resolution in this chapter to the tension between working with Deleuze and Guattari's approach to philosophy as the creation of concepts and the expectation that one provide a clear communication of these concepts to facilitate their 'application'. The compromise here will be to provide an uncreative first repetition of concepts developed in *WIP*, in order to stage a second repetition, inflected by Isabelle Stengers' (2005) reading of *WIP*, which aims at reactivating these concepts in relation to the field of education policy studies.

First repetition: what is philosophy? What is science?

There are many contemporary inheritors of Deleuze and Guattari's work who, in repeating their concepts, have emphasised their transgressive and deterritorialising potential, including feminist poststructuralist thinkers concerned with challenging established categories and concepts to produce new lines of flight and accelerationist thinkers who attempt to take the deterritorialising force of Deleuze and Guattari's concepts to their limit. Here I pursue a more sober engagement with their theory of philosophy and science, emphasising the need to slow down thinking and to give situations the power to force us to think, rather than confirming us in the security of common sense (Stengers, 2005).

As Stengers has observed, *WIP* came as a disappointment to many readers who considered Deleuze and Guattari to be among the more radical philosophers of their generation, and who were not expecting a systematic analysis of science, philosophy and art that tends to sharpen the distinctions between them – each 'discipline must proceed with its own methods' (Deleuze and Guattari, 1994: 17) – rather than celebrating new hybridisations.

> Deleuze and Guattari were associated with the affirmation of productive connexions, the creation of deterritorializing processes escaping fixed identities, transgressing boundaries and static classifications, destroying the power of exclusive disjunction, that is the either/or alternatives, such as, for instance, doing either science or philosophy.
>
> *(Stengers, 2005: 151)*

In response to this disappointment Stengers develops a political reading of *WIP* and argues that Deleuze and Guattari were concerned with resistance to the coming dangers for thought posed by capitalism, including the claims of marketers to be the proper creators of concepts and the demands of technoscience for knowledge that 'works'. From this perspective, the sobriety that Deleuze and Guattari (1987: 344) advocated can be seen as creative strategy for resisting the demands of other practices that do not share the particular obligations of philosophy, science and art, and which place these creative adventures of thought at risk.

Deleuze and Guattari (1994) develop a constructivist and materialist account of philosophy, science and art as modes of thought (the latter will be put to one side here, although its relations to philosophy and science are integral to this conceptual system). Each confronts the chaos, which can be understood as the rapid emergence and disappearance of possibilities for thought that do not form into consistent ideas (what William James characterised as an intensively active gap in consciousness). Deleuze and Guattari (1994: 201) argue that

> [w]e require just a little order to protect us from the chaos. Nothing is more distressing than a thought that escapes itself, than ideas that fly off, that disappear hardly formed, already eroded by forgetfulness or precipitated into others that we no longer master.

Philosophy and science, in their own ways, give consistency to the chaos: philosophy by creating concepts and science by creating functions.

Science and philosophy both struggle against opinion, which shields us from the chaos through the reassurances of orthodoxy and relieves us of the demand to actually think. Deleuze and Guattari characterise opinions as 'functions of the lived' – functions whose arguments are consensual perceptions and affections (Stengers, 2005: 154) – and contrast these to the functions that science constructs and the concepts that philosophy creates through their distinctive processes. Philosophy and science are adventures of thought that require an encounter with the chaos and must therefore also struggle against the 'cliches of opinion' that prevent such encounters: 'the *struggle against chaos* does not take place without an affinity with the enemy, because another struggle develops and takes on more importance – the struggle *against opinion*, which claims to protect us from the chaos itself' (Deleuze and Guattari, 1994: 203).

Philosophical concepts are not discovered preformed: 'the concept is not given, it is created' (Deleuze and Guattari, 1994: 11). Concepts have multiple components and are produced in response to problems. Conceptual systems involve the laying out of concepts on what Deleuze and Guattari (1994: 21) call a plane of immanence and are situated in relationship to other concepts that make up this system.

> The concept is therefore both absolute and relative: it is relative to its own components, to other concepts, to the plane on which it is defined, and to the problems it is supposed to solve; but it is absolute through the condensation it carries out, the site it occupies on the plane, and the conditions it assigns to the problem.

Deleuze and Guattari provide the example the Cartesian *cogito* as a concept of the self. The statement, 'I think therefore I am', expresses a concept comprising three components – doubting, thinking and being – and provides the plane of immanence upon which the *cogito* is the first concept. The *cogito* thus constitutes a beginning point for a modern philosophical thought that does not presuppose other concepts (e.g. God), although it cannot escape reliance on subjective understandings or opinions about what it means to doubt, to think and to exist. This pre-philosophical understanding is the plane of immanence upon which the Cartesian conceptual system is constructed.

Deleuze and Guattari reject the view that philosophy is a matter of reflection, contemplation or the communication of ideas. Philosophy's task is not to provide clear representations of a world onto which the philosopher gazes from a transcendent position. Rather, philosophy involves an 'ontogenesis' because the concept 'posits itself and its object at the same time that it is created' (Deleuze and Guattari, 1994: 22). The creation of concepts calls forth alternative futures to those promised by the conditions and concepts of the present. Philosophical creation proceeds according to a pedagogy of the concept. This concept signal's Deleuze's privileging of learning as a process over knowledge as a product. The pedagogy of the concept designates philosophy's specific adventure of thought as the modification of the thinker through an encounter with concepts: 'The greatness of philosophy is measured by the nature of the events to which its concepts summon us or that it enables us to release in concepts' (Deleuze and Guattari, 1994: 34). Pedagogical encounters of this kind involve a creative violence – what Deleuze often described as 'witch's flight' – from which the thinker emerges (see Biesta, 2005).

While philosophy creates concepts, the vocation of science is the construction of functions (relationships between variables). Science confronts chaos in order to slow it down and to create functions, variables and systems of coordinates on a plane of reference. Through its specific practices and constraints, science translates opinion into matters of fact by establishing variable relationships between quantities. Commensuration is thus an important element of scientific thought. Indeed, 'the entire theory of functions depends on numbers' (Deleuze and Guattari, 1994: 119). In contrast to philosophy, which gives consistency to the chaos but does not exhaust the reserve of possibilities for thought in doing so, science makes certain possibilities actual by fixing them as facts or realities that require considerable effort to challenge.

Stengers (2005) provides a helpful example of science understood in these terms. The first experimental device – Galileo's inclined plane, which enabled the measurement of bodies falling through space – conferred on its user 'the power to transform a usual state of affairs, a consensual function of the lived perception of falling bodies [opinion], into a scientific matter of fact correlated to a scientific mathematical function' (Stengers, 2005: 156–157).

> Indeed, the power of the inclined plane was to transform the fact that heavy bodies do perceptively fall into an articulated fact, defined in terms of independent variables, variables whose value can be modified at will, and the articulation of which produces a functional (state) description.
>
> *(Stengers, 2005: 157)*

Scientific facts are created but they must be hard won and a particular set of conditions must be met before one's colleagues will acknowledge that a new fact has been produced. Science studies scholars have developed detailed accounts of the practices involved in creating scientific facts (e.g. Stengers, 2010; Latour, 1987).

It is important not to confuse Deleuze and Guattari's account of science as creative construction of functions with the strain of social constructivism that aims at demonstrating the relativity of all knowledge and, in doing so, undermines claims to truth. Deleuze and Guattari (1994: 130) make the important distinction between the truth of the relative and the relativity of truth, siding with the latter in their account. Science produces 'truths' from the relative – the chaos – according to its own specific practices and constraints. These truths are *relative* insofar as they are not discovered as preformed facts, but they are *true* insofar as they meet the specific demands of a scientific community of competent colleagues. There are good reasons to avoid critiques of science that represent facts as 'only relative' and as having no greater claim on us than opinions (Latour, 2004). This species of social constructivism proceeds by affirming the power of its deconstruction at the expense of the construction enabled by the obligations of scientific practices.

Much more could be said about Deleuze and Guattari's theory of philosophy and science. However, for the purposes of this chapter there are three important points to be made here. First, philosophy and science constitute different adventures of thought, although they share a struggle with chaos and opinion. Second, philosophical concepts and scientific functions must be constructed through particular kinds of events and when these occur new 'truths of the relative' emerge. Third, and perhaps most importantly here, philosophy and science can communicate in productive divergence with one another, when the methodologies of one discipline modulate those of another and blur overly distinct divisions between them, or when the creations of one discipline become the object of creation in another discipline (e.g. the concepts of scientific functions). In the latter case though, 'the rule is that the interfering discipline must proceed with its own methods' (Deleuze and Guattari, 1994: 217). This rule is aimed at using the creations of one adventure of thought to undermine the legitimacy, and thus the creative force, of another. As Stengers (2005: 158) observes, 'none of these adventures needs to belittle the other ones in order to affirm itself'; or, in other words, we should resist 'belief in the power of proofs to disqualify what they have no means to create' (Stengers, 2010: 82).

Second repetition: towards a politics of method

How might Deleuze and Guattari's theory of thought inform a politics of method that would focus on creating new relations between social theory and the proliferation of data in education policy? In responding to this question the first issue we must confront is Deleuze and Guattari's account of the relation between philosophy and *human* sciences. This response will already implicate us in a politics of method in which Deleuze and Guattari's concepts must be creatively repeated. The human sciences, among which it seems education research should be counted, were seen by Deleuze and Guattari as rivals to philosophy:

> The human sciences, and especially sociology, wanted to replace [philosophy]. But because philosophy, taking refuge in universals, increasingly misunderstood its vocation for creating concepts, it was no longer clear what was at stake. Was it a matter of giving up the creation of concepts for a rigorous human science or, alternatively, of transforming the nature of concepts by turning them into the collective representations or worldviews created by the vital, historical, and spiritual forces of different peoples?
>
> *(Deleuze and Guattari, 1994: 10)*

Deleuze and Guattari are ambivalent about whether human science succeeds in the struggle against opinion and 'wondered whether all the human sciences should be included in this category: however sophisticatedly presented or statistically verified they would constitute just scientific opinion' (Stengers, 2005: 154). We have to acknowledge that, in the assessment of Deleuze and Guattari, human sciences in their theoretical modes may only be pretenders to the creation of concepts and in their empirical modes may not meet the obligations required for the scientific creation of functions.

This assessment raises many questions, but the purpose of this chapter is simply to sketch a response to the following two questions:

1   How might we understand the use of theory in education policy studies in relation to Deleuze and Guattari's discussion of philosophy, science and opinion?; and
2   How might those who feel obliged to the practices of social theory engage with others who are obliged to scientific practices of educational measurement?

The OECD's education work, specifically PISA (see OECD, 2013), provides a helpful example of an influential arena of policy in which data are produced and used for a variety of purposes. PISA is a triennial large-scale educational assessment that was first conducted in 2000 and now covers more than sixty national and sub-national education systems globally. PISA tests the mathematical, reading and scientific literacy of 15 year olds, focusing on their capacity to apply knowledge to real-world problems. The tests include items relating to each of these three domains, as well as a questionnaire that collects information on students' attitudes and social backgrounds. The assessments employ a number of established psycho-metric methods, including matrix sampling and Rasch analysis. PISA data are claimed to be the creation of scientific measurement and this confers upon the data an authority and persuasive force with politicians, policy makers, some sections of the education research community and interested publics.

PISA numbers are generated using scientific methods that enable common sense perceptions of schooling – 'functions of the lived' – to be supplanted by descriptions of systems in terms of variable relationships between different quantities. The success of PISA is attributable to the capacity of the data it generates to confront consensual perceptions of national and sub-national schooling performance with matters of fact based on measurements and comparisons of students' test performance. This confrontation is often described as a 'PISA shock', which can be seen as a confrontation between facts and opinion. Further, PISA and other large-scale international and national assessments are a matter of concern for psychometricians who feel the obligations of a scientific community and who constitute a network of competent colleagues who give their assent or otherwise to the data created through large-scale educational assessments.

If education 'policy as numbers' can be seen to emerge, in part, from the practices of a scientific community, then how might theoretically-informed policy analysts engage with these practices? To respond to this question it is necessary to consider whether social theory can be aligned with philosophy as concept creation. Clearly the affinity between these practices depends on how social theory is defined. Writing about theory in educational research, Anyon (2009: 3) has defined theory as a 'coherent structure of concepts' that 'help us to understand and explain discursive and social phenomenon' and to provide 'a model of the way that discourse and social systems work and can be worked upon'. If we are to find affinities with Deleuze and Guattari's theory of philosophy then some modification of this definition is required. This might be effected through a shift of emphasis to see the development of models and explanations as a process of concept construction oriented toward pragmatic interventions – *working upon the social* – rather than explanatory representations. Social theory can be understood as an encounter with the social that might generate events in which concepts are created, rather than as an overlay of preformed concepts to explain or represent the social. From this perspective, education policy researchers that feel obliged as practitioners of social theory, rather than as producers of data, might find affinities between their practice and that of philosophy as conceived by Deleuze and Guattari.

This brings us to the question of the relationship between scientific practices associated with data production and usage in contexts such as those of PISA and policy analysis as theoretical concept creation to work upon the social. Two aspects of the relations between these practices will be discussed. First, an obligation to theory does not authorise the use of theory to expose the limits of psychometric practices and to denounce the creations of these practices. Rather, social theory can seek to foster 'a vital communication between science and philosophy's diverging adventures' in order 'to give each of them some means to resist their respective and probable destruction' (Stengers, 2005: 160). Here Stengers emphasises the fragility of philosophical and scientific practices in the context of knowing capitalism and the need for a politics of method oriented toward strengthening resistance among practices rather than mutual poisoning.

The concepts of Deleuze and Guattari might thus help to recast the task of *critical* education policy studies as one of engagement with the commensurative work that informs policy insofar as this work constitutes another adventure of thought. This openness may also encourage openness from the side of the scientific practices that are engaged, potentially opening up what Stengers (2005: 166) describes as

> a line of escape from the Great Sad Problem of scientific reductionism, and its poisoning consequence: the very sad role accepted by philosophers when they see their task as that of defending human values, experience, or responsibility against its reduction to scientific explanatory frameworks.

Along this line we might create alternatives to critical encounters between practices that aim to delimit and denounce scientific practices or to defend the chaos against measurement in the name of an alliance between certain philosophical concepts and a particular 'function of the lived': consensual belief in the value of the 'immeasurable'. Whether such alternatives lead to less defensive and reductive conceptions of scientific practices is a matter for experimentation.

This brings us to the second point regarding the relationship between philosophy, science and opinion. Stengers (2005) argues that philosophy first, and then science, have drawn authority from their opposition to opinion, but that this can be dangerous for both. For example, the challenge of social constructivism to science was based on recognition that the legitimacy of science depends on its distinction from opinion and then undermining this distinction. Philosophy and science thus both pay a price for the opposition to opinion from which they derive their legitimacy, insofar as the grounds of this opposition can be eroded through external critiques. Rather than an alliance between philosophy and science based on a struggle against opinion, as suggested in *WIP*, Stengers proposes a reading of Deleuze and Guattari that would lead in another direction. Acknowledgement of the obligations that must be met for philosophy and science to generate their specific creations, and resisting the opportunity to denounce the obligations of others, can also be extended to other communities whose creations have long been dismissed as opinion by philosophy and science.

Theoretically-informed policy analysis might thus support interventions in arenas of policy practice by engaging new publics in the production and analysis of knowledge for and about policy, giving policy arenas the power to force new kinds of thinking about policy problems beyond the often consensual views that prevail in academic communities. For example, researchers in England have drawn on this theorisation of scientific practices to bring the situated knowledge of publics gathered around issues such as flooding into connection with scientific expertise and models, honouring what gives each practice its distinctiveness and finding ways for them to productively interfere with one another in relation to particular problems (see Whatmore and Landström, 2011).

Conclusion

This chapter has introduced concepts drawn from the theory of thought elaborated by Deleuze and Guattari in *WIP*. The chapter aimed to begin conceptualising a politics of method for education policy studies in an era of knowing capitalism. Deleuze and Guattari's concepts of philosophy and science, it has been argued, can help us to pose questions about our intellectual commitments as education policy scholars, how we understand our methodologies and how we relate to the practices of others. One implication of such questioning is the view that social theory and its use in education policy studies risks marginalisation if it provides a reassuring critical distance from which to dismiss or delimit the proliferation of social data and commensurative work in policy arenas. To take the different practices of thought involved in policy processes as an explicit concern of education policy studies is to engage in a politics of method that raises questions about the relationships between these practices, their consequences for policy and the consequences of policy. The repetition of Deleuze and Guattari's concepts, inflected by the commentary of Stengers, is offered here as an example of how we might begin to pursue such a politics.

Theory might play a productive role in negotiations between practices in policy arenas *not* as critical judge, but as an engaged mediator that struggles against authorising divisions between different ways of knowing, creating concepts that might help to spark new connections and interferences between theory, measurement and situated knowledge. Instead of mobilising concepts in an external critique of scientific practices of commensuration that produce numbers for policy, theory might be approached as a means for creating conceptual systems that enable new relations with these practices and new social relations more generally. In the era of knowing capitalism, it would be a mistake to confuse science and public opinion as targets for critiques that preserve the distinctiveness and sophistication of an increasingly marginal practice of theoretically-informed policy analysis. This confusion holds considerable risks for thought at a time when consensual views are being presented as concepts and facts for the purposes of control and profit, enabling those who mobilise them to dismiss the objections of various publics (including academics) as mere opinion.

References

Anyon, J. (2009). Introduction: Critical social theory, educational research and intellectual agency. In J. Anyon, M. Dumas, D. Linville, K. Nolan, M. Perez, E. Tuck and J. Weiss (Eds.), *Theory and educational research: Toward critical social explanation* (pp. 1–24). New York and London: Routledge.

Ball, S. J. (2008). *The education debate.* Bristol, UK: The Policy Press.

Ball, S. J. (2012). *Global education Inc: New policy networks and the neo-liberal imaginary.* London: Routledge.

Ball, S. J. and Junemann, C. (2012). *Networks, new governance and education.* Bristol, UK: The Policy Press.

Biesta, G. (2005). *Beyond learning: Democratic education for a human future.* Boulder, CO and London: Paradigm Publishers.

Bowker, G. C., Baker, K., Miller, F. and Ribes, D. (2010). Toward information infrastructure studies: Ways of knowing in a networked environment. In J. Husinger, L. Klastrup and M. M. Allen (Eds.), *International handbook of internet research* (pp. 97–117). Dordrecht, Netherlands and London: Springer.

Deleuze, G. (1995). *Negotiations, 1972–1990.* New York: Columbia University Press.

Deleuze, G. and Guattari, F. (1987). *A thousand plateaus: Capitalism and schizophrenia.* Minneapolis, MN: University of Minnesota Press.

Deleuze, G. and Guattari, F. (1994). *What is philosophy?* New York: Columbia University Press.

Espeland, W. N. and Stevens, M. L. (1998). Commensuration as a social process. *Annual Review of Sociology, 24*, 313–343.

Latour, B. (1987). *Science in action.* Cambridge, MA: Harvard University Press.

Latour, B. (2004). Why has critique run out of steam? From matters of fact to matters of concern. *Critical Inquiry, 30*(2), 225–248.

Lingard, B. (2011). Policy as numbers: Ac/counting for educational research. *The Australian Educational Researcher, 38*(4), 355–382.

OECD (2013). *PISA 2012 results: What students know and can do (volume I, revised edition, February 2014).* Paris: OECD Publishing.

Rose, N. (1991). Governing by numbers: Figuring out democracy. *Accounting, Organizations and Society, 16*(7), 673–692.

Rose, N. (1999). *Powers of freedom: Reframing political thought.* Cambridge, UK: Cambridge University Press.

Savage, M. and Burrows, R. (2007). The coming crisis of empirical sociology. *Sociology, 41*(5), 885–899.

Stengers, I. (2005). Deleuze and Guattari's last enigmatic message. *Angelaki, 10*(2), 151–167.

Stengers, I. (2010). *Cosmopolitics I.* Minneapolis, MN and London: University of Minnesota Press.

Thompson, G. and Cook, I. (2012a). The logics of good teaching in an audit culture: A Deleuzian analysis. *Educational Philosophy and Theory, 45*(3), 243–258.

Thompson, G. and Cook, I. (2012b). Spinning in the NAPLAN ether: 'Postscript on the control societies' and the seduction of education in Australia. *Deleuze Studies, 6*(4), 564–584.

Thrift, N. (2005). *Knowing capitalism.* Sage: London.

Toscano, A. (2004). Preface: The coloured thickness of a problem. In E. Alliez (Ed.), *The signature of the world: What is Deleuze and Guattari's philosophy?* (pp. ix–xxv). New York and London: Continuum.

Verran, H. (2008). Science and the dreaming. *Issues Magazine, 82,* 23–26.

Verran, H. (2012). The changing lives of measures and values: From centre stage in the fading 'disciplinary' society to pervasive background instrument in the emergent 'control' society. *The Sociological Review, 59*(s2), 60–72.

Webb, T. and Gulson, K. N. (2012). Policy prolepsis in education: Encounters, becomings, and phantasms. *Discourse: Studies in the Cultural Politics of Education, 33*(1), 87–99.

Webb, T. and Gulson, K. N. (2013). Policy intensions and the folds of the self. *Educational Theory, 63*(1), 51–68.

Whatmore, S. J. and Landström, C. (2011). Flood apprentices: An exercise in making things public. *Economy and Society, 40*(4), 582–610.

4

DERRIDA

The 'impossibility' of deconstructing educational policy enactment

Greg Vass

Dear reader,

I am going to think and work with Derrida and the intriguing 'happening' with which he is perhaps most widely associated, *deconstruction*. I am writing this as an open letter, because as suggested by Royle,[1] there is something about this approach that resonates with the nature of deconstruction itself, namely it is a metaphysically disturbing act. What do I mean by this? Most immediately, it unsettles the familiar formal mode of academic writing, while concurrently invoking the sense of privileging the spoken word. Taking up this approach is a performative critique of Western philosophies privileging of the 'metaphysics of presence' and was central to the work of Derrida. Writing a letter also invites the reader to reflect on the temporal and contextual slippage that occurs between (for example) the act of writing, what the writing is focused on, who the reader is, and what they are read-ing for. What do I mean by this? It gestures to an awareness of the sorts of traces that are left unspoken in discursive exchanges; I am writing a letter to and for you, though I don't know you, while in many respects I am also writing for myself. More than this, I am also *now* sitting in my office writing about research, however this 'data' was *from* several years ago, but it is being constructed *for* future use. I may be getting a little ahead of myself, at this stage my point is to simply acknowledge the vague and veiled entanglements between speech, writing and the reading of texts that arguably motivated Derrida to pen *Of grammatology*,[2] which in turn introduced his thoughts on deconstruction to international attention. In addition to exploring this line of thinking in a little more depth, in the remainder of the letter I will consider Derrida's invitation and challenge to engage with concepts such as 'logocentrism', 'absent presence', 'erasure' and 'aporias' in relation to the deconstruction and the work we undertake.

To begin with then, as is widely noted, Derrida vehemently avoided offering a definitive explanation of what deconstruction is, should be or how to go about it;

he was also very clear in making the point that it was not a research method as such. Emphatically articulating this view, in *Letter to a Japanese friend* he explains that deconstruction is not an analysis, a critique, method, act or operation, if it is anything, it is a happening that is ongoing.[3] Perhaps this is why he chose to write about deconstruction on occasion in the form of a letter,[4] a textual style that offers the illusion of a conversation taking place as it is happening – perhaps Derrida even considered writing a letter a form of deconstruction?[5] I hope so! This begs the question however, if Derrida stressed concerns about the take up of deconstruction as a methodological and analytical framework, why put deconstruction forward in the context of a book that explicitly encourages readers to engage with the utility of theory in education research? Answering this will involve telling you a little bit about how and why I came to start thinking about Derrida in relation to my research.

My interest in the work of Derrida stemmed from my uncertainties with analysing interview transcripts with teachers about recent education policy initiatives. The interviews honed in on the recently introduced 'gap' education policies that are concerned with addressing disparities in educational achievements, attendance and retention when Indigenous and non-Indigenous learners are compared.[6] While noting similarities in what was said and how things were expressed, I started noticing what appeared to be cautiously avoided, and I wondered if these discursive patterns and practices might be more important than what the teachers were literally articulating. I was unsure what to methodologically and analytically 'do' with this funny sort of 'non data' – what Elizabeth St. Pierre might describe as 'transgressive data'.[7] I asked myself if this interest was shifting my investigation away from the more familiar sort of tripartite implementation, formulation or product policy analysis, and if so, how was I to account for this? In addition to questioning what is meant by terms such as 'data', St. Pierre suggests that deconstruction can help with questioning the use of language coupled with our researcher reliance on language, and with her encouragement I started considering how some of Derrida's ideas might assist me methodologically with this sort of policy analysis.[8] This line of thinking was highlighted for me in the work of Mazzie,[9] with her approach challenging me to engage with the limits and limitations, the boundaries of what is known and knowable, with what is said and unsaid, during interviews about education policy.

Next however, I am going to talk a little about the broader educational research context (or episteme) that I learnt that deconstruction and policy analysis connects with. The education policy research 'field' has undergone shifting epistemological and methodological influences since the 1970s, creating an impression of the researcher gaze moving from somewhat tangible objects of research (i.e. policy documents), through to more amorphous ebbs and flows of power and influence (i.e. policy as discourse that influences behaviour).[10] While not wanting to be too reductive, the traditional or historical emphasis largely appears to be concerned with what policy is, where it comes from, and what it does. But I am also mindful of the distinction regarding analysis *of* and *for* policy, particularly within the current climate of 'evidence-based' research.[11] Importantly, the move towards poststructuralist approaches like deconstruction enabled asking different sorts of questions such as the 'fundamental question of whether the recipients and readers of policies have a sense of agency'.[12] Focusing on *a sense of agency* strikes me as both an interesting and potentially productive direction to take policy analysis, this is because more attention is needed that concentrates on a broader range of roles and positions involved in working with education policy than is sometimes the case.[13] This seems a significant yet easily overlooked point of concern – with teachers central to this, as clearly the constraints and opportunities they *feel* plays a role in how they go about enacting education policy.

In my case, what teachers said about policy and the actions they undertook were important. However, the stilted, stunted and evasive moments in the responses that punctuated the interviews, communicated an unsettled and unsettling awareness of their role and responsibilities in relation to the enactment of policy. Deconstruction offered me a way of thinking and closely reading these sorts of moments, to explore the instabilities and silences within and outside their textual structures.[14] This is an ephemeral moment that is readily overlooked in research on the policy cycle.[15] Located beyond policy as text, what is explicitly said in relation to policy, or the practices arising from policy, coming to an awareness of my witnessing these deconstructing moments (in the transcripts) helped me to start considering the deeper implications and unintentional effects of policy. For me, these were moments such as when the teachers presented themselves in seemingly contradictory ways as unknowing knowers of the gap policy, or as empowered teachers that were powerless to address the social justice aspirations of the policy. In this sense, the teachers were communicating a complex and contradictory feeling of agency in relation to the education policy framework.

As a closing thought on this part of the letter, it is perhaps salient to raise the point that the time, or context, that the work of Derrida emerged is significant. During the 1960s and 70s, when he and other poststructuralist thinkers were coming to notoriety at the forefront of a wave that questioned and critically challenged the metanarratives that had come to dominate 'modernity', he famously said that 'there is nothing outside the text'. Not without his critics, this is the sort of misunderstood shorthand that resulted in Derrida being viewed by some as nihilistic and potentially dangerous. However, this observation from Derrida goes to the very core of his philosophical concerns and the sort of shift in thinking and awareness he championed. He is referring here to the point that there is no way of getting outside of language; that we need language to explain language. Said another way, we need signs to try and describe or explain the signified, but the signs we rely on are connected to other signifiers. From this sort entanglement is the acknowledgment that there is no way of getting to 'a truth', and that we need more sophisticated understandings of the ways language works, and the ways we put language to work.

Derrida reminds us then, that there is no point of 'origin' for the signs (words) we use, there is no 'transcendental' signifier that is 'absolutely present outside a system of differences'.[16] I like the way Jackson introduces this idea when she says, 'Utterances – either written or spoken – do not have presence or origin; they have both a partial presence and partial absence'.[17] This all stems from Derrida's concern with the 'metaphysics of presence', the 'contract between words and meanings', which rely on a hierarchy of oppositions.[18] This thinking is grounded in Western philosophy and privileges the pursuit and emphasis being placed on a 'full or pure "presence" as the supreme value by which all reality can be judged'.[19] In other words, 'presence' is (assumed to be) the 'essence of the signified', with the proximity of the signified to the signifier impacting on the meaning-making ensembles researchers contribute to (re)constructing.[20]

To try and make this a little clearer, I am now going to turn attention to some of the other ideas linked with deconstruction. I will engage with each of them here separately, however, this should not be read as a marking the ideas out as 'tools' of deconstruction that are to be picked up and analytically put to work for particular purposes. Remembering that Derrida was a philosopher first and foremost, his work aimed to build and contribute to a sum total of thinking and awareness that is greater than the compartmentalised elements when atomised in this way. If I was to try and characterise this branch of his life work, I would tentatively suggest that he was interested in the role and uses of language that make things known and knowable, or said another way, how meaning is constructed in and through discourse. For this, as noted above, the 'sign and the signifier' are important ideas that permeate the concepts I am going to discuss here.

Logocentrism

One of Derrida's central concerns relates to *logocentrism*, the privileging and emphasising of the spoken word over the written as a more genuine or 'truthful' insight into the 'thoughts, conscious or intentions' of people.[21] On the surface of it, this seems to be an important and critical reminder that should raise questions for anybody engaging in interviews as part of their research, as there seems a high risk of logocentrically valuing the sort of 'truths' that are offered by interview data. Even when we present verbatim transcripts, we run the risk of implying that this in some way is a more 'truthful' voice of our participants – this is a discursive sleight of hand that suggests they are 'present' in our texts. For Derrida, the relationship between the written and spoken word is more complex and interactive than accepting that the written is a representation of the spoken.[22] In a moment I will speak a little more about the reliance of logocentrism on the 'metaphysics of the presence', for now, my point is to draw attention to Derrida's criticism of the assumed stability and coherence between the signified and the signifier.[23] This is part and parcel of his broader interests with the role and influence of binary oppositions as shaping Western thinking, so his thoughts on deconstruction can be viewed as a way of interfering with the 'hierarchy of opposition between speech and writing'.[24]

It is with these sorts of concerns in mind that Jackson and Mazzei encourage us to be on the lookout *with* Derrida for openings in our transcripts that 'present a consideration of moments when deconstruction is happening'.[25] This is more to do with the structural arrangements of text, not in a literal way, but in a way that accepts spoken and written language is part of network of differences and relationships.[26] For example, in the context of my research, when the participants spoke of the education policy as seeking to address the 'disadvantage' of Indigenous students, this is part of a meaning-making ensemble. In other words, there cannot be a sense of being 'disadvantaged' without a connecting understanding and awareness of some experiencing 'advantages' in education. By extension, 'disadvantage' is typically 'known' to be linked with markers such as socio-economic status, language, race and so on, which then serves for many as the foundation of the deficit discourse in education. The very prospect of 'knowing' discrimination is relationally reliant on 'knowing' privilege. How does a teacher then talk about and work towards eliminating 'disadvantage' without also eradicating 'privilege'? This seems impossible!

Jackson and Mazzei suggest we need to be on the 'lookout' for moments in our transcripts when the blurring of this sort of binary thinking comes to the surface. These 'happenings' are important and potentially insightful because they offer more than coherence or corroboration, rather, they can help with drawing attention to 'tensions, inconsistencies, omissions, and moments of destabilization'.[27] Within the sort of research I was undertaking, these were moments when concerns with colour-blindness and meritocracy emerged. For me, this meant locating colour-blindness and meritocracy as an institutional and systemic issue, rather than as an aberration of 'extreme' individuals.[28] Importantly then, the intention of this approach is not to unnecessarily critique or question the stories we encounter from participants in our studies, rather it is to look for 'snags' in the broader discursive fabric in which these exchanges are situated, and to then 'tear' at 'that which we have unproblematically come to accept'.[29]

Absent presence

Entangled with this, the role and influence of 'presence' is fundamental to Derrida's concerns about the workings of Western language and thinking. For Derrida, there is no 'original' starting place or point that 'meaning' derives from, but rather, there is the 'production of differences itself'.[30] In other words, the use of language relies on an understanding or awareness of something that is 'absent' in order to render something 'present' (in the utterance) as meaningful. The notion of *absent presence* is a Derridian reference to the 'trace' that already 'inhabits our language before we use it', imprinting our words with meaning prior to their use.[31] This idea can be helpful because it reminds us that the use of signs to represent the signified remains reliant on the absence of the binary partner. This was gestured to above in relation to 'disadvantage', with the absent presence being the unspoken and discomforting notion of 'advantage' that permeated the interviews with the participants in my study.

In some respects, this seems to go to the core of qualitative research itself, as the very idea of observing and listening to others, and then writing about them, evidently involves a sizable distance being travelled between the research 'field' and what is eventually encountered in books and journals. As a result of the research process itself, the signifier becomes far removed from the signified, resulting in binaries such as self–other, researcher–observer, insider–outsider raising concerns about the potential for distorted understandings and misrepresentations in the work we produce. Acknowledging and accepting this problematic understanding of the ways binaries 'work' in relation to the type of work we undertake as researchers, places a set of responsibilities on those involved in research and moves closer to highlighting the sort of political and ethical 'charge' that deconstruction entails.[32]

An awareness and consideration of the influence of absent presence can make a valuable contribution to education policy analysis, particularly in terms of how we go about constructing representations of the work undertaken. There is no avoiding the writing dimension of the research process. However, with writing, we are back with concerns to do with 'truths' and the sorts of 'gaps' that occur between what we see/hear, what we think, what is put down in words/signs, and how this representation is read.[33] As MacLure cautions, 'If research is to tangle with deconstruction, it must be acknowledged that it is always possible for meanings and messages to go astray or awry – to miss their mark – because of the gap that writing interposes'.[34] Despite ten years passing, her worries about the influential pressures of undertaking and presenting 'transparent' and 'evidence'-based research still ring true. Taking up deconstruction, requires a vigilance to remain wary of attempts to make our research 'relevant' and 'accessible',[35] with the reminder of the absent presence helping and encouraging us to reimagine how we go about constructing texts.

Under erasure

One such example of a how we can approach constructing texts in different sorts of ways, is the notion of *sous rapture*, or placing words 'under erasure' by writing them down and then crossing them out. This serves the purpose of simultaneously highlighting the (in)significance *and* questioning the necessity of the words.[36] Spivak explains in the introduction to *Of grammatology*, that this can involve putting a strike through elements of a text, resulting in the words remaining visible and present for the reader at the same time that they are presented as unwanted or problematic, with the example of ~~truth~~ used in this instance.[37] The concept is based upon Derrida's concerns with the slippage in meaning and understanding that occurs between the signified and the signifier. 'Truth' offers a helpful illustration of this idea, as the prospect of there ever being a universal 'truth' is impossible, indeed if/when it emerges in interviews, it raises questions about how we analytically and ethically account for this subjective view. Accordingly, there is always an instability in the meaning-making between what is said and what it refers to, meaning that 'meaning is always elusive, always deferred, always multiple, always somewhat paradoxical'.[38]

There may be a temptation for novice researchers to put 'erasure' to work, as on the surface it appears a readily accessible strategy. Perhaps this is why MacLure offers the reminder to be cautious when working with these sorts of ideas in and for education research, while at the same time suggesting that putting things 'under erasure . . . is one of those impossible things that we cannot do without'.[39] Rather than taking up a literal approach to this concept, she talks about this involving 'putting signifiers (such as data, truth, narrative) under erasure . . . to engage in the process of using them and troubling them simultaneously, rendering them inaccurate yet necessary'.[40] To help illustrate what this looks like and what happens when we approach representations of our research by putting text under erasure, I am going to use a brief example from my study.

In this excerpt, one of the participants explains her understanding of the 'gap' policy context. Within her response, the racialised binary categories used to describe people are put under erasure in a way that opens up different types of thinking and understanding the meaning-making that takes place.

> ~~Indigenous~~ people tend to die earlier than ~~non=Indigenous~~ people, they tend to have lower educational standards than ~~non=Indigenous~~ people, they tend to have . . . umm . . . you know, more health problems than ~~non=Indigenous~~ Australians have, so all of these issues . . . are there as a result of the inequality that still exists in Australia, between ~~Indigenous~~ and ~~non=Indigenous~~ Australians. And that is where the policies are good. [pauses] But . . . are we really, kind of . . . asking these ~~Indigenous~~ people whether they want to . . . live . . . like ~~non=Indigenous~~ people or whether they want to . . . live . . . how they want to live, and what input do they have into . . . the policies and what control do they have over their own lives . . . umm . . . how does it all work?

Reading through the comments, you can get a sense of the teacher struggling to reconcile what she perceives on a deep level to be limitations of the 'gap' policy framework, yet her reliance on the language of the policy itself, entangles her language choices and culminates in a problematic result on the surface. However, putting the text under erasure invites a plurality of readings: the teacher's reliance on making sense of the 'gap' policy as framed by the binary Indigenous and non-Indigenous; her discomfort with this framing as she raises concerns about the inequalities and a lack of understanding and communication between *people*; and gesturing towards a racialised reading of the inequities. In the textual representation with certain terms under erasure, attention is shifted away from the racialised binary underpinnings of the explanation, while simultaneously acknowledging that they remain influential.

When analysing the comments, it might be tempting (or 'easy') to highlight the impossibility of realising the social justice aspirations that underpin the 'closing the gap' framework because they are premised on binary, essentialised and hierarchically framed relationships and understandings. Deconstruction is not an exercise in looking closely at interview comments, pulling them apart, and then critically re-constructing an understanding or view of what is said, what it means, or engaging with the politics of where the comments may or may not have come from. This would be a somewhat crude interpretation of deconstruction for reconstruction, which Derrida was critical of.[41] In their current form, from the perspective of this teacher, it appears as though there is no way for education practices to move towards dismantling the discriminating outcomes the 'gap' policy seeks to address. This seems to be the sort of predicament that Derrida cautions about in relation to the limits and limitations of binary thinking. Putting text under erasure, is an invitation to look for moments and the possibilities beyond this type of thinking, and for me, this is why the teacher's comments are a happening, an 'event' that offers a glimpse of deconstruction taking place.[42] A potentially more productive and constructive view of her comments then, is to embrace the challenge that they present, to think beyond, to push the boundaries and limits, to envisage the possibilities of doing education policy ~~research~~ differently.

Aporias

In a couple of parts of this letter I have mentioned the 'impossibility' of enacting social justice oriented education policy. This understanding is built on my reading of the interview transcripts, when I encountered instances involving explanations that justified inaction in relation to the 'gap' policies. In many cases, the teacher's reasoning argued that enacting these 'special measures' would simultaneously disadvantage other (non-Indigenous) groups. This is a sort of paradox, or what Derrida might describe as an *aporia*.[43] Dimitriadis and Kimberlis explain aporias as 'logical contradictions', they discuss Derrida's thinking in relation to the impossible–possible human conditions such as the ethics of responsibility involved with pursuing social justice aspirations for any one particular group as jointly involving displacing social justice concerns with another.[44]

It is in this sort of space that I think meritocracy and colour-blindness could potentially be viewed as aporias. This is because the motivation and desire to treat everybody 'equally' displaces acknowledging and working towards the sort of socially just equity that accepts education is not a 'fair' playing field, and indeed that there are strong grounds to justify treating people differently as the way forward in realising equality of outcomes. For me, this speaks to the sort of contradiction permeating the silences and discomfort of the teachers I interviewed, as they struggled to reconcile the aspiration of pursuing and emphasising socially just educational practices for Indigenous students in ways that were understood to be at the expense of non-Indigenous students. These are the sorts of deconstructive happenings to be on the 'lookout' for, revealing 'blind spots' or 'points of impasse' that draw attention to the failings of, and complications that can arise from, a reliance on binary frameworks.[45]

The idea of aporias extend well beyond this sort of example though, as they have an important role to play in the responsibilities we take on as researchers, indeed according to Derrida, 'without experiencing aporia, there is no responsibility'.[46] It is then, with half on eye on the politics and ethics of research(er) responsibilities, that deconstruction can potentially play a role in research practices that stimulate or provoke the types of actions that social justice polices attempt to inspire.[47] Derrida describes deconstruction as an 'ethics of affirmation' and charges it with the responsibility of 'changing the world'.[48] Discussing this in relation to education policy, Stronach and MacLure posit that Derrida challenges us to undertake 'deconstructive praxis' as a way forward with this, indeed that it would be 'irresponsible to continue to privilege the escape clauses of a foundational appeal'.[49]

This seems a pretty good spot to start drawing this letter to a close. I have talked through how I came to think about and work with some of Derrida's ideas about deconstruction in relation to my research, and in doing so I have tried to show some of the wider potential for methodologically engaging with some of these ideas in and for education policy analysis. This is of course not complete in the sense that I have not discussed the 'trace', 'differánce' or 'arch-writing' for example, all of which also contribute to engagements with deconstruction – but this will have to wait for another time. My approach has not been an effort in talking about how to 'do' deconstruction, nor have I tried to focus too much on 'why' deconstruction should (or should not) be engaged with – though this is implied. Rather than this, the approach has worked towards contributing to a line of conversation regarding some of the implications for qualitative research once we start asking different sorts of questions about the 'data' we work with. This then, connects with the final element in the brief for the chapter, suggestions for further reading.

Does it go without saying that Derrida himself is notoriously difficult to read? Of course his original texts are in French, so there are implications if this is to be considered as a starting point. He was also fundamentally concerned with words and language, particularly with how discourse works as a meaning-making process, and hence his approach to writing in many ways is dense, abstract, circuitous, vague . . . did I mention it is difficult? Having a firm grasp on a lot of the classic texts he works with would also be helpful, but finding the time to read Husserl, Saussure, Heidegger, and Nietzsche (to name a few) prior to even getting to Derrida in this day and age is a challenge. *Of grammatology* is a key text, at least read the introduction by Spivak, and then selectively make your way through some of the other sections. I have also mentioned a couple of the 'letters' he wrote, then there are some 'interviews' with him, all of which are helpful in many ways as they offer a more concentrated or focused encounter with some of Derrida's thinking. However, I think getting a little familiarity with some of the secondary texts prior to more deeply engaging with Derrida himself has much merit as a strategy.

For me, Maggie MacLure[50] was a helpful starting point and is a text I continue to return too, it helps me more deeply think about deconstruction in relation to the big 'D' types of discourse we encounter and work within as education researchers. More recently she co-wrote with Erica Burman[51] a really helpful shorter piece that also works towards offering a more applied or practical sort of discussion about deconstruction. Alecia Jackson and Lisa Mazzei have written a collection of pieces both individual and collaboratively that work with ideas from Derrida to help illustrate the usefulness and relevance of deconstruction in education research. However, their most recent effort, *Thinking with theory in qualitative research*[52] (2012) is perhaps the most concise in terms of offering clear explanations and examples of how they approach this in practice. Lastly, the offering from

Bradley[53] is a succinct entry point into *Of grammatology* itself, offering a readily accessible 'guide to the text'.

I would like to express my thanks to the editors for this opportunity to consider and talk about the 'impossibility' of working with deconstruction in relation to the education policy research. While far from being an exhaustive discussion, the ideas from Derrida I mention here were particularly helpful in relation to my work and hopefully you can see why this was the case. As such, I now also hope that in some small way this letter is able to offer a useful contribution to your research and you can see some of the potential and possibilities for education policy research that engages with Derrida and his thoughts on deconstruction.

Yours sincerely,
Greg Vass

Notes

1 Royle, 2000: 4.
2 Published in English in 1976 with an Introduction from Spivak, Dimitriadis and Kimberlis (2006: 104) offer the reminder that this was first published in 1967 in French.
3 Derrida, 1998: 3–4.
4 Royle, 2000.
5 For the *Afterword: Toward an ethic of discussion* (in *Limited Inc,* 1988), Derrida once again takes up letter writing, providing three reasons, one of which is most readily identifiable as deconstructive by addressing the 'essential predicament [*trouble*] of all speech and of all writing, that of *context* and of *destination*' (original italics).
6 Here, I am referring to *Closing the gap on Indigenous disadvantage: A challenge for Australia* (DFHCSIA, 2009) and *Closing the gap. Education strategy* (DET, 2009).
7 St. Pierre, 1997.
8 St. Pierre, 1997: 177.
9 Mazzei, 2003: 361.
10 Blackmore and Lauder, 2011: 190.
11 Rizvi and Lingard, 2010.
12 Blackmore and Lauder, 2011: 192.
13 Ball, Maguire and Braun, 2012.
14 Hitchcock, 2008.
15 Ball (1994) coined the 'policy cycle' in reference to the 'messy, often contested and non-linear' facets of policy processes and the contexts they are located within (cited in Rizvi and Lingard, 2010: 6).
16 Derrida, 2007: 249.
17 Jackson, 2009: 168.
18 Burman and MacLure, 2011: 286.
19 Bradley, 2008: 6.
20 Dimitriadis and Kimberlis, 2006: 106.
21 Burman and MacLure, 2011: 287.
22 Dimitriadis and Kimberlis, 2006: 105.
23 Dimitriadis and Kimberlis, 2006: 106.
24 Burman and MacLure, 2011: 287.
25 Jackson and Mazzei, 2012: 16.
26 Bradley, 2008.
27 Jackson and Mazzei, 2012: 16.
28 Castagno, 2014: 6.

29 Jackson and Mazzei, 2012: 17.
30 Bradley, 2008: 73.
31 Jackson and Mazzei, 2012: 19.
32 MacLure, 2003: 179.
33 MacLure, 2003: 165.
34 MacLure, 2003: 168.
35 MacLure, 2003: 170.
36 Dimitriadis and Kimberlis, 2006: 103.
37 Spivak – cited in Derrida, 1976.
38 Dimitriadis and Kimberlis, 2006: 103.
39 Burman and MacLure, 2011: 288.
40 Jackson and Mazzei, 2012: 18.
41 Derrida, 2001.
42 Jackson and Mazzei, 2012: 18.
43 Jackson and Mazzei, 2012: 17.
44 Dimitriadis and Kimberlis, 2006: 107–108.
45 Burman and MacLure, 2011: 287.
46 Cited in Koro-Ljungberg, 2010: 606.
47 Trifonas, 2004: 40.
48 Derrida, 2001: 180.
49 Stronarch and MacLure, 1997: 95–98.
50 MacLure, 2003.
51 Burman and MacLure, 2011.
52 Mazzei and Jackson, 2012.
53 Bradley, 2008.

References

Ball, S., Maguire, M. and Braun, A. (2012). *How schools do policy: Policy enactments in secondary schools*. London: Routledge.

Blackmore, J. and Lauder, H. (2011). Researching policy. In B. Somekh and C. Lewin (Eds.), *Theory and methods in social research* (2nd edn) (pp. 190–197). London: Sage.

Bradley, A. (2008). *Derrida's of grammatology*. Bloomington, IN: Indiana University Press.

Burman, E. and MacLure, M. (2011). Deconstruction as a method of research. In B. Somekh and C. Lewin (Eds.), *Theory and methods in social research* (2nd edn) (pp. 286–294). London: Sage.

Castagno, A. (2014). *Educated in Whiteness: Good intentions and diversity in schools*. Minneapolis, MN: University of Minnesota Press.

Department of Education and Training (DET). (2009). *Closing the gap: Education strategy*. Brisbane: Queensland Government. Retrieved from www.dss.gov.au/sites/default/files/documents/05_2012/closing_the_gap.pdf.

Department of Families, Housing, Community Services and Indigenous Affairs (DFHCSIA). (2009). *Closing the gap on Indigenous disadvantage: The challenge for Australia*. Retrieved from www.fahcsia.gov.au/indigenous/closing_the_gap/default.htm.

Derrida, J. (1976). *Of grammatology*. With translation and introduction by C. Spivak. Baltimore, MD: Johns Hopkins University Press.

Derrida, J. (1988). *Limited Inc*. Evanston, IL: Northwestern University Press.

Derrida, J. (1998). Letter to a Japanese friend. In D. Wood and R. Bernasconi (Eds.), *Derrida and differance* (pp. 1–5). Evanston, IL: Northwestern University Press.

Derrida, J. (2007). Structure, sign, and play in the discourse of the human sciences. In R. Macksey and E. Donato (Eds.), *The structuralist controversy: The language of criticism and the sciences of man*. Baltimore, MD: The John Hopkins University Press.

Derrida, J. with Montefiore, A. (2001). Talking liberties. In G. Biesta and D. Egéa-Kuehne (Eds.), *Derrida and education* (pp. 176–185). Abingdon, UK: Routledge.

Dimitriadis, G. and Kemberelis, G. (2006). *Theory for education*. New York: Routledge.

Hitchcock, L. (2008). *Theory for classics: A student's guide*. London: Routledge.

Jackson, A. Y. (2009). 'What am I doing when I speak of this present?' Voice, power, and desire in truth-telling. In A. Y. Jackson and L. Mazzei (Eds.), *Voice in qualitative inquire: Challenging conventional, interpretive, and critical conceptions in qualitative research* (pp. 165–174). Abingdon, UK: Routledge.

Jackson, A. Y. and Mazzei, L. (2012). *Thinking with theory in qualitative research: Viewing across multiple perspectives*. Abingdon, UK: Routledge.

Koro-Ljungberg, M. (2010). Validity, responsibility, and aporia. *Qualitative Inquiry*, *16*(8), 603–610.

MacLure, M. (2003). *Discourse in educational and social research*. Buckingham, UK: Open University Press.

Mazzei, L. (2003). Inhabited silences: In pursuit of a muffled subtext. *Qualitative Inquiry*, *9*(3), 355–368.

Rizvi, F. and Lingard, B. (2010). *Globalizing education policy*. Abingdon, UK: Routledge.

Royle, N. (2000). What is deconstruction? In N. Royle (Ed.). *Deconstructions: A user's guide* (pp. 1–13). New York: Palgrave.

St. Pierre, E. (1997). Methodology in the fold and the irruption of transgressive data. *Qualitative Studies in Education*, *10*(2), 175–189.

Stronach, I. and MacLure, M. (1997). *Educational research undone: The postmodern embrace*. Buckingham, UK: Open University Press.

Trifonas, P. (2004). The ethics of science and/as research: Deconstruction and the orientations of a new academic responsibility. In Trifonas and M. Peters (Eds.), *Derrida, deconstruction and education: Ethics of pedagogy and research* (pp. 31–41). Malden, MA: Blackwell.

5

EDUCATION POLICIES AS DISCURSIVE FORMATIONS

A Foucauldian optic

Eva Bendix Petersen

The key to my understanding of Foucault, when I first started reading his work, was getting my head around the statement that discourses are practices that systematically constitute the objects of which they speak. This statement appears and is elaborated in *The archaeology of knowledge* (1972) where Foucault comes as close as he gets to explicating a 'discourse theory'. Understanding that discourses no longer merely describe things but actually *make* them entails that any form of meaning-making act needs to be understood as engaged in reality-making.[1] Put differently, discourses are *performative* in that they engender a series of effects. Writing on the matter of 'madness', Foucault (1972: 32) explained:

> It would certainly be a mistake to try to discover what could have been said of madness at a particular time by interrogating the being of madness itself, its secret content, its silent, self-enclosed truth: mental illness was constituted by all that was said in all the statements that named it, divided it up, described it, explained it, traced its developments, indicated its various correlations, judged it, and possibly gave it speech by articulating, in its name, discourses that were to be taken as its own.

With a Foucauldian optic, then, we are not looking for universal essences, absolute truths or other foundations. We are looking for discursive operations, with 'a discourse' being a distinct way of making sense (and sense can be made through speaking, thinking, doing, feeling, enacting, etc.). Following Nietzsche, Foucault argued that there is nothing 'underneath' or 'behind' discourses; all we have are 'surfaces' that constitute our conditions of possibility. He writes, 'we shall not pass beyond discourse in order to rediscover the forms that it has created and left behind it; we shall remain, or try to remain, at the level of discourse itself' (Foucault, 1972: 48). Prevailing notions of depth (e.g. as in 'more authentic') or relevance (e.g. as in 'a more central factor') are discursive effects that work to reproduce particular notions of significance. As Dreyfus and Rabinow (1983: 107) suggest, the coats of arms of Foucault's methods would read: 'Oppose depth, finality, and interiority.' This becomes important for our research foci, as I will discuss a bit later.

If we consider discourses as lodged in 'regimes of truth' (Foucault, 1980) we will recognise how discourses come with particular notions of what is true and right, they will stipulate what knowledges are good and valid knowledges, and they will stipulate, even if implicitly, what ways of being and acting are good and right. A 'regime of truth' shifts our gaze from truth understood in an absolute sense to truth being historically contingent. As others have noted (Bacchi, 2000; Ball, 1994; Hume and Bryce, 2003), this has significant implications for how policies are conceptualised and engaged with. A policy is a 'serious speech act' but it is also a world-making act; it constitutes times, places, problems, relationships, solutions, objects, norms, moralities, subject positions, institutions, etc. The way in which realities are formed has implications for what actions, sentiments, bodies, material arrangements and so on, are deemed appropriate and desirable, and which are not or relatively less so. This is what Foucault catches with the notion of power/knowledge relations. As he writes:

> In a society such as ours, but basically in any society, there are manifold relations of power which permeate, characterize and constitute the social body, and these relations of power cannot themselves be established, consolidated nor implemented without the production, accumulation, circulation and functioning of a discourse. There can be no possible exercise of power without a certain economy of discourses of truth which operates through and on the basis of this association. We are subjected to the production of truth through power and we cannot exercise power except through the production of truth.
>
> *(1980: 93)*

As I have intimated, Foucault's notion of discourse not only concerns language, although language is important. Unfortunately, it is quite common to come across this reduction. As Foucault notes, while we understand that discourses are composed of signs, 'they do more than use these signs to designate things. It is this *more* that renders them irreducible to language and to speech. It is this "more" that we must reveal and describe' (1972: 49). In that way, institutions, material objects, social behaviours or spatial arrangements, for example, are discursive in the sense that they are entangled in historically and culturally contingent power/knowledge relations. What they are and what they do can never be fully determined, yet they act in and on the world, they constitute 'the world' as it were, and they are interacted with by other actors, human and non-human, and in the process everyone involved are constituted – albeit that the constitution is neither unilateral nor predictable. I follow Butler's (1993) reading of Foucault in making the claim that we have no access to either the pre-discursive or the non-discursive, as it were, outside of discourse and, specifically, outside of the discourses that are available to us. This is not the same as saying that the pre-discursive or the non-discursive does not exist; it means that we do not have unmediated access and that the mediation is always already discursive; even when it does its work on us before consciousness and articulation. As Foucault (1972) writes, 'in the end, we're sent back to a setting-up of relations that characterizes discursive practice itself; and what we discover is . . . a group of *rules* that are immanent in a practice, and define its specificity' (p. 46). At this point we should remind ourselves that there are many different readings of Foucault's position on these onto-epistemological questions. There is not one Foucault, nor is it possible to establish in any final or absolute sense the right way to read Foucault.

Policies as official discursive formations

In light of Foucault's discourse perspective policies become incredibly interesting things to study. The specific classroom's bespoke 'rights and responsibilities' chart, the local school's after school pick-up procedures, the State government's student welfare and behaviour management policy recommendations; the Federal government's Higher Education funding structures, the ways notions of 'best practice' policies on all manner of education matters travel across the globe. What becomes apparent is that what counts as a policy is contested in itself. Once again, rather than seeking to define and fix, a Foucauldian optic would have us ask, 'what counts as a policy in this specific context? How are policies constituted? What is included and excluded from that discursive category? What are the effects of those inclusions and exclusions?' If something is deemed to be 'policy' rather than a 'guideline', say, then what does that category boundary work afford? What subject positions become available within and against these categorisations?

If we, as analysts, take our interest to policies that in various ways have been established and stabilised as 'a policy' in a given context the question then becomes how we can conceptualise the creature. First of all we might ponder what a policy does. This question can be explored in many ways, but if we think education policies against the insights Foucault offers in his book *Discipline and punish* (1977), we can consider how policies are part of a modern form of 'governing at a distance'. Foucault describes how governmental technologies changed from the late sixteenth century – from the spectacle of the public execution to the mundane but in some ways no more humane disciplinary technologies of institutions such as prisons and schools. Foucault writes:

> Physical pain, the pain of the body itself, is no longer the constituent element of the penalty [. . .] If it is still necessary for the law to reach and manipulate the body [. . .] it will be at a distance, in the proper way, according to strict rules, and with a much 'higher' aim.
>
> *(1977: 11)*

In this light, we might consider a policy as technology of power that works, or aims to work, in the absence of direct and continual supervision. In this sense the most 'effective' policy is a policy that does what it means to do quietly, invisibly; that inserts itself into the 'common sense', so that its subjects can only think of this policy as fair and reasonable, and therefore are happy to abide by it, even 'own it' and defend it if they feel they need to. Foucault (1977) notes, 'adjust the mechanisms of power that frame the everyday lives of individuals: an adaptation and a refinement of the machinery that assumes responsibility for and places under surveillance their everyday behaviour' (p. 174).

In some take-ups of Foucault's perspective a policy is said to be a discourse. In my view this is a less productive conceptualisation. It invites questions such as 'what is the discourse of this policy?' Given that Foucault (1977) argued that actors such as policies rarely cite and propel just one discourse but rather are heterogeneous, I find it analytically helpful to consider a policy a discursive 'formation', which in my take-up is of a slightly different order to what Foucault (1980) termed a 'dispositif' (variously translated as apparatus or machine), which evokes the heterogeneous ensemble that a policy might be part of (alongside architectural forms, laws, moral propositions, etc.) and different to a 'regime of truth', which I find to be the best concept to catch more over-arching discursive continuities (such as neoliberalism) that may be present in a specific policy.

The notion of formation catches the idea that any policy is both bounded *and* can be composed of multiple and even competing discourses. Take as an example the previous Australian Federal government's National Partnerships programme, which incorporated the National Partnership Agreement for Low Socio-Economic Status Schools Communities, which had as its stated aim to enhance the academic and social outcomes of students from low socio-economic backgrounds. Even a cursory look at the Agreement and its recommended practices for schools and school communities, shows how it cites and constitutes as 'good and right' a number of discourses that could be argued are in tension (i.e. neoliberal new public management discourses of 'effective' school leadership, and more social-democratic discourses of 'social justice' and 'community ownership')[2].

Taking the point that policies are multifarious invites us to think about the relationship between the discourses that appear to be in play, and also their relative 'weight' within the policy. Not all discourses are equal. In our analysis we might want to ask which discourses appear ascendant, and which appear more marginal or given a more minor role? And how does that manifest? Once again, we need to consider how discursive practices are part of a historically contingent dispositif, and how policies in their citational practices further and/or negate prevailing power/knowledge relations. In other words we may ask how they are *of* their time. For instance we might ask whether they seem to speak to and speak for dominant configurations of common sense. And how is that accomplished? What taken-for-granted truths are backgrounded or black boxed, for example, and how are tensions with other possible discourses managed? In other words, we need to remember that whatever speech acts are taken seriously is 'a function only of other serious speech acts' (Dreyfus and Rabinow, 1983: 58).

Methodological strategies

Dreyfus and Rabinow (1983) comment upon Foucault's 'strange and complex attitude', and write that in taking up a Foucauldian approach, as it were, 'one has to take the world of serious discourse seriously because it is the one we are in, and yet one can't take it seriously, first because we have arduously divorced ourselves from it, and second because it is not grounded' (p. 105). In other words, while we recognise 'the weight of reality' so to speak, we have to be ready to let go of and interrogate even the most common-sense and the most deeply felt, we have to attempt to make the familiar unfamiliar; we have to wrest everything from a foundational assumption and treat everything as historically contingent. Nothing is sacred, not even, or perhaps especially not, the analysts' own reality constructions. As Dreyfus and Rabinow (1983: 49) explain:

> Studying discursive formations requires a double reduction. Not only must the investigator bracket *truth* claims of the serious speech acts he is investigating – Husserl's phenomenological reduction – he must also bracket the *meaning* claims of the speech acts he studies; that is, he not only must remain neutral as to whether what a statement asserts as true is in fact true, he must remain neutral as to whether each specific truth claim even makes sense, and more generally, whether the notion of a context-free truth claim is coherent.

Rather than thinking that this leads to the hopeless abyss of relativism, it may be helpful to think of this practice in terms of a double movement. Destabilising everything that is held dear, held true or held significant as discursive effects or accomplishments is the first movement. This is what is sometimes called the anti-Oedipal tradition of poststructuralist thought. But the second movement recognises at the same time our own and others' serious implicatedness and how we as subjects have become subjects to and of these strange discourses, and in the process have become passionately attached to them *and* to ourselves as particular kinds of beings (Butler, 1997). We are in the space of the funny–serious and the unreal–real, not as binary oppositions but as simultaneities. This can be a difficult attitude to exercise, but one I consider crucial in 'Foucauldian scholarship'. In a certain sense, it comes well *before* all manner of research design decision-makings and, ideally, should be carried through in these practices. It is not objectivity; rather it is a productive combination of both radical or irreverent neutrality and embodied, passionate 'situatedness'.

As others have noted, a Foucauldian discourse analytic strategy will tend to be propelled by 'how' questions (Rabinow, 1991). Questions of 'why' compel us to look for causes and for causal relationships, and often let us forget how in this pursuit we are at risk of reproducing prevailing understandings rather than interrogating and destabilising them. Questions of 'when' are difficult too as they ask us to pinpoint and fix things, such as events, whose pinpointing is contested or if it is not is an issue to be interrogated in itself. 'How' questions, on the other hand, take our focus to how actors make sense, how they explain why something happened or how they account for when something happened for example, which will allow us to analyse what modes of sense making is available in this context, which discourses are available, and how realities (such as 'facts') are produced in the process. 'How' questions will guide us to interrogate how things are done and the implications of actions. 'How' questions open up and enable us to explore the discourses at play in whatever context we are interested in. For example:

- How is authority achieved here?
- How are 'the facts of the contemporary status of things' constituted here?
- How is 'common sense' discursively constructed and how is it constructed as a valid or invalid mode of knowing?
- How do actors speak and act and what are the effects of that?

Taking seriously the 'how' focus, that overall we are interested in how x and y are discursively constituted, we can in specific studies also ask 'what', as in 'what seems to be the dominant discourses at play here?', or 'which discourses seem to be relatively more marginal or even silenced?' The 'what' question on its own, though, runs the same risks as the 'why' and 'when' questions.

Following on from the above more general methodological pointers, I think it is possible to distil three different strands in Foucauldian policy analysis. Listing them here as separate does not mean that they should be or could be separated in research designs, but emphasising their different foci might put in relief the different kind of questions that they afford and invite. I am by no means the first 'Foucauldian' to do so, and the below is a synthesis of the work others have done to show the different possibilities (in particular Ball, 1993, 1994; Bacchi, 2000).

Policy-formulation processes

In these kinds of projects the focus is on how specific policy texts come about. By following the human and non-human actors in the process, we get to explore 'discursive activity' and the discourses in play. Both are interesting to follow. As discussed above, it is likely that there are several discourses at play so it becomes interesting to attempt to identify the different discourses, and investigate their relationships: do they converge or contradict each other, and how are similarities and differences between them made sense of and negotiated by involved actors; how are compromises achieved, if they are, or how do particular discourses get to set the agenda and become dominant? For instance, how do the actors shore up the relevance of the discourses they embody (e.g. 'we need to use what was good about the old policy, we shouldn't throw the baby out with the bathwater'); what 'regime of truth' do they draw on to make things seem obvious, natural, given, necessary, important and so on? We are reminded that whenever Foucault heard talk of meaning and value, of virtue and goodness, he looked for strategies of domination (Dreyfus and Rabinow, 1983: 109). Again, the focus for analysis is not so much what specific actors of intentionality are doing to achieve domination (this is where a Foucauldian optic in my reading presents a significant departure from some Bourdieuian and Latourian approaches), it is about analysing which kinds of knowledges, virtues and so on come to be taken for granted, come to be naturalised, and therefore come to be taken more seriously. Subjects, rather than being instigators or authors of power/knowledge relations are subject to/of them, and should be treated as such when we study the 'meticulous rituals of power'. As Foucault elaborates (1980: 98):

> The individual, that is, is not the *vis-à-vis* of power; it is, I believe one of its prime effects. The individual is an effect of power, and at the same time, or precisely to the extent to which it is that effect, is it the element of its articulation. The individual which power has constituted is at the same time its vehicle.

Foucault's 'historical' gaze is more focussed on the discourses that are enacted, carried forward, challenged and maintained (including the one that stipulates that individuals 'of course' act to feather their own nest), than it is in 'personal politics', yet the 'personal politics' may well be starting point for a genealogy/destabilising historical analysis. Foucault (1980: 99) calls it an 'ascending' analysis of power.

Policy-product analysis

A product analysis considers the product of the above process, the operative policy text (present or past). Here we are interested in the discourses and regimes of truth as they manifest themselves in the text. Again, policy texts can be made up of multiple discourses, which may support or challenge each other. The analyst will usually not find that the discourses name themselves so to speak, so it is the analyst's job to identify them working with the policy text as 'data' and showing the reader why they believe it is possible to name various 'discourse snippets' as belonging to a 'larger' discourse. In this work it is helpful to have a sense of how the policy text is lodged in a wider web of discursive continuities and discontinuities, to understand how the policy text is of its time and place (like in the example provided above). It is both true and not true that time and place precedes the policy text; it will not be possible without time and place but it also *makes* the very time and place; in that sense a policy text is a citational and performative practice. Stated differently, it is possible to think of product analysis as 'genealogical'. Thinking 'how did this text come to appear like this?' – not in terms of the process approach described above, but a different form of analysis mapping and tracing kinships and breaks with other policies, from other times and in other places. The understanding is that all policy texts are simultaneously unique and not unique at all.

In Education, the policy product analysis is often dismissed as 'arm chair research' – meaning that it is not 'real' research and that it is useless in its detachment from the 'real' world – and the presupposition is that policy texts (especially non-current ones) do not really matter that much. What matters, this view would have it, is how policies are taken up and 'actually' shape actors' conditions of possibility. While the latter questions are interesting and important, as I will outline below, critical interrogations of policy texts in themselves are significant as they give us insight into the discourses that became officially sanctioned in particular times and places. As a 'significant speech act' it tells us something about the articulable truths and values of a time-place.

Policy-implementation processes

As indicated, 'implementation' studies focus on how policies are 'taken up'; how they are made sense of, engaged with, resisted, etc. The question of 'implementation' and how to conceptualise it has been subject to some sophisticated conceptual scrutiny (e.g. Webb and Gulson, 2012, 2013). As Stephen Ball et al. (2010, 2012) argue, the notion of 'implementation' is a functionalist one, which assumes a fairly straight-forward policy cycle of decision–implementation–evaluation–improvement and which usually overlooks or reduces the messiness and indeterminacy of 'rolling out' policies in that they are interpreted and translated, indeed 'enacted', by very diverse actors. Notwithstanding, it becomes interesting to ask how a policy, whether new or established, help shape actors' conditions of possibility. Recognising, again, that there are often multiple and contradictory discourses at play in any institution or space in which a policy is put to work, it becomes interesting to consider how a policy converges with other and/or already operative policies. Or how it encounters existing norms, traditions, and practices? How are divergences, contradictions, incommensurabilities, negotiated and managed, or resisted and interrupted? How do policies impact on bodies, subjectivities and actors' sense of self; does the policy continue and maintain these actors' passionate attachments, their investments, or does the policy constitute a break of sorts? What actions become possible and impossible, desirable or undesirable, and how do policies affect conduct and practices? Understanding that policies are multiplicities rolled out and into other multiplicities highlight that policy 'implementation' and its effects are, usually, far from straightforward, linear and predictable. It is instructive here to think of this work as 'post-phenomenological', where the central move is asking not 'what is meaningful?' but 'what do the actors take to be meaningful and significant?', and how they discursify meaning into existence.

Conclusion

Needless to say I have only been able to offer a few theoretical and methodological pointers here. Foucault's scholarship is rich and complex and the implications for policy analysis are many. At every turn Foucault himself invited the reader to enact an anti-Oedipal relation to him and his work. He prompted that others took his work to be a set of tools; to break things with, to build with. For me an important question that follows on from this invitation is the question of what we might call 'tool-box alignment'. The notion of 'tool' invites theoretical eclecticism, a concept from here and a concept from there, etc. While some analysts manage to enact a very powerful eclecticism and sometimes in doing so come to create altogether new tools (as Foucault himself did), there also seem to be instances where the various tools controvert each other in unproductive ways. For me a theoretical concept such as 'discourse' sits in a larger methodological ensemble, where some coherence between onto-epistemological perspective, conceptual apparatus, research methods, researcher positioning and so forth is required. In particular, the onto-epistemological perspective that realities are historically contingent and made by various actors means that the concept of discourse that I work with is a particular one that cannot sit easily alongside concepts steeped in more 'realist' onto-epistemologies. Each of us, in our engagement with theory, is required to consider and account for the relationship between the concepts that we pick up.

Finally, in this day and age there is a lot of secondary literature available on Foucault's concepts and methods. Much of this literature is very helpful and I certainly have my own favourites (you would have noted my use of Dreyfus and Rabinow). Yet, ending on a slightly ironic note, I would like to say also that nothing beats reading Foucault's work itself. I find much hope in the idea that as each of us read his work and try to make sense of it lays the possibility of a continuing proliferation of 'take ups', which may counteract movements towards congealment, dogma and deference.

Notes

1 That goes for this text as well. It will constitute a Foucauldian optic in a particular way, and seek to make itself not only intelligible but compelling. The reader is invited to consider, critically, how this is being attempted here.
2 I'd like to acknowledge my Honours student April Chisholm for her analysis of the Agreement. The work is as yet unpublished.

References and further reading

Bacchi, C. (2000). Policy as discourse: What does it mean? Where does it get us? *Discourse: Studies in the Cultural Politics of Education, 21*(1), 45–57.
Ball, S. J. (1993). What is policy? Texts, trajectories and toolboxes. *The Australian Journal of Education Studies, 13*(2), 10–17.
Ball, S. J. (1994). *Education reform: A critical and post-structural approach.* Buckingham, UK: Open University Press.
Ball, S. J., Hoskins, K., Maguire, M. and Braun, A. (2010). Disciplinary texts: A policy analysis of national and local behaviour policies. *Critical Studies in Education, 52*(1), 1–14.
Ball, S. J., Maguire, M. and Braun, A. (2012). *How schools do policy: Policy enactments in secondary schools.* London: Routledge.
Butler, J. (1993). *Bodies that matter: On the discursive limits of 'sex'.* London: Routledge.
Butler, J. (1997). *The psychic life of power: Theories in subjection.* Stanford, CA: Stanford University Press.
Dreyfus, H. L. and Rabinow, P. (1983). *Michel Foucault: Beyond structuralism and hermeneutics* (2nd edn). Chicago, IL: The University of Chicago Press.
Foucault, M. (1972). *The archaeology of knowledge.* New York: Pantheon Books.

Foucault, M. (1977). *Discipline and punish: The birth of the prison*. New York: Vintage Books.

Foucault, M. (1980). *Power/knowledge. Selected interviews and other writings 1972–1977*. Edited by C. Gordon. New York: Pantheon Books.

Humes, W. and Bryce, T. (2003). Post-structuralism and policy research in education. *Journal of Education Policy*, *18*(2), 175–187.

Rabinow, P. (1991). *The Foucault reader*. London: Penguin.

Webb, P. T. and Gulson, K. N. (2012). Policy prolepsis in education: Encounters, becomings, and phantasms. *Discourse: Studies in the Cultural Politics of Education*, *33*(1), 87–99.

Webb, P. T. and Gulson, K. N. (2013). Policy intensions and the folds of the self. *Educational Theory*, *63*(1), 51–68.

6

LACANIAN PERSPECTIVES ON EDUCATION POLICY ANALYSIS

Matthew Clarke

Lacanian psychoanalytic theory[1] is perhaps not the most obvious candidate as a resource for policy analysis. To quote the opening words from the introduction to Yannis Stavrakakis's (1999) book, *Lacan and the political,* 'What does Lacan have to do with the political [policy]? Isn't Lacan that obscure mystical psychoanalyst turned philosopher who has nothing to do with any consideration of the political [policy]?'(p. 1). In responding to his own rhetorical questions, Stavrakakis draws attention to the way Lacan's oeuvre highlights the 'ultimately impossible but, nevertheless, necessary' construction of the unattainable but 'inter-implicated' objects otherwise known as 'identity' and 'society' (1999: 4). The repeated attempts to generate these unachievable objects, whose very necessity is grounded in their impossibility, is, for writers like Stavrakakis and Laclau (1990, 1996), the very stuff of the political.

Clearly, like Stavrakakis, I don't believe that Lacan has 'nothing to do with any consideration of the political'; nor do the significant and growing body of scholars who draw on Lacan's intellectual legacy as part of their critical work in politics and political theory (Copjec, 2002; Dean, 2009; Glynos and Stavrakakis, 2008; McGowan, 2013; Rothenberg, 2010; Stavrakakis, 2007; Vighi, 2010; Žižek, 1989, 1997, 2008a, 2008b, 2009). Psychoanalytically informed work in education policy analysis is a less common but growing field of scholarship (e.g. Clarke, 2012a; Clarke, 2012b, 2013, 2014; Clarke and Moore, 2013; Levine-Rasky and Ringrose, 2009; Moore, 2006). In many ways, the relatively recent uptake of psychoanalytic thought in education policy is not surprising, given that the 'revolution in mind' staged by psychoanalysis in Paris and Vienna began nearly a century after the political revolution that occurred in the former city shook the Western world (Makari, 2008).

In advocating the potential value of a psychoanalytic approach for critical education policy analysis, I am guided by Frosh (2010) in arguing that the significance of key psychoanalytic notions, such as the unconscious, desire and fantasy, is too great to be ignored and that they clearly have insights to offer beyond the clinical encounter.

The challenge then becomes 'not that of justifying psychoanalysis, but rather of deploying it creatively and yet with integrity' (Frosh, 2010: 4). In relation to this point, it is important to bear in mind that not only does psychoanalytic theory speak to wider social and political issues, but policy – something we are tempted to see as purely concerned with the realm of the institutional and the political – is enacted by individuals and is individuating in its governance effects. Hence the potential for critical dialogue between psychoanalytic theory and policy is substantial.

It is also important to stress at the outset that my advocacy of the employment of psychoanalytic theory is not intended to suggest the crude 'application' of its ideas to education for to attempt to do so would be to do both violence and injustice to each domain; rather, one can use such theories 'only as enabling metaphorical devices, not as extrapolated, preconceived items of knowledge' (Felman, 1987: 11). That is to say, psychoanalysis provides a unique and invaluable set of thinking tools for the conduct of critical policy analysis but they demand to be used in concert with, not in place of, creative and critical thought. The section below outlines some of these tools.

Some key concepts in Lacanian psychoanalytic theory

Psychoanalysis differs from many other bodies of thought in that unlike, say, Marxism, it does not provide a positive agenda for change *or* offer an explicit political program that its followers might seek to implement in order to realize the good society; indeed, it rejects the very notion of the 'good society' (McGowan, 2013). Nonetheless, psychoanalysis is far from apolitical, insofar as it is part of a wider tradition of disruptive, 'negative' political theories that share a number of family resemblances. These include an emphasis on 'the vulnerability and contingency of every phenomenon that appears to be fully positive and replete' and a foregrounding of the operations of power in the formation and maintenance and transgression of all identities and practices (Coole, 2000: 231). Furthermore, psychoanalysis offers a distinctive, if counterintuitive, way of thinking about the dilemmas that face us as individuals and as societies, insofar as it advocates the embrace rather than the overcoming of lack, loss and absence. In order to explore this counterintuitive claim further it is helpful to contrast education policy's subject of knowledge with the psychoanalytic subject of desire.

Subjects of knowledge and subjects of desire

Education policy in recent decades has witnessed the replacement of politics by management (Strhan, 2010), with a consequent emphasis on instrumentally conceived knowledge and a focus on the promotion of values of effectiveness and efficiency – 'more, higher, better!' (Ball, Maguire, and Braun, 2012: 74) – with little pause for reflection on the underlying ethical and political purposes of education (Biesta, 2010). The managerialist conceptualization of education, reflected in the neoliberal trope of the 'knowledge economy', is predicated on Enlightenment notions of the autonomous agent capable of calculating and pursuing her/his rational interests in order to achieve the 'good life', as well as on assumptions about the possibilities of limitless economic growth and endless scientific progress. For Lacan, this conception of existence as accumulation, in which human life is devoted to 'the service of goods' (Lacan, 1992), poses a significant obstacle to identification with lack and loss as the paradoxical path to progress (McGowan, 2013).

In addition to his reputation for textual fecundity/obscurity, Lacan is also (im)famous for his 'subversion of the subject' (Lacan, 1977b; Van Haute, 2002), captured in his definition of the signifier as 'that which represents the subject for another signifier'(1977b: 350). In other words, the subject is an effect of language; it comes about through its subjection to the signifier. Subjection to the signifier is linked to lack/loss (the symbolic is structured around absence since the signifier stands in for the always absent object) and hence to desire: 'the subject stands under the mastery of the signifier, which causes the loss which gives life to desire . . . desire is borne along by signifiers that knead and shape our existence' (Van Haute, 2002: 124–125). Thus, in contrast to the subject of (conscious) knowledge that underpins much education policy, Lacanian psychoanalytic theory, following in the footsteps of 'Freud's great revolution in the history of thought' (McGowan, 2013: 17), views the subject as the subject of (unconscious) desire. As Lacan puts it in typically enigmatic fashion, 'There has been no desire for knowledge but . . . a horror of knowing' (1974, cited in McGowan, 2013: 17). How are we to understand this rather cryptic comment? As McGowan points out (2013: 17–18), what we shrink from is not knowledge per se but knowledge of the unconscious (truth), which we avoid in order to remain subjects of desire (conscious knowledge). For Lacanian psychoanalytic theory, conscious knowledge is inherently limited, marked by irreducible gaps and inevitable epistemological shortfalls, suggesting the need to relinquish our obsession with knowledge as a means to full mastery and control (Nobus and Quinn, 2005). In this vein, one way of understanding policy is as a discourse that, like modern science, seeks 'to annihilate the constitutive gap between knowledge and truth, and thus to abolish the unconscious' (Nobus and Quinn, 2005: 50) as part of its aspiration to omniscience and omnipotence.

In order to fully grasp the notion of our being subjects of desire, rather than subjects of knowledge, we need to explore the misrecognition that constitutes the subject from its earliest inception in the mirror stage. Indeed, owing to its status as the most familiar aspect of the Lacanian corpus – Eagleton (2008: 1) notes how no piece of cultural criticism in the 1970s and 1980s was complete without some reference to it – as well as the insights it offers into the distinctiveness of the human psyche, the mirror stage offers a logical point of embarkation for a deeper consideration of the divided nature of the Lacanian subject.

The mirror stage and the three registers of the psyche: imaginary, symbolic, Real[2]

In seeking to articulate the distinctiveness of humans in relation to other animals, the capacity for language is typically noted. The capacity for desire is surely another distinction, insofar as animals may have needs and some, like our pampered pets, may be vocal in making demands; but to talk of animals as subjects of desire is taking anthropomorphism a step too far. The use of language and the capacity for desire are inextricably linked in Lacanian theory and come together in the mirror stage. Initially conceived as a specific stage in infant development and expounded in his first formal contribution to psychoanalytic theory, the mirror stage and the complex vision of the psyche it embodies later became fundamental to Lacan's overall conception of human subjectivity (Evans, 1996). As Bowie (1991) puts it, 'the mirror stage (stade du miroir) is not a mere epoch in the history of the individual but a stadium (stade) in which the battle of the human subject is permanently being waged' (p. 21). That is to say, the mirror stage is both an explanatory narrative and an enduring structure.

The mirror stage involves recognition of self in the specular image of the other perceived in the (literal or figurative) mirror. For the infant, this imag(e)inary identification offers the (illusory) promise of (potential) self-reliance and mastery; at the same time, it entails an alienating separation and distinction between self and other, in which the external other is the paradoxical source of the self. Prior to this distinction there is only primeval existence with no distinction between self and other – what Joan Copjec (1994) characterizes as 'realtight'– which is one interpretation of the Lacanian register of the Real.

Meanwhile, the achievement of individuation through identification entails the simultaneous loss of what is now 'other'; and although this is a paradoxical form of loss, in that prior to self-identification there was no 'self' to suffer any loss (McGowan, 2013), it is nonetheless one source of the enduring desire that seeks to recoup a purportedly lost object. Identification with specular or gestalt formations, through which individuals or groups seek to recapture an imagined, or fantasmatic, prior state of harmony, fullness and completion, is associated with the Lacanian register of the imaginary, a realm which, as Eagleton (2008: 10) notes, 'is a kind of ideology'.

The initial alienation of the mirror stage is compounded on accession to subject-hood through entry into the symbolic register of language, a social system of signification and regulation – the symbolic is also the realm of the law and prohibition – that henceforth mediates the individual's relations with others and with the world. By barring direct access to the objects of the world and to the other, the symbolic entails another experience of loss; indeed, it even mediates and constrains the subject's very possibilities for understanding itself. Entry into the symbolic order not only brings with it prohibitions but also as an awareness of objects and experiences the subject does not have access to.

> In this fashion, the signifier dispels the child's primordial impression of being at one with the world, causing an irreparable rift or division; the very developmental course that empowers the child to materialize as a psychically autonomous entity is also what makes it feel lacking and self-alienated.
>
> *(Ruti, 2009: 93)*

This alienating loss is further underscored by the incapacity of language to fully or adequately convey the individual's intentions and desires, since, owing to the play of difference, the signifier is never fully present and consequently, no signifier can adequately represent the individual's identity; yet at the same time, paradoxically, the symbolic register often conveys more than the individual intended (Chiesa, 2007). In Eagleton's (2008) words, 'we are fated, then, to express ourselves in a tongue which is forever foreign' (p. 86; see also, Derrida, 1998). For these reasons, Lacan designates the subject, $, indicating the impossibility of complete self-knowledge or fully present self-consciousness (Evans, 1996: 192). This split in the subject corresponds to that between (conscious) knowledge and (unconscious) truth (Lacan, 2002: 727).

One consequence of our sense of lack is a pervasive experience of alienation whereby our lives and the world are felt to be somewhat out of joint and where our enjoyment has been lost. One consequence of this experience is an ongoing engagement with fantasy prompted by a desire to recapture the full and harmonious state along with the enjoyment that we purportedly lost and from which we are now alienated. These fantasies may be of the 'beatific' variety – 'if I buy this gym membership I will gain control of my life'– in which the achievement of a specific concrete object is seen as the key to a more generalized state of wellbeing. But fantasies may also adopt a 'horrific' form, in which the non-achievement of an object is seen as a prelude to disaster. Such fantasies typically pivot around an object blamed for stealing or spoiling our enjoyment or representing an obstacle to its realization. Refugees and asylum seekers are frequently positioned as such objects in the national psyche of many wealthy Western nations.

In sum, Lacanian psychoanalytic theory presents us with a view of knowledge as indelibly marked by ignorance and of subjects irremediably split between conscious and unconscious whilst fissured between the three ontological registers of the imaginary, the symbolic and the Real. A key consequence of this division and attendant self-alienation is the resort to fantasy in an attempt to recapture a purportedly lost fullness, to compensate for a troubling absence of completion or harmony. As we will see below, these ideas have considerable purchase in terms of social and educational policy analysis.

Thinking policy psychoanalytically

In my introduction, I noted how, on the one hand, we can view psychoanalytic theory as suggesting social as well as the individual-psychological insights, while, on the other hand, we can see policy as operating at the individual as well as the institutional and political scale in terms of the way it presumes and shapes particular policy subjects. Indeed, at its most basic level policy can be seen as a process of identifying issues and diagnosing problems in order to pose solutions that will address these issues and rectify the problems. In other words, like the psychoanalytic subject for whom a perceived lack, a purported loss, is the object-cause of desire, policy simultaneously posits a problem and a solution. In order to develop these parallels further, the following discussion presents a psychoanalytic reading of some of the key themes presented in the Foreword to the former Australian federal government's signature education policy document, *Quality education: The case for an education revolution in our schools* (Commonwealth of Australia, 2008).

Revolution or repetition: plus ça change . . .

New governments often seek to establish their legitimacy and authority by inaugurating new policy programs to address perceived or constructed problems and issues, reflecting the point that policy is as much a matter of strategic, political positioning as it is about rational analysis of practical problems (Stone, 2012). Seen in this light, the 'case for an education revolution in our schools' argued by the incoming federal Australian government in 2008 was as much a bid for legitimacy as it was a solution to a real and substantial problem. Concepts from Lacanian psychoanalytic theory enable us to identify and deconstruct this phenomenon.

The Foreword opens with a commitment on the part of the government to 'creating and education revolution to build a world-class education system, which would establish Australia as one of the most highly education and skilled nations' (p. 5).[3] The operating assumption here is that Australia is *not* currently among the most highly educated and skilled nation. In other words, the policy goal is premised on an identification of lack as the basis of a proposal for dramatic change (how else can one read the choice of the term, 'revolution'?). We might read this statement as an instance of imaginary identification with an illusory other (those 'most highly educated and skilled nations', against whom Australia is deemed to not yet measure up, yet which are not specified) that is at the same time an instance-source of alienation. In this sense, achieving 'world-class' status is a fantasy that serves to structure reality so as to make it seem harmonious and complete:

> It is to this object that cannot be grasped in the mirror that the specular image lends its clothes. A substance caught in the net of the shadow, and which, robbed of its shadow-swelling volume, holds out once again the tired lure of the shadow as if it were substance.
>
> *(Lacan, 1977b: 349)*

The opening statement is followed by a series of claims about 'the central role that education plays in the economic and social strength of our nation'. Critically, we are informed that 'beyond economic growth, education creates social benefits' and that these benefits, all flowing from of a commitment on the part of society to education, include 'higher levels of civic participation, greater social cohesion, lower levels of crime and disadvantage, and a more trusting, equitable and just society'. This is a very impressive list! Indeed, it is so impressive that it suggests that we are entering the terrain of utopian thinking. This is a realm characterized by beatific fantasies, in which social dislocations and contradictions are smoothed out: in which, for example, inherent tensions between market-based competition and social cohesion are conveniently glossed over (Clarke, 2012b), or in which quality is conflated with equity by reducing the latter to a weak notion of equality of opportunity in order to mask, rather than challenge, actually existing social and economic inequalities (Gillies, 2008).

However, in contrast to the ideological yearnings of the imaginary, policy enacted and *realized* in the symbolically-mediated world of practice is never so simple and straightforward: 'the beatific side of fantasy is coupled in utopian constructions with a horrific side, a paranoid need for a stigmatised scapegoat' (Stavrakakis, 1999: 100). Here, the 'failing schools', the 'incompetent teachers' and the 'unmotivated students' blamed for the failure of education to live up to utopian fantasies in contexts such as the UK and the US (Lyons and Drew, 2009) – policy contexts from which the Rudd and Gillard federal Australian Labor governments drew their educational inspiration – spring to mind. For in Australia, as in other neoliberal contexts such as England, education has moved 'from being a pillar of the welfare state to being a prop for a global market economy' (Tomlinson, 2005: 11). This neoliberal colonization of education and education policy is evident in the remarkable prominence of economic and managerial terminology and concepts, italicized in the following three statements and sub-statements taken from the middle of the Foreword, where the core aspirations of the policy document are laid out:

> Through the Council of Australian Governments, we want to go further than any previous Government in creating a national agenda for *long-term investments* and *innovative approaches* to *building* Australia's *productivity*.

> That is why we have placed education and all aspects of our *human capital* at the very heart of Australia's *economic* and social *investment* priorities.

> The Education Revolution is a key element of the Australian government's *agenda* as it is central to the *goals* we have for this nation:

> - Building a Stronger Future – Increasing Australia's capacity to sustain *higher economic growth* with *low inflation* through increasing the *skills base* of the *labour force* and aligning that *skills base* with the needs of the *economy*.
> - Building a Fairer Australia – Raising the *skills* and *capacity* of all Australians, particularly those with *low skill levels*, is essential to ensuring equity in the *economic*, social and political life of the nation.
> - Preparing for Future Challenges – Australia faces significant changes to its social and *economic* environment through an ageing population and increasing *international competition*. The nation must *invest* in developing a *world-class* education system and *drive development* of a *workforce* that is *highly skilled*, *flexible* and *adaptable* in responding to increasing *global competition* for *skills*.

Framing education in this way, as a conduit for a globalized market economy, entails embracing values of instrumentalism, atomization and competition and no amount of fantasmatic policy rhetoric (Clarke, 2012b) can compensate for the consequences: 'market states must maximize opportunities by encouraging competition, providing incentive structures and draconian penalties' (Tomlinson, 2005: 221). In other words, as Lacan suggests in his Seminar of 1959–1960, *The ethics of psychoanalysis*, 'what is foreclosed in the symbolic reappears in the real' (Lacan, 2007: 131). The Foreword may symbolically juxtapose 'Building a Stronger Future' with 'Building a Fairer Australia' but the impossibility of reconciling the latter with the neoliberal competitive and instrumental individualism of the former reappears in the Real of what Kenway (2013) describes as '*the deplorable social inequalities in Australia's education system*' (p. 293, emphasis in original).

Conclusion

The above discussion provides only a sketch of some possible lines of analysis but I hope it has served to whet the reader's appetite for further entanglements with policy analysis and psychoanalytic theory. Such work may focus, for example, on identifying the fantasmatic or sublime object-causes of desire around which particular policy discourses 'pivot' (Hook, 2008: 400; see Clarke, 2012b, 2013, for examples) or on identifying the defensive strategies of disavowal adopted by policy discourses (Clarke, 2012a).

In concluding, I would suggest that Lacanian psychoanalytic theory, by shifting the focus from subjects/societies of knowledge to subjects/societies of desire striving to compensate for alienation and loss, allows policy analysis to foreground the workings of the libidinal, rather than just the material, economy – that is, for example, to recognize how the operation of fantasy and fantasmatic fears and yearnings can be used to explain such phenomenon as neoliberal policy's obsessional and repeated fixation on signifiers such as 'productivity' and 'growth' as fantasmatic object-causes of desire organizing the social and symbolic field.

Suggestions for further reading

I need to begin by saying something about reading Lacan, for if he is (im)famous for subverting the subject, Lacan is equally notorious for the impenetrability of his writing, something Nobus and Quinn (2005: 71) generously describe as 'a ludic dream world of language':

> It is as if Lacan eventually managed to overcome the force of gravity which had kept him firmly on Freudian ground during the first ten years of his seminar, and, once airborne, celebrated his freedom of movement with the creation of a new idiom, bristling with infinite semantic pluralism and reflecting virtuoso stunt work on the connotations of his own conceptual inventions.

Alas, for the newcomer this 'infinite semantic pluralism' and 'virtuoso stunt work' can be decidedly off-putting. However, for those keen to enter the Lacanian labyrinth,

Écrits: A selection (Lacan, 1977a) is a good place to begin containing as it does a number of seminal essays such as: *The mirror stage as formative of the function of the I; The agency of the letter in the unconscious or reason since Freud* and; *The subversion of the subject and the dialectic of desire in the Freudian unconscious.* Reading these essays hand in hand with such insightful guides as Bruce Fink's (2004) *Lacan to the letter: Reading Écrits closely;* Phillipe Van Haute's (2002) *Against adaptation: Lacan's 'subversion' of the subject;* Joël Dor's (1998) *Introduction to the reading of Lacan: The unconscious structured like a language* or; Slavoj Žižek's (2006) *How to read Lacan,* will make the journey less daunting, more informative and more enjoyable. Beyond this, any of the Lacanian psychoanalytic texts in the reference list below will reward further exploration.

Notes

1 For many readers, Freud, not Lacan, is the first name that springs to mind in association with psychoanalysis. Central to Lacan's innovations in relation to Freudian theory are his stress on the central significance of language and of the Other in the construction of the subject, as well as his emphasis on the failures and deficiencies inherent to symbolization, structure and the Law, which have led many to label him as 'post' structuralist. In this chapter, I use Lacanian and psychoanalytic interchangeably.
2 I am following the practice of Žižek and others in capitalizing the Real to emphasize its distinctness from 'reality', unless quoting from authors who do not follow this practice.
3 This and all subsequent unattributed references are to the Foreword of *Quality education: The case for an education revolution in our schools* (Commonwealth of Australia, 2008).

References

Ball, S. J., Maguire, M. and Braun, A. (2012). *How schools do policy: Policy enactments in secondary schools.* London: Routledge.

Biesta, G. (2010). *Good education in age of measurement: Ethics, politics, democracy.* Boulder, CO: Paradigm Publishers.

Bowie, M. (1991). *Lacan.* Cambridge, MA: Harvard University Press.

Chiesa, L. (2007). *Subjectivity and otherness: A philosophical reading of Lacan.* Cambridge, MA: The MIT Press.

Clarke, M. (2012a). The (absent) politics of neo-liberal education policy. *Critical Studies in Education, 53*(3), 297–310.

Clarke, M. (2012b). Talkin' 'bout a revolution: The social, political and fantasmatic logics of education policy. *Journal of Education Policy, 27*(2), 173–191.

Clarke, M. (2013). The sublime objects of education policy: Quality, equity and ideology. *Discourse: Studies in the cultural politics of education,* (iFirst), 1–15.

Clarke, M. (2014). Dialectics and dilemmas: Psychosocial dimensions of ability grouping policy. *Critical Studies in Education,* (iFirst), 1–15.

Clarke, M. and Moore, A. (2013). Professional standards, teacher identities and an ethics of singularity. *Cambridge Journal of Education, 43*(4), 487–500.

Commonwealth of Australia (2008). *Quality education: The case for an education revolution in our schools.* Canberra: Department of Education, Employment and Workplace Relations Retrieved from www.deewr.gov.au/Schooling/Programs/Pages/QualityEducation-Theca seforanEducationRevolutioninourSchools.aspx.

Coole, D. (2000). *Negativity and politics: Dionysus and dialectics from Kant to poststructuralism.* London: Routledge.

Copjec, J. (1994). *Read my desire*. Cambridge, MA: The MIT Press.

Copjec, J. (2002). *Imagine there's no woman: Ethics and sublimation*. Cambridge, MA: The MIT Press.

Dean, J. (2009). *Democracy and other neoliberal fantasies*. Durham, NC: Duke University Press.

Derrida, J. (1998). *Monolingualism of the other, or, the prosthesis of origin* (P. Mensah, Trans.). Stanford, CA: Stanford University Press.

Dor, J. (1998). *Introduction to the reading of Lacan: The unconscious structured like a language* (S. Fairfield, Trans.). New York: Other Press, LLC.

Eagleton, T. (2008). *Trouble with strangers: A study of ethics*. Chichester, UK; Malden, MA: Wiley-Blackwell.

Evans, D. (1996). *An introductory dictionary of Lacanian psychoanalysis*. London: Routledge.

Felman, S. (1987). *Jacques Lacan and the adventure of insight: Psychoanalysis in contemporary culture*. Cambridge, MA: Harvard University Press.

Fink, B. (2004). *Lacan to the letter: Reading Écrits closely*. Minneapolis, MN: University of Minnesota Press.

Frosh, S. (2010). *Psychoanalysis outside the clinic: Interventions in psychosocial studies*. London: Continuum.

Gillies, D. (2008). Quality and equality: The mask of discursive conflation in education policy texts. *Journal of Education Policy, 23*(6), 685–699.

Glynos, J. and Stavrakakis, Y. (2008). Lacan and political subjectivity: Fantasy and enjoyment in psychoanalysis and political theory. *Subjectivity, 24*(1), 256–274.

Hook, D. (2008). Articulating psychoanalysis and psychosocial studies: Limitations and possibilities. *Psychoanalysis, Culture & Society, 13*, 397–405.

Kenway, J. (2013). Challenging inequality in Australian schools: Gonski and beyond. *Discourse: Studies in the Cultural Politics of Education, 34*(2), 286–308.

Lacan, J. (1977a). *Écrits: A selection* (A. Sheridan, Trans.). London: Routledge.

Lacan, J. (1977b). The subversion of the subject and the dialactic of desire in the Freudian unconscious (A. Sheridan, Trans.). In J. Lacan (Ed.), *Écrits: A selection* (pp. 323–360). London: Routledge.

Lacan, J. (1992). *Seminar VII: The ethics of pyschoanalysis* (D. Porter, Trans.). New York: Norton.

Lacan, J. (2002). *Écrits* (B. Fink, Trans.). London: Norton.

Lacan, J. (2007). *Seminar XVII: The other side of psychoanalysis* (R. Grigg, Trans.). New York: Norton.

Laclau, E. (1990). *New reflections on the revolution of our time*. London: Verso.

Laclau, E. (1996). *Emancipation(s)*. London: Verso.

Levine-Rasky, C. and Ringrose, J. (2009). Theorizing psychosocial processes in Canadian, middle-class, Jewish mothers' school choice. *Journal of Education Policy, 24*(3), 255–269.

Lyons, W. and Drew, J. (2009). *Punishing schools: Fear and citizenship in American public education*. Ann Arbor, MI: University of Michigan Press.

Makari, G. (2008). *Revolution in mind: The creation of psychoanalysis*. New York: Harper Perennial.

McGowan, T. (2013). *Enjoying what we don't have: The political project of pyschoanalysis*. Lincoln, NE: University of Nebraska Press.

Moore, A. (2006). Recognising desire: A psychosocial approach to understanding education policy implementation and effect. *Oxford Review of Education, 32*(4), 487–503.

Nobus, D. and Quinn, M. (2005). *Knowing nothing, staying stupid: Elements for a psychoanalytic epistemology*. London: Routledge.

Rothenberg, M. A. (2010). *The excessive subject: A new theory of social change*. Cambridge, UK: Polity Press.

Ruti, M. (2009). *A world of fragile things: Psychoanalysis and the art of living.* Albany, NY: State University of New York Press.

Stavrakakis, Y. (1999). *Lacan and the political.* London: Routledge.

Stavrakakis, Y. (2007). *The Lacanian left.* Edinburgh, UK: Edinburgh Univesity Press.

Stone, D. (2012). *Policy paradox: The art of political decision making* (3rd edn). New York: Norton.

Strhan, A. (2010). The obliteration of truth by management: Badiou, St. Paul and the question of economic managerialism in education. *Educational Philosophy and Theory, 42*(2), 230–250.

Tomlinson, S. (2005). *Education in a post-welfare society* (2nd edn). Buckingham, UK: Open University Press.

Van Haute, P. (2002). *Against adaptation: Lacan's 'subversion' of the subject* (P. Crowe and P. Vankerk, Trans.). New York: Other Press.

Vighi, F. (2010). *On Žižek's dialectics: Surplus, subtraction, sublimation.* London: Continuum.

Žižek, S. (1989). *The sublime object of ideology.* London: Verso Books.

Žižek, S. (1997). *The plague of fantasies.* London: Verso.

Žižek, S. (2006). *How to read Lacan.* London: Norton.

Žižek, S. (2008a). *For they know not what they do: Enjoyment as a political factor* (2nd edn). London: Verso.

Žižek, S. (2008b). *Violence: Six sideways reflections.* London: Profile Books.

Žižek, S. (2009). *In defense of lost causes.* London: Verso.

PART II
Concepts and theories

7

SITUATED, RELATIONAL AND PRACTICE-ORIENTED

The actor-network theory approach

Radhika Gorur

Researchers of policy who are interested in policy processes, doings and enactments, and who seek to explore the messiness and uncertainty that attends the lives and careers of policies, would be drawn to actor-network theory (ANT). Although ANT is not a 'policy theory' as such, it has much to offer a policy researcher who wishes to:

> focus on how different people, materials, and practices meet to somehow cobble together shared worlds, worlds that are always under negotiation and always dynamic, yet somehow manage to cohere.
>
> *(Spinuzzi, 2003)*

ANT is a material-semiotic approach that offers theoretical and methodological resources that direct attention to the practices that create, mobilise, sustain or challenge relations between actors in any social phenomenon. Using empirical case studies, ANT researchers describe the mundane and everyday practices through which, eventually, ideas are stabilised, systems are established and actors become powerful. It does not use power as an *explanation,* as is common in many forms of sociology – rather, it seeks to explain *how power is achieved.*

Origins

ANT grew out of Science and Technology Studies (STS), which have drawn together historians and philosophers of science; sociologists; anthropologists; economists; and scholars in political and legal sciences. Regarding 'science' (used in the sense of 'knowledge') as a human endeavour as well as a social system, STS scholars reject dichotomies such as nature and science, and society and culture. ANT was conceptualised by Michel Callon, an economist; Bruno Latour, a philosopher; and John Law, a sociologist, in the late 1970s and the early 1980s

(Law, 2009a). Law traces several influences to the origins of ANT, including systems studies in engineering and management, such as the historical studies of technology of Thomas Hughes and Michel Callon; studies of laboratory practices and other makings of science, including the theories of Thomas Kuhn and the laboratory studies of Bruno Latour; the influence of Michel Serres and his work on order, disorder and translation; and the influence of poststructuralism, particularly the work of Michel Foucault. But whereas Foucault attends to 'the productively strategic and relational character of epochal epistemes', ANT focuses on 'the strategic, relational, and productive character of particular, smaller-scale, heterogeneous actor networks' (Law, 2009a: 145). ANT is also closely related to Deleuze's 'nomadic philosphy' (Deleuze and Guattari, 1998), as Law explains:

> Latour has observed that we might talk of 'actant rhizomes' rather than 'actor networks', and John Law has argued that there is little difference between Deleuze's agencement (awkwardly translated as 'assemblage' in English) and the term 'actor network' (Law 2004). Both refer to the provisional assembly of productive, heterogeneous, and (this is the crucial point) quite limited forms of ordering located in no larger overall order. This is why it is helpful to see actor network theory as a particular empirical translation of poststructuralism.
>
> *(Law, 2009a: 145–146)*

Whilst the term 'actor-network' was useful in early ANT accounts to express the relational productions of actors and networks, it soon became a liability – the term 'network' too often evoked a kind of structure (such as a transport network or a communication network), which did not evoke the precariousness, contingency and relationality that 'actor-network' sought to convey (Latour, 1999a). Some scholars of ANT – which is itself increasingly being referred to as 'material semiotics' – have switched to using the term 'assemblage' as an alternative to 'actor-network' (Law, 2009a). In this chapter, the two are used interchangeably.

How is ANT located in relation to sociology more broadly? One important point of departure between traditional sociologies and ANT is that the two have very different conceptualisations of the meaning and composition of 'the social'. For ANT researchers, 'the social' is an assemblage made up of heterogeneous elements held together through a series of associations. The material is an important participant of the social. Latour distinguishes it from traditional sociologies, especially critical sociologies, by designating traditional sociologies as 'sociology of the social' and ANT as 'sociology of associations'. ANT is also not concerned with 'why' and steers clear of ascribing intentions to actors. Instead, concerned with 'how', it focuses on the practical accomplishments of power.

ANT eschews the use of the standard sociological categories such as race and gender as *a priori* explanations, instead focusing on the socio-material relations that enable such categories to be established and stabilised. In this regard, and in its insistence on a post-humanistic approach, it differs from other theories of policy enactment, and makes a distinct contribution to policy studies.

Theory, methodology or analytical toolkit?

Although ANT has the word 'theory' in it, it is more usefully conceptualised as a 'sensibility' or a 'set of tools' rather than a theory:

> actor network approach is not a theory. Theories usually try to explain why something happens, but actor network theory is descriptive rather than foundational in explanatory terms, which means that it is a disappointment for those seeking strong accounts. Instead it tells stories about 'how' relations assemble or don't . . . [I]t is better understood as a toolkit for telling interest-ing stories about, and interfering in, those relations. More profoundly, it is a sensibility to the messy practices of relationality and materiality of the world. Along with this sensibility comes a wariness of the large-scale claims com-mon in social theory: these usually seem too simple.
>
> *(Law, 2009a: 142–143)*

Understanding ANT as a sensibility and a set of tools rather than a theory has important analytical implications. ANT offers no ready-made explanatory frame-work with which to approach social phenomena. Rather, it provides concepts with which one can trace associations that make up the empirical phenomena one is studying. In other words, it is not a theory that one *applies*, throwing it like a web over a situation in order to explain it; rather it is a sensibility that is *deployed* to describe and understand how a phenomenon coheres or fails to do so (Latour, 2005). Latour (2005: 17) describes ANT as a kind of 'travel guide':

> 'where to travel' and 'what is worth seeing there' is nothing but a way of saying in plain English what is usually said under the pompous Greek name of 'method' or, even worse, 'methodology'. The advantage of a travel book approach over a 'discourse on method' is that it cannot be confused with the territory on which it simply overlays. A guide can be put to use as well as forgotten, placed in a backpack, stained with grease and coffee, scribbled all over, its pages torn apart to light a fire under a barbecue. In brief, it offers suggestions rather than imposing itself on the reader.

In turn, the researcher also does not impose herself on the terrain studied. Nothing is taken for granted. Setting out like anthropologists studying an exotic land, ANT researchers make the familiar strange so that they may learn from the actors them-selves how they make sense of their worlds. In the words of Latour (2005: 30):

> If I had to provide a checklist for what is a good ANT account – this will be an important indicator of quality – are the concepts of the actors allowed to be stronger than that of the analysts, or is it the analyst who is doing all the talking?

ANT researchers, then, approach their empirical sites armed with a few tools, and prepared to abandon the most basic held notions, such as the nature of groups and the nature of 'the social'.

Actors in ANT

ANT regards social phenomena as networks of relations between actors. 'Actors' are themselves not pre-formed – both the actors and the networks are simultaneously and reciprocally performed (hence the hyphen in the term 'actor-network' – actors and networks co-produce each other). Characteristics of actors are never pre-supposed or essential – they are always an empirical and contingent matter.

ANT researches pay attention to human as well as non-human entities, refusing an a priori distinction between the two in their capacity to act. Anything that 'acts' is taken to be an 'actor' (or, more correctly, an 'actant'). ANT proposes that objects have agency and 'do' things: forge relations, configure users, act as mediators, translate interests and perform politics. Non-humans may participate as delegates of humans – for instance, the untiring and always-there 'sleeping policeman' (speed bump) stands in for its less robust and more easily fatigued (and more easily ignored) human counterpart (Callon and Latour, 1992), and the hydraulic door-closing system proves to be a more reliable actor than a human 'groom' (Latour, 1988). Here, non-humans assist humans in gaining the ability to act at a distance. Non-humans are thus deeply implicated in technologies of governance. Not only do such objects as 'sleeping policemen' stand in for human counterparts, they also translate drivers' interests and regulate their behaviour: drivers may not respond to the injunction not to endanger pedestrians, but they may be more inclined to slow down to avoid damaging their car's suspension, as Latour (1992) explains. Thus not only do humans delegate tasks to non-humans, non-humans also impose behaviours – and even morals – on humans. The attention to non-humans in ANT is thus not mere whimsy; it has deep implication for the politics of its critique.

The symmetrical treatment of entities and the refusal to distinguish between 'human' and 'non-human' as prior categories is an analytical stance that facilitates the observation of which actants act (Latour, 1992, 1999a), and what relations or movements make action possible. By attending impartially to all the active entities in assemblages – what Latour (2005) calls 'mediators' – the performative or empirically agentic participation of things previously considered uninvolved and unimportant come to be recognised.

Shifting the focus from human actors to *socio-material practices* allows the ANT policy researcher to attend to the *performative functions* of socio-material inscription devices such as evaluative tools, computer software, forms and surveys in such processes as standardisation, commensuration and universalisation that are so important in the spread of innovations and knowledge practices.

Translation

Actors enter into relations with other actors through processes of 'translation'. These processes have been elaborated famously by Michel Callon (1986) as consisting of four 'moments':

1   problematisation, where a problem is articulated in such a way that the articu-
    lators can then become indispensable to the solution;
2   interessement, in which actors come between other actors and their desired goals;
3   enrolment, in which actors are assigned specific roles and relationships; and
4   mobilisation, a process by which one set of actors gains the ability to become
    spokespersons for the collective (Gorur, 2013).

Actors may become powerful in their capacity to translate other actors by setting up 'obligatory passage points' through which actors must pass in order to
become relevant. Some actors may gain the power to become spokespersons with
the authority to speak on behalf of other actors. Some actor-networks may become
'centres of calculation', (Latour, 1987) and occupy positions that allow them to
have a grand overview of the domain they are interested in controlling and the
authority to produce credible knowledge (Gorur, 2011a; Latour, 1999b).

Although the 'four moments' offers a convenient heuristic, and the notion of
translation remains central to ANTish approaches to understanding relations
between actors, Latour, Law and even Callon himself do not 'apply' the 'four
moments' explicitly in their studies – precisely because ANT is not a theory that
one applies as a ready-made explanation. Theory and the empirical are always in
dialogue in ANT accounts.

Stabilisation of actor-networks: one way of thinking about power

ANT does not regard power as an essential or inherent property of any actor,
phenomenon or object. Actor-networks gain strength as they involve more actors
and become imbricated and embedded in more practices. The stronger the
actor-network and the harder it is to displace it, the more easily it travels, entering
other actor-networks and insinuating itself into more places and practices. The
naturalisation and ubiquity of the Christian calendar to calculate a person's age is
an example: this way of understanding age is now embedded deeply into how
students are grouped in schools, the setting of literacy standards, and the categorisations
of 'special needs' and 'giftedness'. The more the networks in which age is calculated
based on chronology, the more natural the practice appears, displacing other forms
that once existed, and may still exist on the margins in some communities.

ANT studies attempt to open up the black boxes of the taken-for-granted and
reclaim their tentativeness and contingency by tracing their routes to naturalisation.
This makes possible the introduction of other calculations and practices. This
taken-for-grantedness and naturalisation is the source of power in ANT studies.

Power is thus not offered as an explanation in ANT studies; it is the processes
by which power is achieved that ANT seeks to describe. ANT studies reveal unexpected conduits of power and thus open up multiple possibilities for interfering in
relations that sustain and stabilise power.

Whenever someone speaks of a 'system', a 'global feature', a 'structure', a 'society', an 'empire', a 'world economy', and 'organization', the first ANT reflex should be to ask: 'in which building? In which bureau? Through which corridor is it accessible? Which colleagues has it been read to? How has it been compiled?' Inquirers, if they accept to follow this clue, will be surprised at the number of sites and the number of conduits that pop up as soon as those queries are being raised.

(Latour, 2005: 183)

This turning around of what are seen as explanations for phenomena in traditional sociologies – such things as 'system', 'structure' or even 'society' – as themselves needing explanation is a major contribution of ANT to policy studies (Latour, 2005). The focus of the analysis is on how these phenomena are materialised in and through practices, and how they gain the ability to exert power. As a result, global policy phenomena that appear monolithic and difficult to displace are broken down into specific, mundane practices (Law, 2008; Gorur, 2008). And this opens up possibilities of interference and intervention:

This, then, is the leitmotif . . . It is to refuse to be overawed by seemingly large systems, and the seeming ontological unity of the world enacted by large systems. It is, instead, to make the problem smaller, or better, to make it more specific. To deal with the materialities of specific practices. To discover difference. And then to intervene in ways that might make a difference to those differences.

(Law, 2008: 637)

ANT researchers focus on discursive and material practices, rather than linguistic representations. ANT does not accord language the unique power of being able to access some prior reality that is otherwise unavailable. Instead, it sees realities as socio-material assemblages that cohere through practices. ANT takes instruments, methodologies and concepts to be agentic in the production of phenomena. Instruments – whether laboratory instruments such as measuring flasks, or survey instruments such as questionnaires – afford the recognition of certain entities and attributes while excluding others from the reckoning. The work of categorisation and standardisation that is achieved through forms, questionnaires and surveys is particularly highlighted in the work of Bowker and Leigh Star (see, for instance, Bowker and Star, 2000; and also Law, 2009b).

The focus on socio-material practices and the attention to the accomplishments of mundane interactions in particular practices turns up unexpected sets of actors. The attention moves from:

the traditional characters that were supposed to occupy the political stage – citizens, assemblies of 'mini-kings', ideologies, deliberations, votes, elections; the traditional sites of political events – street demonstrations, parliaments, executive rooms, command and control headquarters; and the traditional passions we spontaneously associate with the political – indignation, anger, back room deals, violence, etc. . . . [to] white coated technicians, corporate room CEOs, mathematicians scribbling at the blackboard, patent lawyers, surveyors, innovators, entrepreneurs and experts of all sorts, all of whom were carrying out their activities in sites totally unrelated to the loci of political action and through means that were absolutely different from the maintenance or the subversion of law and order. A vaccine, an incandescent lamp, an equation, a pollution standard, a building, a blood screening procedure, those were the new means through which politics was being carried out.

(Latour, 2007: 812–813)

Thus the politics of ANT looks somewhat different from more traditional accounts of power, and often it is not the 'usual suspects' that feature in ANT stories.

Because ANT researchers trace how practices enact realities, their focus is not epistemology but ontology. The analytical stance is performative rather than representational (Pickering, 1995). The shift to the idiom of performativity demands that researchers regard their own practices as a moral enterprise, which necessitates the asking of the question 'what types of worlds are being brought into being, and with what consequences?' A crucial corollary to that question is 'What kinds of worlds do we want to bring into being?'

Methodology: telling ANTish tales

There are no set rules about how ANT is 'done'. However, one methodological implication of thinking of realities as assemblages or networks of practices, is that researchers must get in amongst the practices. As Law (2010: 2) puts it:

There is an immediate methodological consequence [of thinking in terms of practices]. We need to proceed empirically. If we are to do philosophy, metaphysics, politics, or explore the character of knowledge, we cannot do this in the abstract. We cannot work 'in general', because there is no 'in general'. All there is are: specific sites and their practices, and then the specificities of those practices. So philosophy becomes empirical. Abstraction is always done in some practice or other.

This means that ANT accounts are necessarily case studies (Law, 2009a). ANT cases come in a very wide variety – from studies of successful or failed innovations, to the practices of knowledge making, to the study of markets, to workplace practices, and to the spread of ideas.

One frequently cited (and often frowned upon) exhortation in ANT is to 'follow the actors' as they go about accessing resources, making associations, subjectifying themselves and rendering things stable. Sometimes this takes a very literal meaning, as it did in Latour's studies. For example, in his seminal study of laboratory life (Latour and Woolgar, 1979), he literally followed the scientists in the

Salk Laboratory in San Diego to document how they went about 'doing science'. Such research would entail participant observation, conversations and interviews, and note taking. Sometimes ANT research involves tracing actions in history, through the study of historical documents, letters and other artefacts (Law, 1986). Accounts in education policy studies typically involve analyses of policy documents, studying media reports, observation and interviews. For instance, Koyama (2011) studied how principals coped with the imposition of external agencies for managing tutoring programs for students who were 'underperforming'. Over three years of ethnographic research, Koyama interviewed a range of principals, parents, administrators and private tutoring company officials; followed media reports as controversies became mediatised; and explored policy documents. My studies of policy (Gorur, 2008, 2011a, 2011b, 2013, 2014; Gorur and Koyama, 2013) have involved interviewing a number of policy makers and measurement experts to understand how they go about their practices, what challenges and dilemmas they encounter and how they are managed.

Latour (2004, 2005) draws clear distinctions between ANT (the sociology of associations) and critical sociology. He says that the purpose of ANT is not 'unveiling, behind the actors' backs, the "social forces at work"' (p. 136), he insists that ANT accounts must refrain from making sense of research sites *on behalf of* the actors on the site. ANT researchers don't seek to deconstruct, unmask or expose:

> The critic is not the one who debunks, but the one who assembles. The critic is not the one who lifts the rugs from under the feet of the naive believers, but the one who offers the participants arenas in which to gather.
>
> *(Latour, 2004: 246)*

Putting ANT to work in education policy studies

Researchers from a variety of philosophical, epistemological and methodological persuasions have been exploring the possibilities offered by ANT in a range of substantive areas, such as animals and nature, medical practice, economics, the political economy, gender, organisation and work, technology, and, increasingly, education policy.[1] However, ANT is still relatively novel in the field of education. Fenwick and Edwards' (2010) *Actor-network theory in education* provides an introduction to ANT, showcases exemplary ANT studies in education, and provides suggestions on how ANT concepts can be used to study issues in education. Their edited collection (2012), *Researching education through actor-network theory*, based on a special issue of the journal *Educational Philosophy and Theory*, provides a collection of ANT accounts in education. Fenwick (2010: 131) explains what an ANT sensibility can bring to the study of education policy:

> ANT sensibilities ask: How do powerful networks (particular stabilized knowledge, accountability systems, evaluative practices) emerge? What connections assemble objects and people into these extended networks that

can wield so much influence? What and who becomes included and excluded? What individual identities and behaviors are translated in becoming part of the network? What negotiations occur as individual elements take up, resist, or compete with the attempts to enroll and mobilize them into particular patterns of action and knowledge? The policy analysis then becomes a question of how things like standards – that is, the assemblies of texts, objects, bodies, practices, and desires that instantiate what we recognize as 'standards' – become enacted.

The recent focus on 'enactment' in the study of education policy (e.g. Ball, McGuire and Braun, 2012) has also led to an attention to materiality, and to the networked nature of dominant actors in national and transnational policy terrains. These accounts share with ANT post-structuralist leanings and an interest in power. However, some fundamental differences remain between these accounts and ANT studies. These include ANT's conceptualisation of 'the social' as a hybrid entity, rather than as composed of humans, its refusal to make an a priori distinction between a phenomenon and its 'context', and its post-humanist understandings of performativity.

ANT lends itself to the study of a variety of aspects of policy. Three are outlined below.

Big things

Big things and established phenomena invite ANT researchers to explore and describe how their size and scale are achieved. There are several 'big things' in education policy today – ideas and practices that have 'gone global', like large-scale comparisons, the practices of providing 'school choice', accountability practices and the involvement of transnational organisations such as the OECD and the EU. These are 'big things' for two reasons – first, they represent practices that have become widespread and normalised; and second, they dovetail into one another so that they are 'networked' – disturbing any one of these destabilises the other – and as a corollary, it is difficult to destabilise any one of these things as it is too well enmeshed in related practices. Change thus becomes costly to implement. Nevertheless, such networks remain precarious and always subject to falling apart or becoming modified.

ANT accounts can challenge the apparently monolithic nature or hegemony of 'big things' in education by following the practices that render them big. Some studies of big things in contemporary phenomena such as accountability measures and evidence include those of Koyama (2010); Gorur (2011a, 2013); Gorur and Koyama (2013); and Decuypere, Ceulemans and Simons (2014).

ANT studies may also show how apparently singular phenomena are in fact 'multiple' – i.e. a range of logics and modes are folded into what may appear to be 'one' thing (Law, 1994; Mol, 2002). For example, 'standards' often seek to regulate and singularise practices. But several ANT studies trace the doing, undoing multiple enactments of standards, challenging dominant policy accounts (e.g. Fenwick, 2010; Hamilton, 2011; Mulcahy, 2011).

'Matters of concern'

Latour (2004) has famously spoken of converting 'matters of fact' into 'matters of concern' as one of the main purposes of ANT research. Here, taken-for-granted and apparently self-evident phenomena are examined closely to discover how it is that they came to be taken-for-granted. The idea is not to discredit or debunk, but to make visible the various translations and negotiations and compromises and controversies that attended the phenomena before they became taken-for-granted. Such descriptions make it possible to keep some of the underlying questions and assumptions open for revisiting as new actors appear and new information presents itself. In these studies, matters that appear settled are reclaimed as sites of contestation and debate. See for example, Gorur (2014).

Studying controversies and innovations

Controversies and innovations are potential 'big things' or 'matters of fact' in the making. Sites of innovation and controversy provide attractive sites for an ANT researcher, since it is seething with a variety of points of view and a heterogeneity of practices, the outcomes of which are not known. They offer a rich mix of facts, objects, people, rhetoric, institutions, protocols and a number of other actors all bidding to translate each other, impose their view on the scene, become spokespersons and so on.

Bigum and Rowan (2004), Rowan and Bigum (2009) and Nespor (1997, 2011) provide instructive accounts of how ANT can be deployed to follow the fates and careers of innovations in education. In addition, Nespor's work provides exemplars for how ANT researchers may conduct school and classroom ethnographies.

Suggested Reading

The works referenced in this paper include some of the seminal ANT works. In particular, Latour's *Reassembling the social* serves well as an ANT textbook, and Fenwick and Edwards' *Actor-network theory and education* provides a very useful guide to how ANT might be deployed in education.

Note

1 A very useful resource for those interested in ANT is the Actor Network Resource website maintained at Lancaster University, initiated by John Law (www.lancaster.ac.uk/fass/centres/css/ant/ant.htm).

References

Ball, S. J., Maguire, M. and Braun, A. (2012). *How schools do policy: Policy enactments in secondary schools*. New York: Routledge.

Bigum, C. and Rowan, L. (2004). Flexible learning in teacher education: Myths, muddles and models. *Asia Pacific Journal of Teacher Education, 32*(3), 213–226.

Bowker, G. C. and Star, S. L. (2000). *Sorting things out – classification and its consequences*. Cambridge, MA and London: The MIT Press.

Callon, M. (1986). Some elements of a sociology of translation: The domestication of the scallops and the fishermen of St Brieuc Bay. In J. Law (Ed.), *Power, action and belief: A new sociology of knowledge?* Boston, MA and London: Routledge & Kegan Paul.

Callon, M. and Latour, B. (1992). Don't throw the baby out with the bath school! A reply to Collins and Yearly. In A. Pickering (Ed.), *Science as practice and culture*. Chicago: The University of Chicago Press.

Decuypere, M., Ceulemans, C. and Simons, M. (2014). Schools in the making: Mapping digital spaces of evidence. *Journal of Education Policy, 29*(5), 617–639.

Deleuze, G. and Guttari, F. (1998). *A thousand plateaus: Capitalism and schizophrenia*. London: Athlone Press.

Fenwick, T. (2010). Un-doing standards in education with actor-network theory. *Journal of Education Policy, 25*(2), 117–133.

Fenwick, T. and Edwards, R. (2010). *Actor-network theory and education*. London: Routledge.

Fenwick, T. and Edwards, R. (Eds.) (2012). *Researching education through actor-network theory*. Chichester, UK: Wiley-Blackwell.

Gorur, R. (2008). *Explaining global policy phenomena using the small and the mundane: A network analysis of PISA*. Paper presented at the AARE 2008 International Education Research Conference Brisbane.

Gorur, R. (2011a). ANT on the PISA Trail: Following the statistical pursuit of certainty. *Educational Philosophy and Theory, 43*(5–6), 76–93.

Gorur, R. (2011b). Policy as assemblage. *European Educational Research Journal, 10*(4), 611–622.

Gorur, R. (2013). My school, my market. *Discourse: Studies in the Cultural Politics of Education, 34*(2), 214–230.

Gorur, R. (2014). Towards a sociology of measurement technologies in education policy. *European Educational Research Journal, 13*(1), 58–72.

Gorur, R. and Koyama, J. P. (2013). The struggle to technicise in education policy. *Australian Educational Researcher, Online*. doi: 10.1007/s13384-013-0125-9.

Hamilton, M. (2011). Unruly practices: What a sociology of translations can offer to educational policy analysis. *Educational Philosophy & Theory, 43*(S1), 55–75.

Koyama, J. (2010). *Making failure pay: High stakes testing; for-profit tutoring and public schools*. Chicago: The University of Chicago Press.

Koyama, J. (2011). Principals, power, and policy: Enacting 'supplemental educational services'. *Anthropology & Education Quarterly, 42*(1), 20–36.

Latour, B. (1987). *Science in action: How to follow scientists and engineers through society*. Cambridge, MA: Harvard University Press.

Latour, B. (1988). Mixing humans and nonhumans together: The sociology of a door-closer. *Social Problems, 35*(3), 298–310.

Latour, B. (1992). Where are the missing masses? The sociology of a few mundane artifacts. In W. Bijker and J. Law (Eds.), *Shaping technology / building society: Studies in sociotechnical change*. Cambridge, MA: The MIT Press.

Latour, B. (1999a). On recalling ANT. In J. Law and J. Hassard (Eds.), *Actor network theory and after* (p. 256). Oxford, UK: Blackwell Publishers.

Latour, B. (1999b). *Pandora's hope: Essays on the reality of science studies*. Cambridge, MA and London: Harvard University Press.

Latour, B. (2004). Why has critique run out of steam? From matters of fact to matters of concern. *Critical Inquiry 30*(Winter 2004), 227.

Latour, B. (2005). *Reassembling the social: An introduction to actor-network-theory*. Oxford, UK: Oxford University Press.

Latour, B. (2007). Turning around politics: A note on Gerard de Vries' paper. *Social Studies of Science, 37*(5), 811–820.

Latour, B. and Woolgar, S. (1979). *Laboratory life – the construction of scientific facts*. Princeton, NJ: Princeton University Press.

Law, J. (1986). On the methods of long distance control: Vessels, navigation, and the Portuguese route to India. In J. Law (Ed.), *Power, action and belief: A new sociology of knowledge?* (pp. 234–263). Henley, UK: Routledge.

Law, J. (1994). *Organising modernity*. Oxford, UK and Cambridge, MA: Blackwell.

Law, J. (2008). On sociology and STS. *The Sociological Review, 56*(4), 623–649.

Law, J. (2009a). Actor network theory and material semiotics. In B. S. Turner (Ed.), *The new Blackwell companion to social theory* (pp. 141–158). Oxford, UK: Blackwell-Wiley.

Law, J. (2009b). Seeing like a survey. *Cultural Sociology, 2*(2), 239–256.

Law, J. (2010). Collateral realities. Retrieved from http://heterogeneities.net/publications/Law2009CollateralRealities.pdf.

Mol, A. (2002). *The body multiple: Ontology in medical practice*. Durham, CA and London: Duke University Press.

Mulcahy, D. (2011). Assembling the 'accomplished' teacher: The performativity and politics of professional teaching standards. *Educational Philosophy and Theory, 43*(S1), 94–113.

Nespor, J. (1997). *Tangled up in school: Politics, space, bodies, and signs in the educational process*. Mahway, NJ: Lawrence Erlbaum.

Nespor, J. (2011). Devices and educational change. *Educational Philosophy and Theory, 43*(S1), 15–37.

Pickering, A. (1995). *The mangle of practice: Time, agency, and science*. Chicago, IL: University of Chicago Press.

Rowan, L. and Bigum, C. (2009). 'What's your problem?' ANT reflections on a research project studying girls enrolment in information technology subjects in postcompulsory education. *International Journal of Actor-Network Theory and Technological Innovation, 1*(4), 1–20.

Spinuzzi, C. (2003). More than one, less that many: A review of three 'post-ANT' books. *Currents in Electronic Literacy, 7*.

8

THINKING EDUCATIONAL POLICY AND MANAGEMENT THROUGH (FRICTIONAL) CONCEPTS OF AFFECTS

Dorthe Staunæs and Justine Grønbæk Pors

> [T]o attend to affective atmospheres is to learn to be affected by the ambiguities of affect/emotion, by that which is determinate and indeterminate, present and absent, singular and vague.
>
> *(Anderson, 2009: 80)*

In this chapter, we will explore a methodology of reading through concepts of affects in empirical research of education policy. Concepts of affects direct our attention to the specific character, or you may call it the specific quality of an atmosphere (for instance, the heated atmosphere in a room where educators and politicians are in discussion). The concept of affects makes us think of overwhelming passions ('Oh, yes, I love numbers and graphs!') and of nearly felt sentiments and senses ('something is not really right here, but I am not sure what the problem is. I just feel uncomfortable'). Concepts of affects do, however, also allow for an attention to more specific feelings of anger, shame, joy, trust, e.g. they allow one to think very broadly in terms of tensions and the charging of energies, of being touched and moved for instance by a Programme for International Student Assessment (PISA) shock (Sellar and Lingard 2013; Staunæs and Pors, 2011).

In several countries, the term 'PISA shock' has been used when international comparisons of students' performances are published. Without going into the content or quality of either PISA or student performances, we find that the term 'PISA shock' can open up our analytical gaze for making an affective turn in methodologies in education studies. The use of the word 'shock' in the media and among educators and politicians indicates that PISA results do not exclusively strike at rational or reflexive indexes, but also at affective registers. Thinking with Brian Massumi, 'shock' is a term for the tiny affective charges, we experience, when something unexpected – whether it is good or bad – hits us (Massumi, 2009). Shock arises out of sudden disturbances of current connections. A shock is the moment when one affective state of mind transforms into another state of mind, and when the power and the potential to affect or be affected is induced in new, indefinite ways – thus contributing to a change of experience, focus and attention (Massumi, 2002: 15). In this theoretical framework, being affected by a PISA shock is not necessarily something bad. It may hit a negative as well as a positive register. However, one may wonder what kind of action potential a shock implies, and how a shock affects enactments of educational policy.

With this chapter, we aim to provide a tentative analytical framework for studying the production and reconfiguration of affect in education policy. We ask:

- How can empirical data on education policy be analysed through different concepts of affects?
- What kinds of insights do these concepts of affect allow?
- How may these differing concepts be used simultaneously and frictionally and yet productively in empirical analysis?

We present conceptual elements of what have been termed the affective turn in the humanities and social sciences (Clough, 2007; Hemmings, 2005; Stenner and Greco, 2008) as a resource for asking analytical questions and pursuing certain movements and lines in empirical data. We do not attempt to work towards a model representing what affects are. Rather we try to elaborate the analytical strategies that emerge from thinking through different concepts of affects/affectivity. The way in which we relate theory and empirical data can be characterised by the term 'thinking through theory', coined by Lisa Mazzei and Alecia Youngblood Jackson (2012). This terminology points to a long tradition in post-structuralism and post-constructionist work emphasised with words like 'thinking technologies', 'diffractive readings', 'transfiguration', 'analytical methodologies', 'reflexive second order readings' and 'plugging one theory' into another (Brown and Stenner, 2009; Lykke, Markussen and Olesen, 2008; Mazzei and Jackson, 2012). Instead of asking the question of whether this knowledge is true or not, these approaches have developed analytical tools and employed them to reach objectives such as destabilising what is already known, and to explore how knowledge is performative in the sense of having effects, and finally to emphasise that conceptualisation and transfigurations may do something to our understandings and thereby our possibilities of action (Sedgwick, 2003). As Mazzei and Jackson (2012: 8) write:

> We characterize this reading-the-data-while-thinking-the-theory as a moment of plugging in, of entering the assemblage, of making new connectives. We began to realize how plugging in creates a different relationship among texts: they constitute one another and in doing so create something new.

One may also name this reading strategy a diffractive methodology (Barad, 2007; Juelskjær and Swennesen, 2012). This is a terminology emphasising that insights from different frameworks are read through one another. Diffraction refers to the turn (light) waves takes when they pass from one kind of material to another (Haraway, 1992). Diffraction is not reflection or miming. To read diffractively means to let different materials and concepts pass (actively) through one another and deflect. Thus, theoretical concepts are understood as an opportunity to compose methodological strategies by which empirical material can be deflected and thereby reconfigured. This way it becomes possible to pursue certain routes through empirical data and to grasp the peculiarity of what seems familiar and taken for granted.

In this chapter, we present both Deleuzian/Massumian concepts of indeterminate affectivity and potentiality and concepts of more determinate and linguistically captured affects, specifically the concept of shame developed by queer-theorists Eve Sedgwick, Sara Ahmed and Elspeth Probyn. These two approaches may seem mutually inconsistent, but, as we will argue, bringing them together can be a fruitful methodological strategy when engaging with educational policy, exactly because of the potential for friction (Hvenegaard and Staunæs, 2014; Puar, 2007, 2012). In order to unfold the kinds of research questions that thinking with (different) concepts of affect triggers, we engage with a specific Organisation for Economic Co-operation and Development (OECD)-report entitled Teaching and Learning in Primary and Upper Secondary Education (TALIS) and its reception in Denmark.

Affective turn(s)

The affective turn is an attempt to invite the energetic, the physical, and the sensual back into the humanities and social sciences (Wetherell, 2012). The affective turn implies discontinuities as well as continuities with the methodologies provided by the linguistic turn. Rather than reading the shift to affects as a turning away from the linguistic turn, we propose that an affective turn should not be viewed as a rejection of, but rather as complicating reversions of the original outsets in the linguistic framework, namely the performative outset, that explored how the world is 'done', 'enacted' and 'performed' rather than represented (Barad, 2003; Butler, 1990, 2010). The turn to affect is an attempt to open up the analytical perspective to matter and energies by including 'more than' merely linguistic components as constituents of worlds and subjectivities. Thus, the object of analysis is not solely linguistics, words and subject positions (highlighted in post-structuralism), and relations, identities and language (highlighted in social constructionism), but also affective qualities and tensions in and beyond what is recognised as the social.

At least two interesting additions are produced when these concepts of affectivity enter our methodological repertoire. First, concepts of affect disturb some of the dichotomies often produced in common sense thinking, but also in academic theories, such as dichotomies between emotional and rational, human and non-human. Concepts of affects involve, transgress and are entangled with both matter and discourse, both human and non-human, both content and form. The second addition resulting from an affective turn is the possibility of moving our reading of data from identities towards intensities. This concerns intensity as tensions, energies and forces. It concerns how intensity may charge for instance non-human subjects, matters and relations, and thereby making something and someone capable of moving and being moved, touching and being touched, affecting and being affected. Affectivity is not installed in somebody or something; rather affectivity is the capacity of influencing on and through somebody/something. However, the effect of affect can be in the form of human bodily expressions such as blushing, increased heartbeat, chills and shivers, sweaty palms, clammy mouth, nervous twitches.

It is misleading to talk about an affective turn in singular, since it seems there are (at least) two distinct and important landmarks – one stemming from the position initiated by Brian Massumi's book *Parables for the virtual* (2002) and another taking its point of departure in the eye-opening introduction 'Shame in the cybernetic fold: Reading Silvan Tomkins' in *Shame and its sisters* (1995) by Eve Sedgwick and Adam Frank (1995). Let us begin with the Massumian approach on indeterminate affectivity.

Reading through the concept of in/determinate affectivity

The affective turn of Massumi (2002) builds on the philosophies of Gilles Deleuze and Benedicto Spinoza. In contrast to approaches that regard emotions as belonging to human individuals, this framework coins affectivity not as something someone is or has. Rather, affectivity is conceptualised as autonomous, non-individual or pre-individual forces that may hit and transform individual beings. These may broadly be known as atmosphere, sentiments, sensations, senses, emotions and feelings.

Massumi's affective turn is an example of a terminology that persistently insists on 'the moment before' entities come into being, and which in addition highlights the intensity of these processes. It is an attempt to think along connective lines, their intensity and mutual tension. Affectivity is vibrant and always about to become something else. The focus is not on the actual and the given, but on another very real aspect of the world and of being, namely the virtual (Deleuze, 1996). Rather than foregrounding, what may be termed, actuality, gridlocks and entities, the Massumian approach can be read as a way of focusing on affective indeterminacy and pinpointing the way in which coming into existence happens in a field of potentiality, always on the move (see also, Braidotti, 1994; Colebrook, 2009). As Massumi (2002: 7–8) writes in *Parables for the virtual*:

> when positioning of any kind comes a determining first, movement comes a problematic second. After all is signified and sited, there is the nagging problem of how to add movement back into the picture.

For Massumi (2002), the very distinction between affect and emotion is a cardinal point. Affect is the indeterminate moment before this capacity becomes a linguistic seizure of already known and 'conceptualised' emotions. But what is this moment before then? Massumi imports evidence from the neurosciences where 'a missing half second' before affects come into consciousness has been measured. However, as we will address in the following, this may neither be entirely unproblematic nor analytically fruitful.

A frictional framework

In 1995, Sedgwick and Frank criticised cultural studies for having prioritised language/symbolisation and foregrounded binaries i.e. of nature/culture in order to escape from essentialism: the enemy of political and cultural change. Since 1995, Papoulias and Callard (2010) argue, a remapping of the conceptual terrain of theory and a recalibration between (cultural) theory and 'science' has taken place. They argue that an import of evidence from neuro-science and developmental psychology are 'part of a strange and partial (mis)translation of complex scientific models into epistemologically distinct space of the humanities and social sciences' (p. 31). This may mean that the ideal of 'good theory' in cultural studies is turned upside down: Sedgwick and Frank were destabilising the everything-is-a-social-construction point of view by inviting biology into the picture, whereby not only language but also biology was conceptualised as performative (Ibid; 31). However, Papoulias and Callard propose, since then, that much work on affects has used and misused biology. Often, affect is privileged over feelings/emotions, and thus (only) biology is favoured as the unpredictable, fluid and dynamic. Perhaps such an approach is caught in its own ontology of movement and positive valuation of movement. A question emerges of why movement and intensity should stop because affects turn into linguistic captured feelings (see, Wetherell, 2012). Could linguistically captured feelings like for instance shame or anger not call upon an urge to act and thereby incite movement?

Two critical remarks seem relevant here:

1   When affect is conceptualised as autonomous, subjectivity as well as ideology/habitus/hexis are by-passed.
2   When affects are thought of as (only) matter and energy but not discourse.

The poaching of concepts from biology may demand a forgetting of the discursive system and modes of argumentation that have given rise to it and of the specific network of relations that give it meaning.

Following these critiques, our worry is that by privileging the non-discursive, the affective turn closes methodological and analytical possibilities in advance. Rather than just following the preference for neuroscience, we propose that 'the moment before' can be an invitation to read ambivalence, friction and indeterminacy as central moments in empirical material. As a methodological strategy, we follow the distinction between undefined affectivity and linguistically defined emotions. In order to do this kind of reading, we need different theoretical apparatuses to plug into and we need different sets of conceptual tools to enable us to follow the fluidity and increase/decrease of affectivity and the processes of affective circulations and transmission in the empirical material. We also ask for tools that make us able to examine the (momentary) halt of the social-material-discursive quality and intensity of specific affects and how particular determinate affects may charge and move us in specific ways. And finally, how indeterminate intensity is transformed into and circulates as determinate affects such as for instance shame, thrill or joy.

Reading through determinate affects and registers: shame as example

In order to provide an example of how to think with a concept of determinate affects, we now present another strand in affect studies initiated by queer theorists. In particular, there seems to be an appeal in returning to and reworking the social psychologist Silvan Tomkins's affect theory on shame (Ahmed, 2004; Bjerg and Staunæs, 2011; Probyn, 2005) and his different affective registers. Tomkins does not make a sharp distinction between emotions and affects, but uses the word 'affect' to describe biological intensities that are always socially entangled. Tomkins narrows affectivity down to nine distinct affects: interest/excitement, enjoyment/joy, surprise/startle, distress/anguish, anger/rage, fear/terror, contempt/disgust and shame/humiliation. In each case, the first term describes the mild manifestation and the second the more intense (Tomkins in Sedgwick and Frank, 1995).

In Tomkins's empirical studies, interest and desire are closely linked to shame. In order to feel ashamed of something, one must have initially invested oneself in or engaged oneself in it: 'Only a situation which offers enjoyment and involvement can make you blush'. According to Tomkins, shame is a decisive affect because shame confronts us with ourselves. Shame is your own experience of yourself, in that shame is the most reflexive of all affects. Shame is concerned with the affective experience of individual un-deservedness, of rejection and alienation. Shame profits from the positive investment in the object that activates the shame. An individual who has shown interest in another individual has operated under the impression that he/she may receive something positive in return. When shame is felt as an exposing affect, one tries to hide, to cover one's face. But because shame is connected to interest and engagement, it makes us desire some sort of self-improvement (Probyn, 2005: 23). Thus, shame becomes not just a negative or destructive affect, but also an affect which produces action and can lead to attempts to mend, repair and do something over again.

The next step is what kinds of analytical question these concepts of more determinate affects can lead us to and how they may add something to the Massumian framework of indeterminate affects. In the following, we will develop our methodology of diffractive reading by bringing the different concepts of affect (and the tensions between them) into conversation with a particular piece of empirical data, namely the OECD report, TALIS.

What does losing feel like? Affective shocks and shame in TALIS

Over the last decade, educational scholars have provided a range of studies of the adverse and irrational effects of the construction of a global commensurate space of school performance and of a hegemonic logic of governing by numbers (Henry, Lingard, Rizvi and Taylor 2001; Martens, Rusconi and Leuze, 2007; Ozga and Lingard, 2007; Sellar and Lingard, 2013). Studies have shown how testing data and indicators prompt politicians, policy-makers, the media, the schooling sector, and the public more broadly, to be concerned about performance and request actions to improve performance. Although there is an increasing awareness of the role of emotions in the curious ways in which international comparison modulates and tunes public and political agendas (Blackmore, 2009, 2011; Ratner and Pors, 2013; Staunæs, 2011), more insight may still arise from thinking through concepts of affect. Reading through a framework of affect, political reactions to national comparisons are not studied as the will, intent or agency of human beings, but rather as micro-political onto-power (Massumi, 2009). In the following, we will briefly present the TALIS report and discuss how thinking through concepts of affects open up possibilities of analytical inquiry.

TALIS is an initiative to examine and compare school management in 16 OECD countries and seven other nations. With a point of departure in a questionnaire survey completed by school managers, these countries are measured and compared on two variables; 'administrative management' and 'instruction management'[1] National performance is represented in numbers and graphs. This makes it possible not only to rank one country in relation to others but also to visualise the resulting hierarchies of countries. The hybridising of the language of nations, numbers and visual depictions of performance in TALIS, at least to us, is reminiscent of a sports match commentary, a sort of 'League of Nations'. One can almost hear TV commentators speaking when the report concludes which countries scored more points, '11 countries, including Denmark, Ireland and Portugal, are below the TALIS average' (OECD, 2008: 194) and that 'Denmark and Iceland are among the least involved with this type of management' (OECD, 2008: 194).

In a study of this report, a framework of affect turns the research interest from questions such as whether there is a good reason to be shocked when PISA results are poor, or whether the shock is strategically staged by powerful actors to legitimate policy change. Instead, the methodological curiosity is directed towards the shock itself, the intensity and quality of the affective shock and the performative effect. Thinking through affectivity makes it possible to analytically pursue the affective performativity of educational policy, as well as (for instance) the language of comparison and competition. An affective methodology is an invitation to explore how connections between numbers, visual graphs, and national imaginaries produce affective shocks, and how these affects may prompt a desire for improvement, and perhaps move politicians and bureaucrats to engage in rapid and ambitious action.

Steven Brown (2007) helps us to understand the potential shock-creating ability of reports when he writes: 'Words themselves are physical beings with their own particular affective force', and continues: 'Words strike us and in doing so, they establish a connection and put the things of the world in order' (p. 216). Thinking about words as affective devices allows us to focus on the maelstrom of affects

OECD-reports may trigger. Words, graphs and percentages are not just objective entities representing reality – they are also components in a potent number language. These components can strike us affectively and influence the way we understand and make sense of the world so that specific options and actions are perceived as threatening, tempting or necessary. Thus, thinking through concepts of indeterminate affects allows for an analytical methodology sensitive to the curious ways in which visualities and language of policy documents strikes at affective indexes through micro shock and works as small indecisive inductions of tension and intensity – even though intensities may remain indefinite even as they effect (Anderson, 2009: 78).

With the diffractive approach we have presented, it also becomes possible to draw attention to how affects are translated as these travel through public media, political negotiations, government practices and local school management initiatives and how they may be reconfigured into more determinate affects, such as shame. Thus, the next question is what an affective methodology has to offer in terms of unfolding the ways in which unpleasant and pleasant affective registers intermingle and how this mixture tunes and tones the energy put into a redesign of a national education system.

When, in TALIS, Denmark was placed in a corner of a diagram, an atmosphere of shame on behalf of the nation emerged, as a former Danish Minister of Education bluntly proclaimed: 'It is shameful for the nation.' The present Minister of Education concurred:

> Apparently we came in dead last in the whole world, when it comes to school management. We do not normally attach high priority to school management and the training of leaders, but we will have to do so from now on.
>
> *(Danish news magazine Danish Municipalities, March 2010)*

The academic experts also took part in the production of intensity, for instance with statements such as the following: 'it was very shameful for Denmark to be ranked at such a low level' (Danish educational magazine *Asterisk*, 53, June 2010, 11).

Thinking through the concept of shame allows for particular research questions of how there is a specific pattern, a qualitative differentiation of the affectivity that involves connections between shame and nation, which can be investigated further. Referring to Elspeth Probyn, shame can be analysed as the bodily sense of being incorrectly placed. It is a shame born out of the desire to fit in, an interest or desire to be part of something (Probyn, 2005: 38). Inspired by Probyn, one could explore how national shame may emerge out of a sense of feeling incorrectly placed in relation to the OECD diagrams in which advance welfare states are compared to and even beaten by countries they do not 'normally compare themselves with'. Research questions emerge of how an evoking and disturbing of imaginary hierarchies of industrial and development countries may trigger national shame and perhaps also renewed self-assertion and othering. One possible reading, which could be explored further, is how TALIS (or other international comparisons) creates an atmosphere of national self-reflection, which then in turn prompts an urge for self-improvement. Thus, an affective methodology may ultimately make it possible to explore how the international comparisons that were supposed to provide policy makers with facts, information and knowledge also produce an intensive urge for rapid action. An urge which may make it less likely for questions such as 'Do we want to win the administrative management competition?' to be raised.

Analytically, here, there is also a possibility of drawing on already known analysis of Western fear of Southeast Asia (Moisi, 2010; Sellar and Lingard, 2013). This would involve looking for worries of being eaten by the Asian tiger and reading the data with a focus on how fear instils a desire to flee or attempts to regain control of the situation. Moreover, an affective and frictional methodology is an invitation to follow how this indeterminate discomfort, which gradually becomes shame, may also take another turn. One could pursue how it may also become a passage of potentiality enabling more comfortable and hopeful states. Perhaps the determinate affect of shame also becomes a qualitative re-tuning of the body that regenerates and unfolds the capacity to think and feel.

Conclusion

In this chapter, we have presented concepts of affects and affectivity and made some preliminary steps towards an affective and frictional methodology by combining key-concepts from two seemingly different strands in newer affects studies. Through what we have termed a frictional methodology we have argued it becomes possible to look for and accept both movement and arrest, indeterminacy and determinacy, representations/categories and non-representations. It becomes possible to analyse how affects, energy and tensions are constantly created in simultaneous and mutually entangled processes of grids happening and grids unhappening.

Our aim has been to show how thinking through both indeterminate affectivity and determinate affects can trigger insight into how international comparisons may not only provide politicians with facts and documented knowledge, but also provoke affective spaces in which certain actions become threatening, tempting or necessary.

Note

1 Administrative management refers to practices such as administrative procedures, reporting to authorities, etc.; and instructional management to supervision of teaching, implementation of goals, etc.

Further reading on theories/tools

MacLure, M. (2013). Researching without representation? Language and materiality in post-qualitative methodology. *International Journal of Qualitative Studies in Education, 26*(6), 658–667.

Taguchi, H. L. (2012). A diffractive and Deleuzian approach to analysing interview data. *Feminist Theory*, *13*(3), 265–281.

Thrift, N. (2004). Intensities of feeling: Towards a spatial politics of affect. *Geografiska Annaler*, 86B, 57–78.

References

Ahmed, S. (2004). *The cultural politics of emotions*. Edinburgh, UK: Edinburgh University Press.

Anderson, B. (2009). Affective atmospheres. *Emotion, Space and Society*, *2*, 77–81.

Barad, K. (2003). Posthumanist performativity: Toward an understanding of how matters comes to matter. *Journal of Women in Culture and Society*, *28*(3), 801–831.

Barad, K. (2007). *Meeting the universe halfway: Quantum physics and the entanglement of matter and meaning*. Durham, NC: Duke University Press.

Bjerg, H. and Staunæs, D. (2011). Self-management through shame: Uniting governmentality studies and the 'affective turn'. *Ephemera: Theory & Politics in Organizations*, *11*(2), 138–156.

Blackmore, J. (2009). Measures of hope and despair. Emotionality, politics and education. In E. Samier and M. Schmidt (Eds.), *Emotional dimensions of educational administration and leadership* (pp. 109–124). Abingdon, UK: Routledge.

Blackmore, J. (2011). Lost in translation? Emotional intelligence, affective economies, leadership and organizational change. *Journal of Educational Administration and History*, *43*, 207–225.

Braidotti, R. (1994). *Nomadic subjects: Embodiment and sexual difference in contemporary feminist theory*. New York: Columbia University Press.

Brown, S. D. (2007). After power? Artaud and the theatre of cruelty. In C. Jones and R. ten Bos (Eds.), *Philosophy and organization* (pp. 201–223). London: Routledge.

Brown, S. D. and Stenner, P. (2009). *Psychology without foundations. History, philosophy and psychosocial theory*. London: Sage.

Butler, J. (1990). *Gender trouble. Feminism and the subversion of identity*. New York. Routledge.

Butler, J. (2010). Performative agency. *Journal of Cultural Economy*, *3*(2), 147–161.

Clough, P. (Ed.) (2007). *The affective turn: Theorizing the social*. Durham, NC and London: Duke University Press.

Colebrook, C. (2009). On the very possibility of queer theory. In C. Nigianni and M. Storr (Eds.), *Deleuze and queer theory* (pp. 11–23). Edinburgh, UK: Edinburgh University Press.

Deleuze, G. (1996). L'actuel et le Virtuel. In G. Deleuz and C. Parnet (Eds.), *Dialogues*. Paris: Flammarion.

Haraway, D. (1992). The promises of monsters. A regenerative politics for inappropriate/d others. In L. Grossberg, et al. (Eds.), *Cultural studies* (pp. 295–337). New York: Routledge.

Hemmings, C. (2005). Invoking affects. Cultural theory and the ontological turn. *Cultural Studies*, *19*, 548–567.

Henry, M., Lingard, B., Rizvi, F. and Taylor, S. (2001). *The OECD, globalisation and education policy*. Oxford, UK: Pergamon Press.

Hvenegaard-Lassen, K. and D. Staunæs (2015). And then we do it in Norway. Learning leadership through affective contact zones. In R. Andreassen and K. Vitus (Eds.), *Affectivity and race. Studies from a Nordic context*. London: Ashgate Publishing.

Juelskjær, M. and Swennesen, N. (2012). Intra-active engtanglements: An interview with Karen Barad. *Kvinder, Køn & Forskning* nr 1–2: 10–24.

Lykke, N., Markussen, R. and Olesen, F. (2008). 'There are always more things going on than you thought!' Methodologies as thinking technologies, interview with Donna Haraway. In A. Smelik and N. Lykke (Eds.), *Bits of life. Feminism at the intersections of media, bioscience and technology* (pp. 32–41). Washington, DC: University of Washington Press:

Martens, K., Rusconi, A. and Leuze, K. (Eds.) (2007). *New arenas of education governance*. Basingstoke, UK: Palgrave Macmillan.

Massumi, B. (2002). *Movement, affect, sensation: Parables for the virtual*. Durham, NC: Duke University Press.

Massumi, B. (2009). Of microperceptions and micropolitics. *Inflexions: A Journal for Research-Creation, 3*, October 2009. www.Inflexions.org.

Mazzei, L. and Jackson, A. Y. (2012). *Thinking with theory in qualitative research: Viewing data across multiple perspectives*. New York: Routledge.

Mehlsen, C. (2010). Output: hvad fører de komparative undersøgelser med sig? (Output: What do comparative assessments lead to?). *Asterisk, 53*, 10–11.

Moisi, D. (2010). *The geopolitics of emotion: How cultures of fear, humiliation, and hope are reshaping the world*. New York: Anchor Books.

OECD (2008). Improving school leadership, education and training policy. By Beatriz Pont, Deborah Nusche and Hunter Moorman: OECD (2009) Teaching and Learning International Survey. TALIS. www.oecd.org/document/0/0,3746,en_2649_39263231_38052160_1_1_1_1,00.

Ozga, J. and Lingard, B. (2007). Globalization, education policy and politics. In B. Lingard and J. Ozga (Eds.), *The RoutledgeFalmer reader in education policy and politics* (pp. 65–82). London: Routledge.

Papoulias, C. and Collard, F. (2010). Biology's gift: Interrogating the turn to affect. *Body & Society, 16*(1), 29–56.

Probyn, E. (2005). *Blush: Faces of shame*. Minneapolis, MN and London: University of Minnesota Press.

Puar, J. (2007). *Terrorist assemblages: Homonationalism in queer times*. Durham, NC: Duke University Press.

Puar, J. (2012). 'I would rather be a cyborg than a goddess': Becoming-intersectional in assemblage theory. *philoSOPHIA, 2*(1), 49–66.

Ratner, H. and Pors, J. G. (2013). Making invisible forces visible: Managing employees' values and attitudes through transient emotions. *International Journal of Management Concepts and Philosophy, 7*(3/4), 208–223.

Sedgwick, E. (2003). *Touching feeling: Affect, pedagogy, performativity*. Durham, NC and London: Duke University Press.

Sedgwick, E. and Frank, A. (Eds.) (1995). *Shame and its sister – a Silvan Tomkins reader*. Durham, NC and London: Duke University Press.

Sellar, S. and Lingard, B. (2013). The OECD and the expansion of PISA: New global modes of governance in education. *British Educational Research Journal*. doi: 10.1002/berj.3120.

Staunæs, D. (2011). Governing the potentials of life itself? Interrogating the promises in affective educational leadership. *Journal of Educational Administration and History, 43*(3), 227–247.

Staunæs, D. and Pors, J. G. (2011). Hvordan føles det at tabe i OECD? Chok og skam som affektiv motor i uddannelsespolitik og – ledelse [How does it feel to lose in OECD? Chock and shame in education policy and management]. *Unge Pædagoger 4*, 18–36.

Stenner, P. and M. Greco (2008). *Emotions: A social science reader*. London: Routledge.

Tomkins, S. (1995). Shame – humiliation and contempt – disgust. In E. K. Sedgwick and A. Frank (Eds.), *Shame and its sister – a Silvan Tomkins reader*. Durham, NC and London: Duke University Press.

Wetherell, M. (2012). *Affect and emotion. A new social science understanding*. London: Sage.

9

ASSEMBLAGE THEORY AND EDUCATION POLICY SOCIOLOGY

Deborah Youdell

From policy sociology to assemblage ethnography

Education policy sociology offers a critical account of the makings and effects of contemporary education policy. In much of this scholarship Foucault's work is the key conceptual resource. Foucault's understandings of multivalent forms of power, the productive force of discourse, and techniques of governmentality have been brought together to provide compelling analyses of the operations and reach but also the uncertainties of policy (see, for instance, Ball, 1990, 2009, 2013; Davies, 2005; Lipman, 2004; Ozga, 2000). This body of research has established a reading of the neoliberal state, its policy orientations and networks, and it's modes of governance that are now broadly accepted in scholarly, if not policy-making, communities. This work shows that education policy tendencies that embed neoliberal forms of governance and transform the public sector into a commodity and the public into individualized consumers have shifted what education is and what it means and are implicated in the ordering of students and the creation of educational inequalities. These readings of policy and its effects have been extremely powerful in unsettling prevailing technicist accounts of policy development and implementation – they engage with policy as produced not simply by the state but through complex and multifarious networks and the nuanced ways in which policy circulates and is enacted inside institutions.

My own research has contributed to this body of thinking and substantive analysis (Gillborn and Youdell 2000; Youdell, 2004, 2006). Yet the certainty that policy should be foregrounded as *the principle object of analysis*, and that critical readings of neoliberalism generated through the lens of governmentality yield the necessary insights, have begun to be augmented with other points of entry and further conceptual devises (McGimpsey, 2013; Webb and Gulson, 2015; Youdell, 2011; Youdell and McGimpsey 2015). As mobile capital and its corporations effect profound global economic realignments; as 'austerity' beds in as the only position taken by Western states; as 'public' education and 'public' services continue to undergo complex transformations; and as civic engagement is appropriated by mainstream politics and detached from protest, I and other writers have become increasingly inclined to approach education policy, and public policy in general, as just one part of a much wider ensemble of factors and forces.

To do this I engage Deleuze and Guattari's idea of assemblage (1983, 2008). The point of this move is to understand the productive forces of ever-shifting, complex, social formations *of which policy is just one component*. In this sense assemblage ethnography is not a new competitor or alternative to policy sociology – it is a different orientation to the 'problem', in which the focus of analysis is the social formation and the 'things', including policy, that produce this, rather than policy itself. This is not to suggest that policy sociology which connects policy to a wider set of influences, sites and actors does not offer nuanced accounts of policy's relationships to social formations. But is it to suggest a different point of departure in which the assemblage, not policy, is the object of study. Thinking with assemblage, I believe, offers new analytic potential by placing policy processes in wider forces of assemblage, and indeed, disassembly.

In this chapter, I outline Deleuze and Guattari's thinking, and examine some instances of the use of assemblage as a conceptual framing and method for interrogating a range of substantive contemporary social phenomena both inside and outside education. I move beyond education purposefully to highlight some emerging ideas and to show how the notion of assemblage invites us to look beyond domain and discipline boundaries and make connections – see assemblage – across these.

Assemblage

Deleuze and Guattari's (1983, 2008) idea of assemblage helps us to conceptualize the complex terrain of education. They use notions of 'ensembles', 'arrangements' and 'assemblages' to think about the multiplicity of diverse and moving elements that combine to form complex social formations. They suggest that apparently whole entities, and 'education' might be one such entity, can be understood as assemblages of heterogeneous components that cross-cut economic, political, state, social, institutional, linguistic, semiotic, representational, discursive, subjective and affective orders. Such components have often treated as separate or of differential significance in social science, but for Deleuze and Guattari (1983: 52) these are inseparable:

> An arrangement in its multiplicity necessarily works at once on semiotic, material, and social flows [...] There is no longer a tripartite division between a field of reality (the world), a field of representation (a book), and a field of subjectivity (the author). Rather, an arrangement connects together certain multiplicities caught up in each of these orders.

In education this might mean mapping the detail of the characteristics, movements and productive interplays between a range of components that include money, political orientations, media and popular climates, policy and legislation, institutional arrangements, formal and informal knowledges, subjectivities, pedagogies, everyday practices and feelings. Thinking about 'education assemblage' helps us to recognize and analyze the interconnectedness and potentialities of this variety of mobile parts.

Rhizome

To understand assemblage/s we move away from hierarchical or 'arborescent' forms of thinking (Deleuze and Guattari, 1983) and scramble these with the 'rhizome' which posits social formations as multi-directional and never ending: '[t]here are no points or positions in a rhizome, as one finds in a structure, tree or root. There are only lines' (Deleuze and Guattari, 1983: 14). Thinking rhizomatically, an assemblage is not hierarchically organized with 'macro' elements such as the state, economy or policy at the 'top', dominating productive forces and bearing down on the 'micro' elements below. Instead, the productive forces of components, and the productivities of the relationships between them, are undecided and mobile – capital may prove to limit the productivities of an assemblage in particular temporal and spatial arrangements, but so might affectivities.

Line

Deleuze and Guattari's notion of the 'line' helps us to think about the ways that assemblages move. They suggest a range of lines: the 'molar', rigid and segmented working as a 'plane of organization' (Deleuze and Guattari, 1983: 80); the 'molecular', supple and segmented creating thresholds, flows and flux; and the 'line of flight', described as a line of 'becoming' (ibid.: 81). The idea that the rhizome moves in and from a middle 'through which it pushes and overflows' (ibid.: 47) invites us to imagine the immediacy and indeterminacy of the movements of these lines. For instance, the image of rigid molar lines can help us to understand the endurance and fixity of notions of intelligence in education and the selection and setting practices that flow from these; molecular lines can help us to make sense of schools' and teachers' attempts to find ways of working with notions such as 'multiple intelligences' or 'abilities' that are not generalized across all areas of learning, or strategies for organizing schools, classrooms and pedagogies that are not predicated on prior assessments of 'ability'; and lines of flight can help us to imagine the sorts of practices that might be possible if schools and teachers discarded 'intelligence' and its associated practices altogether.

Affect

Affectivities – the eruptions and flows of bodily intensities and the encounters between these eruptions and flows – are suggested by Deleuze and Guattari (2008) as components of assemblages. While education studies has increasingly engaged with questions of feeling (Bibby, 2011; Britzman, 1998; Boler, 1999), the psychic and affective are not common aspects of policy sociology, in particular when these are understood as 'outside' or 'before' the subject and her/his emotions. Anna Hickey-Moody and Peta Malins (2007: 9) explain:

> Affect is that which is felt before it is thought; it has visceral impact on the body before it gives subjective or emotive meaning. [. . .] Affect is . . . very different from emotion: it is an a-subjective bodily response to an encounter. Emotion comes later, a classifying or stratifying of affect.

Thinking about affectivities as assemblage components invites us to add to our understanding of the significance of subjectivated subjects a consideration of the potentialities and productive flows of pre-personal feelings and bodies for an education assemblage.

Uses

In the remainder of this chapter I show assemblage being put to work in a range of ways and across a number of areas of substantive focus – we see a variety of assemblages as they assemble and are assembled. One generative aspect of working with/from assemblage is the way it enables, or even insists on, movement across academic and political fields – for this reason I include work whose concern is outside education. The examples that I draw on here are inevitably selective, and other work might have been selected (see, for instance, Allan, 2008; Hickey-Moodey, 2009; Ringrose, 2011; Webb, 2009). My aim here is to offer a flavour of what assemblage can show us and what it can be made to do.

Youth service assemblage

Ian McGimpsey's work on 'youth service assemblage' (McGimpsey, 2013) approaches policy as a component of the assemblage. Moving across and interweaving analyses of multiple orders, including economics, a whole raft of national policy, and the discourses and practices of people in particular spatial and affective relations, this work demonstrates the interrelation and productive force of these components. McGimpsey's work also situates education policy sociology pursued as assemblage analysis in a clear political economy by fore-grounding capitalism and monetary and labour flows as significant components of youth service assemblage.

Particularly helpful is McGimpsey's use of the 'molecular' and 'molar' to consider the variant potentialities that components might have – not all components have the same productive force, or have consistent productive force across space and time. At the molar level, he offers a sense of youth service assemblages as formations that imply the existence and reproduction of various categorized populations of organizations, educator subjects, young people and so on. While the molecular level serves as a distinction not only of scale, but of 'quality of production':

'trajectories to and from sameness in discursive, affective, and material orders' (McGimpsey, 2013: 119).

By making these distinctions of productive forces in relation to social formations, McGimpsey's assemblage analysis offers policy sociology a distinction between 'neoliberalism' and 'capitalism'. He suggests that neoliberalism within policy analysis has largely been understood as a 'territorializing' policy force that reforms and regulates spaces of education practice in terms of the market. Working from Deleuze and Guattari's characterizations of capitalism, McGimpsey (2013: 120) argues for an openness to changing forms of neoliberalism, or 'post-neoliberalism' that *are nevertheless capitalist* in the sense of being:

> the simultaneous process of decoding and deterritorialization of existing social formations, and the formation of new productive connections through recoding and reterritorialization that take up recognisable cultural objects and norms [such as education, youth services, schooling and so on] . . . it is not straightforwardly the case that capitalist policy is therefore a force that reinscribes neoliberal categories.

As well as illustrating an assemblage analysis of the contemporary youth service terrain which includes but does not foreground policy, McGimpsey's work offers policy sociology a way of thinking again about neoliberalism; the distinction and relationship between neoliberalism and capitalism; and the variant potentialities of these.

Pedagogic assemblage

Deana Leahy (2009) draws on Nikolas Rose's thinking about contemporary governmental practice in terms of assemblages (Rose 2000 in Leahy 2009) to extend her analysis of the governmental project of school-based health education. Leahy does this by understanding school-based health education as a 'pedagogic assemblage' whose 'bio-pedagogies' 'contribute to the classroom assemblage' and are part of a 'wider governmental assemblage' concerned with the control of obesity (Leahy, 2009: 176). She argues:

> Classrooms are indeed complex spaces, made up of a vast assemblage of objects, bodies, curriculum imperatives, and pedagogic practices bodies, curriculum imperatives, and pedagogic practices that are connected to broader assemblages. There is much value I suggest in conceptualizing the field as a governmental assemblage and, in so doing, considering all of what is going on in that assemblage.
>
> *(2009: 181)*

Rather than move from a concern with health education policy and its effects, Leahy moves from these interconnecting assemblages in order to engage and map 'the messiness that characterizes contemporary projects of governance' (p. 177). Leahy suggests that assemblage provokes us to engage factors and forces that are beyond the expert knowledge or prevailing discourses – often enshrined in policy – that are usually centred in analyses of health education as a governmental project. She suggests that moving from assemblage brings into play 'other dynamics and affects' (p. 180), exposing the 'convergences, hybridizing and morphing of knowledges in the classroom, processes of subjectivation and the provocation and recruitment of affectivities into the pedagogical assemblage that fold expert knowledges into and onto the body' (p. 181).

Art education assemblage

Maria Tamboukou (2008, 2010) deploys the notion of 'art education assemblage' to engage with 'a complex assemblage of interrelations between social structures, economic conditions, power/knowledge relations, architectural and spatial arrangements, forces of desire and pleasure seductions' (Tamboukou, 2008: 369). As she considers a particular nineteenth-century woman art educator and artist, Tamboukou (2008: 6) argues that with a rhizomatic framing:

> Becoming an artist cannot be pinned down within a specific space/time block, it would rather be seen as a continuum that needs to be mapped on a grid of intelligibility, a machinic rather than a linear model of transformations, that allows for rhizomatic connections to be seen working together.

In this art education assemblage, the artist 'emerges as an effect of disparate, co-existing elements, producing the real: subjects and their social milieus' (Tamboukou, 2008: 369). Tamboukou argues that the becoming-artist of the woman art educator whose biography she reconstructs suggests the deterritorialization of the art education assemblage that would foreclose the possibility of artist for this woman educator. Tamboukou charts the narratives and social milieus of women artists and educators, their relationships to art, education and a range of social spaces, as well as 'power relations and forces of desire' (Tamboukou, 2010: 679). As she does this she shows a series of components and their interrelations, demonstrating the significance of understanding art education as assemblage as well as the utility of the notion of 'lines of flight' for considering the imminence of resistance. 'Policy' *per se* is not part of this analysis, not because it has been overlooked but because moving from assemblage orientates Tamboukou to an array of components, interrelations and productivities of which 'policy' is not a part. A possibility that in itself may offer new potentialities.

Childhood sexuality assemblage and re-assembly

Mindy Blaise (2013) uses assemblage to think beyond the prevailing developmental accounts of childhood sexuality and connected moral panics over 'sexualization'.

Blaise's aim is not to map an assemblage, but to initiate 'a different dialogue about curiosities, human and non-human bodies, and desires, to chart new territories about childhood sexuality in the early years classroom' (Blaise, 2013: 801). Working with assemblage Blaise shows media, policy and expert accounts as molar lines that invoke childhood innocence/development and child sexualization and risk. Rather than focusing on critique or deconstruction of these knowledges and their effects, Blaise argues that they 'must be re-assembled', a re-assembly that 'requires a new set of concepts that may generate different logics about childhood gender and sexuality' (ibid.: 804). Blaise aims to generate 'postdevelopmental perspectives' that allow children both 'sexual agency' and 'meaning-making' (p. 802). Blaise (2013: 805, emphasis added) states:

> A Deleuzo-Guattarian idea of assemblage focuses on the processes of bring-ing together heterogeneous elements in order to produce something new (Deleuze and Guattari 1987). [...] The point of this style of logic is not about determining and defining the assemblage. Rather, *it is about exploring what the assemblage can do or produce* that makes it possible to re-imagine childhood sexuality.

Blaise's focus here is the inchoate nature of components and the newness and potentialities of what they assemble. Her analysis at once exposes the assemblage of childhood development and sexualization and enacts a re-assembly of childhood sexuality. Belt buckles, plastic dolls, picture books, children's curiosities and feelings, moving and colliding bodies, loitering mums and self-scrutinizing researcher are shown together in mobile assemblage and re-assemblage. This suggests a shift for policy sociology – from the interrogation of policy processes, enactments and effects to the movements of components in assembly and re-assembly.

Economics and risk/safety assemblages

Away from education, Hillier (2013) uses assemblages in her 'cartographic tracing' of spatial planning practices. Following Deleuze and Guattari, she positions her concern as being 'not what is a thing? But, how does it come into being? How was/is it actualized?' (p. 868). Hillier's empirical instance is the controversial instal-lation of Antony Gormley's iron men, entitled 'Another Place', on Crosby beach, north-west England. To undertake her cartographic tracing Hillier brings together Foucault and Deleuze through their shared interest in the 'generative' and 'engagement with both discursive and material worlds' (p. 862) and, specifically, their respective notions of *dispositif* and assemblage. For Hillier assemblages are multiple and 'nested' but most notable for her analysis are 'economics (regenera-tion)' and 'risk/safety (to humans and birds)'. These assemblages include a range of forces – political, statutory, scientific, economic, and popular and the movements of a range of 'actants':

> Sefton Council planning and leisure services officers, Sefton Councillors, local residents, organizations such as Liverpool08 and the Maritime and Coastguard Agency (MCA), 'celebrities' including Tony Blair, and nonhuman actants including the beach, the ocean, waterbirds and dead worms! [. . .] The iron men themselves were members of all the assemblages simultaneously. They possessed material agency (potentially attracting economic investment, starving birds or drowning humans) as they connected to other elements in various assemblages.
>
> *(Hillier, 2013: 862)*

Here, then, human and non-human actants come into productive relationships as assemblages are made and remade. Hillier moves through a series of analyses organized by the concepts of

- assemblages;
- actants;
- territorializations;
- materialities; and
- expressivities.

At the same time, there remains a strong thread of engagement with the formalities of planning processes and their legislative underpinnings. In this way the piece continues to be recognizable as a study of planning in which policy is a core concern even as it endeavours to extend recognition of multiple actants and the productive forces in/of assemblages. This suggests a way in which education policy sociology might borrow assemblage to augment and enrich its analysis.

Blackout assemblage

My final example is Jane Bennett's (2010) engagement with the power blackouts that occurred across Canada and the USA in 2003. The project of Bennett's influential 2010 book, *Vibrant matter*, is to make a case for what she calls 'thing-power' (p. 20) – the capacity of all sorts of non-human 'actants' to make things happen through what she calls 'congregational' or distributive agency (p. 21). With this in mind, and in the context of readings of social complexity on global scales, assemblages are drawn on to develop 'new conceptualizations of the part-whole relation' (p. 23). Bennett (2010: 24) defines assemblages as:

> ad hoc groupings of diverse elements, of vibrant materials of all sorts. Assemblages are living, throbbing confederations that are able to function despite the persistent presence of energies that confound them from within. [. . .] The effects generated by an assemblage are, rather, emergent properties, emergent in their ability to make something happen (a newly inflected

materialism, a blackout, a hurricane, a war on terror) is distinct from the sum of the vital force of each materiality considered alone.

With this framing, Bennett examines the electricity blackout from a 'vital materialist' perspective. She identifies a series of human and non-human actants: 'coal, sweat, electromagnetic fields, computer programmes, electron streams, profit motives, heat, lifestyles, nuclear fuel, plastic, fantasies of mastery, static, legislation, water, economic theory, wire and wood' (p. 25). And as she moves to interrogate how the blackout might be understood through the productive interplay of this list of actants, she demonstrates productive force of electricity and of the deregulation enabled through the Federal Energy Regulatory Committee. Bennett argues that 'responsibility' for the blackout cannot be placed finally with any agent or agency. Instead she argues that 'the locus of political responsibility is a human–non-human assemblage' (p. 36) – 'harmful effects' have 'sources' but 'the notion of confederate agency [. . .] broadens the range of places to look for sources' (p. 37). This reading of the blackout through assemblage, then, not only calls on us to refocus our thinking about the relative significance of policy and legislation, it also aims refocus our thinking about politics and political responsibility.

Conclusions

Assemblage offers a generative conceptual framework for investigating the complexity of social formations. The engagements with the uses of assemblage offered in this chapter go some way to demonstrate how thinking in its terms invites us to move across – and encounter movements across – a whole range of orders, domains and substantive concerns. These examples have shown that 'education assemblage' is neither singular nor a complete system. Assemblages may well include a thing we call 'policy', but they may not, and when they do 'policy' will no longer be in its usual place as the central substantive concern and item for analysis. The assemblages mapped here begin to show the multiplicity of assemblages that we might find as we begin to investigate education. From McGimspey we have a whole sub-domain of education 'youth service', from the despair of workers to the money no longer available. From Leahy a field of educational philosophy and practice – a pedagogic assemblage – as intersects with classroom and governmental assemblages. From Tamboukou a curricular area – Art Education – but assembling the productive connections of much more than a curriculum. From Blaise a domain of knowledge, social-cultural practice, subjectivity and regulation – childhood sexuality assemblage – to be reassembled and, perhaps, let loose. From Hillier, two assemblages of quite different characters – economics and risk/safety to/of seabirds – both assembled through the spatial planning process. Finally from Bennett, an event – blackout assemblage – that lasted for three days but whose lines spread out along multiple planes. Assemblages, then, are unpredictable, they traverse scale, space and time. They are as much the process of assemblage and the near future that can be diagnosed from that, as they are the thing made.

Approaching the study of assemblages as ethnography suggests an emphasis on the actually existing, on movements as they happen, and on the diagnosis of the near future (Deleuze, 1992); an unlimited orientation to things and/as actants and data; and a need for the fine grained, the forensic following of lines and productivities. As we develop assemblage ethnography to map education assemblages the components we encounter may be of varying familiarity:

- a global economic order of untethered capitalism;
- affectivities, as pedagogic devices and erupting unbidden and despite prohibition;
- mobile international and trans-national geo-political setups, nation states and local states;
- subjectivities and identifications, and recognitions and identifications made possible, provoked and excluded;
- legislative and policy frameworks;
- new technology and new media;
- buildings new, old and absent;
- privatization and deregulation, markets, accountability, choice, performance management, effectiveness, efficiency, investment;
- institutions and institutional forms;
- social movements and social networks;
- individualism and instrumentalism;
- diverse school forms;
- National Curriculum;
- regimes of school inspection and intervention;
- selection, sorting and setting;
- measurements of 'ability' and diagnoses of 'special needs';
- the rhetoric of economic imperative, commodity, private goods, meritocracy, deprivation and responsible citizens;
- school exclusions, 'special schools', 'alternative provision', the education 'mainstream'.

Of course, this list is not exhaustive and the danger of such a list is that it threatens to foreclose the components that we see and impose an arborescence where we sought a rhizome. Assemblages are, as much as anything else, about the productive interplay of the unexpected – components we didn't see coming, movements that could not be anticipated.

The work of Deleuze and Guattari often feels abstract and impenetrable to new readers. As we shift between assemblages, the arborescent, the rhizomatic, the molecular and molar, lines of flight, and becoming their ideas move. Yet this movement is itself rhizomatic; constantly moving, ideas avoid cementing, territorialization, capture. Using Deleuze and Guattari to think in terms of an education assemblage suggests movements and productive encounters, human and non-human actants, the new and emergent. As an incitement to more assemblage ethnography in education, I finish with an invitation from Deleuze and Guattari (1983: 23):

Always follow the rhizome by rupturing, lengthening, prolonging, taking up the line of flight, make it vary, until it produces the most abstract and tortuous line in n dimensions and scattered directions. Combine the deterritorializing flows. Follow the plants: begin by fixing the limits of a first line according to circles of convergence around successive singularities; next see if new circles of convergence are established along the interior of this line, with new points situated outside its limits and other directions. To write, form rhizomes, expand your own territory by deterritorialization, extend the line of flight to the point where it covers the whole plane of consistency in an abstract machine.

Acknowledgments

I would like to acknowledge the contribution to the thinking in this chapter made by a number of my friends and colleagues through the *Public Service Academy Reading Group* at the University of Birmingham, especially Ian McGimpsey, Tina Hearne, Stephen Jeffares and Paula Lamau and the Canadian Research Council/ University of British Columbia seminar, *Poststructural Theory and Education Policy,* especially Kalervo Gulson and Taylor Webb. Some elements of the material offered here appeared in an earlier form in Youdell (2011) 'Theorizing political subjects' in *School trouble: Identity, power and politics in education*, pp. 36–56. London: Routledge.

References

Allan, J. (2008). *Rethinking inclusion: The philosophers of difference in practice*. Dordrecht, Netherlands: Springer.

Ball, S. J. (1990). *Politics and policy making in education: Explorations in policy sociology*. London: Routledge.

Ball, S. J. (2009). Privatising education, privatising education policy, privatising educational research: Network governance and the 'competition state'. *Journal of Education Policy, 24*(1), 83–99.

Ball, S. J. (2013). *Foucault, power and education*. London: Routledge.

Bennett, J. (2010). *Vibrant matter: A political ecology of things*. London: Duke University Press.

Bibby, T. (2011). *Education – an 'impossible profession'?: Psychoanalytic explorations of learning and classrooms*. Abingdon, UK: Routledge.

Blaise, M. (2013). Charting new territories: Reassembling childhood sexuality in the early years classroom. *Gender and Education, 27*(5), 801–817.

Boler, M. (1999). *Feeling power: Emotion and education*. London: Routledge.

Britzman, D. (1998). *Lost subjects, contested objects: Towards a psychoanalytic inquiry of learning*. Albany, NY: State University of New York Press.

Davies, B. (2005). The (im)possibility of intellectual work in neoliberal regimes. *Discourse: Studies in the Cultural Politics of Education, 26*(1), 1–14.

Deleuze, G. (1992). What is a dispositif. In T. J. Armstrong (Ed.), *Michel Foucault philosopher* (pp. 159–168). London: Havester Wheatsheaf.

Deleuze, G. and Guattari, F. (1983). Rhizome. In G. Deleuze and F. Guattari (Eds.), *On the line*. New York: Semiotext(e).

Deleuze, G. and Guattari, F. (2008). *A thousand plateaus*. London: Continuum.

Gillborn, D. and Youdell, D. (2000). *Rationing education: Policy, practice, reform and equity.* Buckingham, UK: Open University Press.

Hickey-Moody, A. (2009). *Unimaginable bodies: Intellectual disability, performance and becomings.* Rotterdam, Netherlands: Sense.

Hickey-Moody, A. and Malins, P. (2007). *Deleuzian encounters: Studies in contemporary social issues*. Basingstoke, UK: Palgrave.

Hillier, J. (2013). Encountering Gilles Deleuze in another place. *European Planning Studies, 19*(5), 861–885.

Leahy, D. (2009). Disgusting pedagogies. In V. Wright and V. Harwood (Eds.), *Biopolitics and the 'obesity epidemic': Governing bodies* (pp. 172–182). London: Routledge.

Lipman, P. (2004). *High stakes education: Inequality, globalisation and urban school reform*. London: RoutledgeFalmer.

McGimpsey, I. (2013). *Youth Service Assemblage*. (PhD), Institute of Education, London.

Ozga, J. (2000). *Policy research in educational settings: Contested terrain*. Buckingham, UK: Open University Press.

Ringrose, J. (2011). Beyond discourse? Using Deleuze and Guattari's schizoanalysis to explore affective assemblages, heterosexually striated space and lines of flight online and at school. *Educational Philosophy and Theory, 43*(6), 598–618.

Rose, N. (2000). Government and control. *British Journal of Criminology, 40*, 321–339.

Tamboukou, M. (2008). Machinic assemblages: Women, art education and space. *Discourse: Studies in the Cultural Politics of Education, 29*(3), 359–375.

Tamboukou, M. (2010). Charting cartographies of resistance: Lines of flight in women artists' narratives. *Gender and Education, 22*(6), 679–696.

Webb, T. (2009). *Teacher assemblage*. Rotterdam, Netherlands: Sense.

Webb, T. and Gulson, K. N. (2015, forthcoming). *Policy Scientificity 3.0: Policy Geophilosophy and Education*. Rotterdam, Netherlands: Sense.

Youdell, D. (2004). Engineering school markets, constituting schools and subjectivating students: The bureaucratic, institutional and classroom dimensions of educational triage. *Journal of Education Policy, 19*(4), 408–431.

Youdell, D. (2006). Diversity, inequality and post-structural politics for education. *Discourse: Studies in the Cultural Politics of Education, 27*(1), 33–42.

Youdell, D. (2011). *School trouble: Identity, power and politics in education*. London: Routledge.

Youdell, D. and McGimpsey, I. (2015). Assembling, disassembling and reassembling 'youth services' in austerity Britain. *Critical Studies in Education, 56*(1), 116–130.

10

COUNTERPUBLICS, CRISIS AND CRITIQUE

A feminist socio-historical approach to researching policy

Jessica Gerrard

Policies saturate educational practices. From international inter-agency and government white papers, to the institutional policies of schools, universities, libraries, workplaces, welfare services and community centres: educational policy documentation proliferates. In many ways, policies represent official instantiations of meaning and intent. Governments and institutions use policies as a means to shape and direct practice, and to indicate particular positions or meanings. Notwithstanding diverse interpretations and enactments (and even rejections) of policies in practice, policies are governing mechanisms. However, policies are also influenced by – and products of – wider social, cultural and political struggles over the purpose, practice and meaning of education. In this chapter, I outline an approach to analysing policy in relation to these wider struggles. I suggest the value in researching policy reform within the context of crises in, and critique of, capitalism – past and present. To do this I draw primarily upon contemporary political philosopher Nancy Fraser, who works at the nexus of feminist, Marxist and critical theory. Fraser's theory of justice has already attracted a range of research engagements by educational researchers (e.g. Apple, 2011; Arnot, 2006; Huttunen, 2007; Keddie, 2012). Here, however, I turn to Fraser's most recent examination of the adaptive capacity of capitalist reforms (Fraser, 2013) and her conceptualisation of subaltern counterpublics (Fraser, 1990, 1997, 2007; see also Gerrard, 2014a, 2014b; Mirza and Reay, 2000; Reay and Mirza, 1997).

First, I outline Fraser's conceptualisation of subaltern counterpublics as a means to examine these wider social, cultural and political dimensions of policy-related practice. Following with Fraser's feminist critique of Jurgen Habermas's theory of the public sphere, I suggest the value of extending policy research beyond the processes and practices that appear within the legitimated public policy field. Second, extending upon the notion of counterpublics, I consider the broader dynamics of hegemony and social change under neoliberal capitalism. Drawing on

Fraser's recent consideration of the relationship between second wave feminism and neoliberal capitalist reform, along with critical theorists Eve Chiapello and Luc Boltanski, I explore the capacity for reforms to have a recuperative function in the maintenance of capitalist hegemony. I propose that focus on the diverse social and historical struggles over – and crises in – educational policy and practice provides generative research avenues to understand the contested and messy processes of policy as a political object.

Public debate, subaltern counterpublics and policy research

Policy production is undoubtedly characterised by public debates and consultation processes. White papers, press releases, opinion pieces and formal responses by academics and teacher unions, are all part of the attempt to influence policy agendas. This public sphere of educational policy activity is of paramount importance for researching the relations of power that characterise policy production, and the public contestations of meaning that surround it. Yet, at the same time, there is a range of activities that lie beyond that which is rendered publicly visible. Glossy policy documents, for instance, reveal little about the processes of drafting and negotiation that occur in their production (Gerrard and Farrell, 2013). Moreover, policies are embedded in much wider processes of social change and relations, which create the conditions to make some policies pragmatically possible, and others not. The legitimated public stage in which policy production is set – white papers, formal written responses, media coverage – does not represent the full range of social activities and struggles over education. Importantly, continuing – and shifting – power relations of gender, race, class and hetereonormativity underpin the exclusions and marginalisations that characterise public politics and policy. It is therefore important to critically reflect upon the limits of research that focuses solely on that which is already legitimated within the formal policy field, and to seek insight into that which may not be immediately visible.

One way in which to understand the broader social relations surrounding policy production is Nancy Fraser's notion of subaltern counterpublics. Fraser puts forward subaltern counterpublics as a means to conceptualise an expansive, and dynamic, conception of the public sphere. Her conceptualisation arises from her critical feminist engagement with Jürgen Habermas's theory of the public sphere. For Habermas, the public constitutes the space in which 'private individuals' come together as a 'public body' to make decisions on common issues (Habermas, 1974: 49; Fraser, 1997). It has 'open, permeable and shifting horizons', drawing 'its impulse from the private handling of social problems that resonate in life histories' (Habermas, 2002). Highly critical of the ways in which the 'democratic' compromise of capitalism in the 'West' enables political elites to reproduce their privilege, Habermas (1989) posits that rational discourse creates a more radically inclusive public. This rational discourse of private individuals, Habermas asserts, provides a means to subvert the political authority of the state to the public sphere's own democratic demands.

Fraser suggests there is a profound inadequacy in the way Habermas's public sphere understands its purpose (Fraser, 1985, 1997). By delineating the public sphere as the province of participatory dialogue, and the state as the potential site of influence, Fraser (1997) argues Habermas's model discredits those public movements or social issues that are not readily incorporated into (or deemed too confrontational for) a rational dialogical model of public action. For instance, his model of the public fails to challenge the 'gender-based separation of the state-regulated economy of sex-segmented paid work and social-welfare, and the masculine public sphere, from privatized female childrearing' (Fraser, 1985: 120). In other words, Habermas's diverse rational dialogue may cloak the power relations and the contestations within the public sphere, and between the public and private (see also, Canovan, 1983).

Correspondingly, Fraser contends that Habermas's public does not make clear to what extent widespread support is necessary for a particular issue to have political salience: Habermas suggests that the 'public of citizens' must be convinced of the issues it finds relevant. In Habermas's model, therefore, there is an implicit presumption that the range of positions represented in the formal public debates on policy corresponds with the diversity of relevant opinions and positions. Thus, preoccupied with developing itself as a rational sphere of influence on the established political apparatuses, Habermas's public sphere overlooks actions that do not immediately fit its rational pragmatic remit, and which may encircle, though not directly target, the state and its policies. As a consequence, dissent outside of recognised and legitimated public spaces and institutions become side-lined (Fraser, 1997). Fraser (1985) constructs her critique most saliently when considering the symbolic burden, and material contribution of women's ('private') unpaid labour. Her criticism highlights how some contributions to public activity and debate are deemed too confrontational, emotive, private or are struck down as being based on impossible or unpragmatic demands. Such judgements have been levelled at many movements for change, from women's to refugee, workers' and LGBTI rights, past and present.

Fraser's criticism raises significant questions surrounding the ability of a rational singular public sphere to adequately recognise and respond to wide range of dissent outside of its parameters. She writes, 'The problem is not only that Habermas idealizes the bourgeois public sphere but also that he fails to examine other, nonliberal, nonbourgeois, competing public spheres' (1997: 72). Fraser's analysis suggests simplistic expansions of public action or space can simply exacerbate existing exclusions and power dynamics. In other words, Fraser contends with generations of feminist thinkers, for the need to fundamentally rethink what is counted as 'valuable' public activity rather than just expand the existing public. Writing on educational contexts, feminist scholar Carol Luke (1992) illuminates this dilemma:

> Granting voice to girls in the public sphere of the democratic classroom is an add-on tactic of incorporation . . . For, without a rewriting of the masculine public subject, women end up doubly inscribed in marginal public positions and in 'natural' caretaking positions in the private.

Similar criticisms have long been levelled at critical education scholars for lacking analysis of the gendered dimensions of teachers' work (e.g. Ellsworth, 1992; Jackson, 1997; Santoro Gomez, 2008). For policy research, these critiques highlight how legitimated fields of policy activity include particular practices and understandings, whilst exclude others.

Drawing on histories of social change, the concept of subaltern counterpublics attempts to represent the multifarious ways people who are oppressed have formed alternative publics. Fraser (1990) writes, 'The history records that members of subordinated social groups – women, workers, peoples of color, and gays and lesbians – have repeatedly found it advantageous to constitute alternative publics' (p. 67). These publics offer a means to 'invent and circulate counterdiscourses' and to 'formulate oppositional interpretations of their identities, interests and needs' (Fraser, 1990: 67). They are, in part, recognition that no single model of the public sphere can adequately represent the diversity of social and political activity. They are also a means to understand the ways in which oppositional politics often require spaces of 'withdrawal and regroupment' alongside 'agitational activities directed toward wider publics' (Fraser, 1990: 68).

Subaltern counterpublics and policy research

For policy research, the feminist critique of the public suggests the need to investigate social practices and contestations that lie beyond the obvious public interplay characterising policy production. At the very least, then, the notion of subaltern counterpublics point to the significance of 'interpretations and situation definitions that cannot at first gain a hearing in mainstream public spheres' (Fraser, 2007: 327). Subaltern counterpublics therefore signal the relationships of power between the state (and other forms of institutional and policy governance) and activities 'on the margins'. In this way it has correspondences with the postcolonial interrogation of the social relations between the colonial centre (or metropolis) and the colonised periphery (or margins). As with postcolonial theory, counterpublics both recognises relations of power and dominance, whilst also troubling normative judgements made about the legitimacy of activity on the 'margins' (see, Mukherjee, 2006). Indeed Fraser borrows from postcolonial literary theorist Gayatri Spivak's influential paper, 'Can the subaltern speak?', in formulating the term 'subaltern counterpublics' (Fraser, 1990).

Within educational research, subaltern counterpublics have proved useful in conceptualising educational activities outside of formal education (e.g. Gerrard, 2014a, 2014b; Kelly, 2003; Mirza and Reay, 2000; Reay and Mirza, 1997). Here, researchers explore how teachers and students in educational counterpublics reclaim space, knowledge and power through often 'covert and quiet ways' (Mirza, 2006). For instance, Diane Reay and Heidi Mirza found in their exploration of contemporary Black Supplementary Schooling in England (Mirza and Reay, 2000; Reay and Mirza, 1997), that 'marginal' educational activity provides opportunity to develop independent educational agency and authority alongside oppositional political cultures of blackness, particularly for the women teachers. Such research unveils how the long-standing policy focus on so-called disinterested and failing students and parents, can obfuscate the various endeavours of these students and parents to create educational opportunities (see also, Gerrard, 2014a).

Turning policy research attention to counterpublics provokes us, as researchers, to consider educational practices outside of the terms of reference of the policy field. Practices, for instance, that may seek spaces outside of the reach of policy directives, or do not exclusively orient their activates towards policy reform, are deemed too confrontational, or attempt to blur and push the boundaries of legitimated political discourse. For instance, my own research into the history of community-based working-class education in Britain signals the complex relationship between counterpublics and policy reform. Created in distinct socio-historical contexts and by very different communities, Socialist Sunday Schools (est. 1892) and Black Supplementary Schools (est. 1967) both represent the claim of parents and community, including large numbers of women, to their own educational agency (Gerrard, 2014a; see also, Mirza and Reay, 2000; Reay and Mirza, 1997). Despite their many differences, these two schooling movements shared a common concern to create independent spaces of (working-class or black) educational authority and political identity, alongside a desire to challenge the inequalities embedded within state schooling (Gerrard, 2014b).

These movements can be easily misrepresented as an addendum to the politics of policy work. Yet, both of these supposedly marginal educational activities produced significant criticisms of the state that influenced policy reform, including issues surrounding poverty and welfare (Socialist Sunday Schools) and inequality and institutionalised racism (Black Supplementary Schools). Nevertheless, these educational counterpublics had a contested and complex – and at times ambivalent – relationship to the state. Reforms often represented significant concessions in their actual demands, and for instance, in the case of the Black Supplementary Schooling movement accepting funding from the state was perceived by many as a double edged sword: in part a necessary right to address the state's own unequal systems of education, but also a potential means for the state to regulate and govern their activities (Gerrard, 2014a). These histories indicate the diversity of activity related to policy, and a non-linearity between such activity and reform. Researching educational counterpublics therefore provides a means to understand the ways in which different contestations gain (or do not gain) attention within the wider, and more readily recognisable, public policy debates.

Thus, counterpublics are not about providing neat romantic countervailing examples of dissent against an image of policy reform dread. Nor are they 'necessarily virtuous' (Fraser, 1990: 67). Indeed, exploration of the educational subaltern counterpublics reveals the diversity and contestations within their own educational practices and meanings (Gerrard, 2014a).

Correspondingly, whilst Fraser's specific conceptual expression of the subaltern counterpublics is interested in understanding the possibility for critical social action, her feminist problematisation of the public sphere has repercussions for understanding the fluidity and diversity of social activity more broadly. As with Antonio Gramsci's theory of hegemony, Fraser's theorisation brings attention to the multifarious, flexible, transient and at times contradictory social relations that lies behind – and in – policy discourses, reform events, and educational practices (see also, Johnson, 2007). This brings into focus the wide range of social and political activity that occurs in the struggle over meanings and practices in education: activities that at times direct themselves to policy reforms, whilst at other times do not, or do so in ways not immediately (or ever) recognisable by the legitimated practices of reform. This includes activity and contestation from a whole range of political perspectives and positions. Indeed, it highlights the ways in which conservative movements for change also create alternative publics, identities and meanings in their attempt to influence policy reform (see Apple, 2007).

Fraser's (1990) notion of a multiplicity of publics, and a subsequent widening of discursive contestation (p. 67), has important ramifications for policy research. The conceptualisation of subaltern counterpublics shifts research attention from the production of policies within the legitimated (albeit fluid) public sphere (e.g. white papers, parliamentary debate, media coverage, and the various formalised responses from teacher unions, parent organisations and professional associations), to the processes of social and political contestation that surround educational practice and policy. It suggests, in other words, a need for a consideration of the broader social, political and historical dimensions of the ways in which ideas for policies gain (or do not gain) traction and legitimacy. This may mean looking beyond departments of education, parliamentary debates and formal educational institutions, to the wider social and historical practices that may appear at first glance marginal to the policy field 'proper'.

Capitalism in/is crisis, subaltern counterpublics and feminist critique: implications for researching policy

As argued above, I suggest there is value in expanding the research focus for policy research beyond the legitimated field of public policy activity. Subaltern counter-publics provide one conceptual avenue for such research foci. Most importantly, however, Fraser's feminist critique of Habermas's model of the public points to the broader dynamics of social change, critique and crisis under capitalism and their relationship to policy activism and reform. Fraser develops this further in her recent exploration of the adaptive capabilities of capitalism. In *The fortunes of feminism* (2013) Fraser suggests there are discursive coalescences between the rise of neolib-eralism in the 1980s and 1990s and the demands of second-wave feminism. For instance, she (2013) asserts the second-wave feminist challenge to the family wage unwittingly converged with the neoliberal policy reform agenda that created the casualisation of work and the emergence of the two-earner family. Her point is not that there is congruence between feminism and neoliberal policy. Rather, capitalism constantly adapts and reforms in response to criticisms and crises, and does so in complex ways. This analysis complicates a romantic or idealistic conceptualisation of subaltern counterpublics, policy reform, and social change. 'In a fine cunning of history', Fraser suggests, second-wave feminist 'utopian desires found a second life as feeling currents that legitimated the transition to a new form of capitalism: post-Fordist, transnational, neoliberal' (2013: 211). Notwithstanding legitimate criticisms of Fraser's glossing over of the diversity of feminism (see, Bhandar and Ferreira da Silva, 2013), Fraser's analysis raises important questions surrounding the nature of policy reforms, pointing to the messy entanglements between subaltern counterpublics, critique and the development of capitalism.

Luc Boltanski and Eve Chiapello (2005) put this point in a slightly different way in *New spirits of capitalism*. They argue that the reform window post-1968, throughout the 1970s and 1980s, became open to some criticisms of the oppressive nature of Fordist economic cultures and technologies. Policy reforms allowed (and incorporated) notions of personal creativity, freedom and wellbeing within the 'new, liberated, and even libertarian way of making profit' (Boltanski and Chiapello, 2005: 201) in the globalising markets of neoliberal capitalism. For instance, neoliberal reforms transformed work conditions, such as flattened management structures and flexible working hours, in ways that spoke discursively (and disturbingly) to progressive criticisms of industrialised capitalism (ibid). As Eve Chiapello (2013) writes, 'The history of capitalism cannot be separated from the history of its criticisms' (p. 60). Reforms are often a result of the 'recuperation of critical ideas, often in a time of crises when the search for alternatives intensifies because the usual remedies are no longer working' (ibid).

Thus, capitalism is highly adaptive and recuperative: diverse socio–political crises, cultural contestations, and economic booms and busts, characterise the history of capitalism, and characterise its reform and development. Such crises provide windows of policy reform opportunity by creating 'a sense of urgency predicated on the assumption that already serious problems will be exacerbated by inaction' (Keeler, 1993: 441). Most recently heightened by both 9/11 and the global financial crisis policy reform is couched in a political discourse of urgency and necessity: from the need for the 'Education Revolution' to border control, policies are presented as vital, imperative, and inexorable. Contemporary policy, therefore, is predominantly (and urgently) present and future preoccupied. Policies routinely address declared 'states of emergency' (in test scores, in teacher accountability, in the global competitiveness of schools and universities), and present reform as inevitable for this emergency to be overcome. The challenge, then, for educational policy research is to examine not only the content and effect of such policies, but also the contours and constitution of this policy-imperative culture and the social struggle that surrounds it.

Crisis, subaltern counterpublics and policy research

Fraser and Boltanski and Chiapello's analyses highlight how neoliberal policy reform is complexly intertwined with various struggles over, and contestations of, the limits and exclusions within previous 'policy settlements' under capitalism, including the post-WWII welfare state. This is not to discount the import of state governance, capital, conservative ideology, and the economic crises of the 1970s in the take-up of neoliberalism (Harvey, 2005). Rather, exploration of the complex intersections between critiques of capitalism and policy reform, attempts to find ways to understand the wider circumstances and public discourses that surround shifts in political (and policy) governance and techniques. This includes seeking to understand the diversity and ambiguity of the various practices that have come to be collectively understood as 'neoliberalism', such as 'choice', 'market' and 'entre-preneurship' (du Gay and Morgan, 2013: 2; see also Rowlands and Rawolle, 2013).

This has significant repercussions for research concerned with the socio-historical dimensions of education policy production and effects. It points to the ways in which struggles under capitalism – including subaltern counterpublics – can contribute to capitalism's own recuperative reform agenda. When faced with crisis, capitalism often recuperates by incorporating and co-opting particular demands. This suggests that in order to understand, for instance, the policy articulations of equity, competition, achievement or diversity, it is necessary to look beyond policy documentation to the various – past and present – struggles over meanings and practices that occurred outside of, surrounding, or oriented towards, the policy field. Fraser's critique of Habermas's gender-blind conceptualisation of the public therefore provokes us to rethink the political boundaries of policy and reform in ways that move beyond criticism of the power dynamics of the policy field towards the multitude of activities that seemingly occur on the margins.

To give an historical example, in the UK in the late 1960s and into the 1970s there emerged a new conservative challenge to schooling, exemplified in the writings of the 'Black Papers' (e.g. Cox and Boyson, 1975). Galvanising public concern over the lack of class social mobility, the writers of the Black Papers centred their challenge on the authority of teachers, and argued for greater parental choice and accountability for teachers. In policy terms, this was supported by the infamous Ruskin speech, delivered by the then Labour Prime Minister James Callaghan in 1976, which also questioned the authority and influence of educators on schooling curriculum and pedagogy. At the same time, with very different political aims and orientations, black parents led significant campaigns against institutionalised racism in British schools as a part of broader activities of the black educational counter-public (Gerrard, 2013, 2014a). These parents also called for tighter practices of accountability for schools and teachers, but in order to address systemic injustice and prejudice. Supported by a wider political radicalism (inside and outside of schools), campaigns were varied, including in some instances targeting particular teachers or head teachers and leading protests outside school gates (Gerrard, 2013).

These parallel – but unmistakably distinct – challenges to schooling practices converged to interrupt the previous policy settlements and practices in education (see Ball, 2008; Baron et al., 1981). They therefore do not indicate congruence in meaning or intent. Rather they point to the messy discursive entanglements, and the multiple meanings and struggles, that hang upon particular ideas (such as teacher accountability), which then become picked up, adapted by, and shaped for, policy.

Exploration of such multiple contestations sheds light on the constant struggle for capitalist hegemony through, and in, relationship with its critics, including subaltern counterpublics. This is not to suggest that capitalism is a complete system that simply feeds criticism into an endless 'reform loop'. Rather, social (and policy) change occurs in and through the multifarious points of contestation/consent/ambivalence/dissent/fluctuation/doubt. In pointing the research gaze beyond the specific horizons of particular policy texts and paradigms, it is therefore possible to explore the social processes that extend beyond, and perhaps eventually underpin, policy reform.

At a time when policy is presented as present and future preoccupied and necessary, it is important to historically contextualise analysis of the contemporary policy field and to question what is deemed to be rational, pragmatic, productive. Borrowing from Foucauldian genealogical approaches, a feminist socio-historical approach is interested in understanding the (re)iteration of ideas across time and context in order to understand their diverse historical mobilisations, and how particular ideas and practices gain and loose salience (see also, Gale, 2001). Genealogy aims to understand the historical mutations, shifts, continuities and ruptures, of ideas and practices (Foucault, 1980: 119). It aims to problematise the taken-for-granted centrality of the subject, and thus opens enquiry to consider how particular subjects (at-risk students, successful students, accountable teachers, engaged parents) come to be constructed within policy, *and* have varying meanings and practices beyond formal policy documentation and its enactment. This includes exploration of the reforms that dominate current political agendas, as well as ideas and practices that had only fleeting (or no) impact or visibility in the legitimated policy field. As Kathi Weeks (2011) writes in reference to feminist history, paraphrasing Barbara Taylor, the history of struggle 'is not only a story of progress but also sometimes . . . of forgotten ideas and stifled aspirations' (p. 116).

Conclusion

In this chapter, I have explored an approach to policy research that seeks to understand the broader social, political and historical dimensions to policy. Openings for reform are often generated through (real or perceived) social, cultural, political and economic crises. Crises provide windows of reform possibility, as well as avenues for the contestation and critique of prevailing policy discourses and practices. At the same time, policies can provoke crises and thus engender periods of contestation and reform. Of course, much policy production occurs within a bureaucratic field characterised by an on-going, and at times routine, imperative to write, review and survey policies. Policies are not only created in times of crisis and contestation. Yet, positioning policy analysis within a consideration of broader social and historical dynamics within research, I suggest, offers a fruitful means to understand how some policies gain traction, and are deemed pragmatically possible.

This approach takes its lead from the feminist critiques of the public sphere, and thus takes as its starting point an analysis of the limitations of – and latent exclusions contained within – the legitimated field of policy action. In response, I suggest the value in researching beyond official policy documentation, to the multifarious struggles surrounding educational practices and meanings. Following Nancy Fraser's conceptualisation of subaltern counterpublics, this approach seeks to understand the relationship of seemingly 'marginal' social activity to the wider dynamics of social change, and with this policy reform. At the same time, such an approach positions policy analysis within the broad complex processes of social change that underpin neoliberal capitalism. This involves, on the one hand, exploring the ways in which criticisms and contestations are inflected, and at times incorporated, within policy reforms, with varying – and at times contradictory – effects, as explored in Fraser's analysis of second-wave feminism and neoliberalism (2013). On the other hand, it also involves a turn to the history of educational ideas and practices and the ways in which they became taken up (or not) within reform moments.

A feminist socio-historical approach to policy research also recognises that policies are never the full representation of educational experience. The sheer volume of policy production can make the policy field appear endless and all encompassing. This is a view supported by the notion that the utility of educational research lies in providing alternative (but pragmatically possible) 'evidence-based' policy solutions (see, Lingard, 2013). Researching policy reform within the context of the multifarious (and at times marginalised) struggles over education highlights historical difference, whilst at the same time wards against nostalgia for a bygone equitable past in the critical analysis of contemporary neoliberal policy reform. There are always 'policy gaps, silences, and disjunctions between rhetoric and embodied encounters and the lived effects of policy imperatives' (McLeod and Allard, 2007). Moreover, not all policies carry the same power or weight. The meaning and power of policy documents, and policy discourses, is constituted through the social relations of power within which they are positioned (see Smith, 2005). Thus, researching policy through these wider relations provides a means to understand the social, political and economic dynamics of educational practice and policy reform, including the ways in which experiences are marginalised from representation and recognition through powerful gender, race, sexuality and class relations. In so doing, it is also possible to explore the 'gaps', 'silences', 'disjunctions' of policies, and the social relations and processes of social change that ultimately underpin them.

References

Apple, M. W. (2007). Social movements and political practice in education. *Theory and Research in Education, 5*(2), 161–171.

Apple, M. W. (2011). Global crises, social justice and teacher education. *Journal of Teacher Education, 62*(2), 222–234.

Arnot, M. (2006). Gender equality, pedagogy and citizenship: Affirmative and transformative approaches in the UK. *Theory and Research in Education, 4*(2), 131–150.

Ball, S. J. (2008). Some sociologies of education: A history of problems and places, and segments and gazes. *The Sociological Review, 56*(4), 650–669.

Baron, S., Finn, D., Grant, N., Green, M. and Johnson, R. (1981). *Unpopular education: Schooling and social democracy in England since 1944.* London: Hutchinson.

Bhandar, B. and Ferreira da Silva, D. (2013). White feminist fatigue syndrome: A reply to Nancy Fraser. *Critical legal thinking: Law and the political.* http://criticallegalthinking.com/2013/10/21/white-feminist-fatigue-syndrome/ (accessed 9 May 2014).

Boltanski, L. and Chiapello, E. (2005). *New spirits of capitalism.* London and New York: Verso.

Canovan, M. (1983). Distorted communication: A note on Habermas and Arendt. *Political Theory, 11*(1), 105–116.

Chiapello, S. (2013). Capitalism and its critics. In P. du Gay and G. Morgan (Eds.), *New spirits of capitalism? Crises, justifications, and dynamics* (pp. 60–81). Oxford, UK: Oxford University Press.

Cox, C. B. and R. H. Boyson (Eds.) (1975). *Black paper 1975.* London: J. M. Dent & Sons.

du Gay, P. and Morgan, G. (2013). Understanding capitalism: Crises, legitimacy, and change through the prism of *The new spirit of capitalism.* In P. du Gay and G. Morgan (Eds.), *New spirits of capitalism: Crises, justifications, and critiques* (pp. 1–42). Oxford, UK: Oxford University Press.

Ellsworth, E. (1992). Why doesn't this feel empowering? Working through the repressive myths of critical pedagogy. In C. Luke and J. Gore (Eds.), *Feminisms and critical pedagogy* (pp. 90–119). New York: Routledge.

Foucault, M. (1980). *History of sexuality, Vol I.* New York: Vintage Books.

Fraser, N. (1985). What's critical and critical theory? The case of Habermas and gender. *New German Critique, 35,* 97–131.

Fraser, N. (1990). Rethinking the public sphere: A contribution to the critique of actually existing democracy. *Social Text, 25/26,* 56–80.

Fraser, N. (1997). *Justice interrupts: Critical reflections on the 'postsocialist' condition.* London and New York: Routledge.

Fraser, N. (2007). Identity, exclusion and critique: A response to four critics. *European Journal of Political Theory, 6*(3), 305–338.

Fraser, N. (2013). *Fortunes of feminism: From state-managed capitalism to neoliberal crisis.* London and New York: Verso.

Gale, T. (2001). Critical policy sociology: Historiography, archaeology and genealogy as methods of policy analysis. *Journal of Education Policy, 16*(5), 379–393.

Gerrard, J. (2013). Self help and protest: The emergence of black supplementary schooling in England. *Race, Ethnicity and Education, 16*(1), 32–58.

Gerrard, J. (2014a). *Radical childhoods.* Manchester, UK: Manchester University Press.

Gerrard, J. (2014b). Counter-narratives of educational excellence: Free schools, success and community-based schooling. *British Journal of Sociology of Education* (ifirst).

Gerrard, J. and Farrell, L. (2013). 'Peopling' curriculum policy production: Researching educational governance through institutional ethnography and Bourdieuian field analysis. *Journal of Education Policy, 28*(1), 1–20.

Habermas, J. (1974). The public sphere: An encyclopaedia article (1964). *New German Critique, No. 3*(Autumn), 49–55.

Habermas, J. (1989). *The new conservatism: Cultural criticism and the historian's debate* (S. W. Nicholson, Ed.). Cambridge, MA: The MIT Press.

Habermas, J. (2002). Civil society and the political public sphere, in C. Calhoun, J. Gerteis, J. Moody, S. Pfaff and I. Virk (Eds.), *Contemporary sociological theory* (pp. 358–376). Oxford, UK: Blackwell.

Harvey, D. (2005). *A brief history of neoliberalism.* Oxford, UK: Oxford University Press.

Huttunen, R. (2007). Critical adult education and the political-philosophical debate between Nancy Fraser and Axel Honneth. *Educational Theory, 57*(4), 421–433.

Jackson, S. (1997). Crossing borders and changing pedagogies: From Giroux and Freire to feminist theories of education. *Gender and Education*, *9*(4), 457–467.

Johnson, R. (2007). Post-hegemony? I don't think so. *Theory, Culture & Society*, *24*(3), 95–110.

Keddie, A. (2012). *Educating for diversity and social justice*. London: Routledge.

Keeler, J. T. S. (1993). Opening the window for reform: Mandates, crises, and extraordinary policy making. *Comparative Political Studies*, *25*(4), 433–486.

Kelly, D. M. (2003). Practicing democracy in the margins of school: The teenage parents program as feminist counterpublic. *American Educational Research Journal*, *40*(1), 123–146.

Lingard, B. (2013). The impact of research on education policy in an era of evidence-based policy. *Critical Studies in Education*, *54*(2), 113–131.

Luke, C. (1992). Feminist politics in radical pedagogy. In C. Luke and J. Gore (Eds.), *Feminisms and critical pedagogy* (pp. 25–53). New York: Routledge.

McLeod, J. and Allard, A. C. (2007). *Learning from the margins: Young women, social exclusion and education*. Abingdon, UK: Routledge.

Mirza, H. S. (2006). Transcendence over diversity: Black women in the academy. *Policy Futures in Education*, *4*(2), 101–113.

Mirza, H. S. and Reay, D. (2000). Spaces and places of black educational desire: Rethinking Black supplementary schools as a new social movement. *Sociology*, *34*(3), 521–544.

Mukherjee, M. (2006). Whose centre, which periphery? In M. Ghosh-Schellhorn (with V. Alexander) (Eds.), *Peripheral centres, central peripheries: India and its diaspora(s)* (pp. 37–46). Berlin: Lit Verlag.

Reay, D. and Mirza, H. (1997). Uncovering genealogies of the margins: Black supplementary schools. *British Journal of Sociology of Education*, *18*(4), 477–499.

Rowlands, J. and Rawolle, S. (2013). Neoliberalism is not a theory of everything: A Bourdieuian analysis of illusion in educational research. *Critical Studies in Education*, *54*(3), 260–272.

Santoro Gomez, D. (2008). Women's proper place and student-centred pedagogy. *Studies in the Philosophy of Education*, *27*, 313–333.

Smith, D. E. (2005). *Institutional ethnography: A sociology for people*. Oxford, UK: Alta Mira Press.

Weeks, K. (2011). *The problem with work: Feminist, Marxist, antiwork politics, and postwork imaginaries*. Durham, NC and London: Duke University Press.

11

EMBODYING POLICY STUDIES

Feminist genealogy as methodology

Wanda S. Pillow

> Pregnancy discrimination is the new frontier.
>
> *(Mason and Younger, 2013: 1)*

> The teen pregnant body has proven to be a body that cannot be simply contained or fixed; it is excessive and leaky, not easily predicted or programmed for under traditional policy studies.
>
> *(Pillow, 2003: 149)*

Title IX, the preeminent US federal civil rights law prohibiting sex discrimination in education reached its 40th anniversary in 2012. This marker provided an opportunity to consider the impact and effectiveness of gender equity policies. While Title IX is widely known for influencing access to and establishment of athletics for women, it also speaks to issues of sexual harassment; single-sex education; equal educational opportunity across science, technology, engineering and mathematics (STEM); and explicitly addresses educational rights of pregnant/parenting youth. Despite the importance of these topics, debate focused on Title IX as an outmoded entitlement policy allowing favouritism toward females and hurting males.

Various women's organizations responded by arguing that Title IX is *not* about girls and women. Consider this statement by the National Coalition for Women and Girls in Education (NCWGE, 2012: 1):

> Contrary to the opinion of critics, Title IX is not an entitlement program; it offers no special benefits or advantages for girls and women. Rather, it is a gender-neutral piece of legislation designed to ensure equality in education for *all* students by eliminating sex-based discrimination.

While NCWGE attempted to shift focus from unfair entitlement for some to equal education opportunity for all, the US is far from 'gender neutral' in educational access and outcomes. Despite gains, girls and women continue to lag behind in all of Title IX's emphasis areas. In this climate, how can policy studies make sense of sex equity policy – how can gender as a variable that impacts access and outcomes be recognized yet have 'neutrality'?

This chapter explores this conundrum by looking at a particularly gendered component of Title IX, the educational rights of pregnant students. What happens when 'gender-neutral' criteria are applied to pregnancy? How have educational rights of pregnant/parenting students been defined since the passage of Title IX? What is most impacting case law, or the lack of case law, in this area? Such questions cannot be taken up without tools of feminist theory.

Three main terms are introduced in this chapter: 'feminism,' 'embodiment' and 'genealogy'. These terms are conceptualized into *feminist genealogy* as a policy studies methodology. An overview of Title IX case law, which is necessary to determine enforcement and regulation of educational policy and practice, provides a working exemplar to apply feminist genealogy. The chapter concludes with a discussion of the utility of *feminist genealogy* for influencing policy discourse and change.

Feminist poststructuralism: feminism, embodiment, and genealogy

The feminisms I work with and think from are committed to an analysis of power and patriarchy by centring women's experiences and voices while simultaneously remaining suspicious of essentialist foundational claims about the category of woman. For example, while early feminist research on women's leadership styles seemed empowering because it promoted the idea of women's innate capabilities at communication and caring, this research allowed essentialized ideas about women leaders to proliferate and explain away inequalities: 'If women are *naturally* more caring then men' they are naturally 'better suited for . . . service oriented, low-paying positions' (Pillow, 1997a: 141). Such discourses become normalized and deeply engrained as 'truth'. Poststructural feminist thought is particularly helpful as it provides a 'continued skepticism about regimes of truth' (St. Pierre and Pillow, 2000: 1) wherever regimes of truth may appear.

As Elizabeth St. Pierre and I wrote in 2000, we place feminist theory and post-structuralism beside each other to utilize 'how the two theories/movements work similarly and differently to trouble foundation ontologies, methodologies, and epistemologies' (p. 2). In this way, feminist theories informed by poststructuralism are able to trace and demonstrate 'structural failures in some of foundationalism's most heinous formations – racism, patriarchy, homophobia, ageism, . . .' (St. Pierre and Pillow, 2000: 2). The feminist poststructuralism I employ is indebted to Black feminist thought and Chicana/Indigenous feminisms (Anzaldúa, 1987; Dilliard, 2000; Lorde, 1984; Moraga and Anzaldúa, 1981). To think and analyze without feminist race theory would yield an ethnocentric gap in analysis. These works are necessary to deeply question and identify what is formed through intimate relations of colonial power and formation of nation-states (Arvin, Tuck and Morrill, 2013; Pillow, 2007, 2012).

This approach requires a focus upon tracing power and discourses through the body. The body has been important to feminist theory and practice as 'a place from which to theorize, analyze practice, and critically reconsider the construction and reproduction of knowledge, power, class and culture' (Pillow, 1997b: 349). As Elizabeth Grosz (1995) notes: 'bodies are essential to accounts of power and critiques of knowledge' (p. 32) and a focus on the body 'is a refiguring of the body so that it moves from the periphery to the center of analysis' (Grosz, 1994: ix). Bodies 'bear the weight of discursive representations' (Pillow, 2003: 148). We can understand bodies not as 'ahistorical, precultural, or natural'; they are 'inscribed, marked, engraved' by external structures and discourses yet are also 'the products, the direct effects, of the very social constitution of nature itself' (Grosz, 1994: x).

Feminist theories of the state refer to a 'body politics' – most familiarly understood as 'the personal is political' – meaning women's and men's sexuality, practices and domestic home relations are part of 'the public sphere of power relations, citizen rights, and public policy' (Mazur, 2002: 137). In this way:

> the teen pregnant body is a site of state regulation and control not only of the teen mother, but also a site for the regulation and reassertion of societal norms, morals, and values on issues such as female sexuality, single-parenting, welfare, birth control and abortion. Teen pregnancy as an educational policy issue specifically challenges norms, morals and values around adolescent sexuality, female sexuality and sex education.
>
> *(Pillow 2003: 149)*

Attention to the embodied lived experience of, in this case the young mother, alongside public discourses about and constructions of the 'teen mother' alters what is meant by policy studies. Instead of focusing on evaluating outcomes, thinking and analyzing from the body includes investigation of discourses surrounding and embedded in constructions of the subject of policy, of the body that is a problem.

For instance, there is an obvious physicality to the pregnant body; a physicality that impacts the young woman who is pregnant, but also marks how others interact with her. Is she to be feared, reviled, protected? These visceral responses to the teen pregnant body work their way into policy – is the young mother best served in a separate class, separate school? What services, if any, is the young mother entitled to? Policy seeks to contain and regulate bodies – this body goes to this place, receives these services under certain conditions – but the pregnant body is a shifting changing body; it 'extend(s) the frameworks which attempt to contain' and 'seep(s) beyond . . . domains of control' (Grosz, 1994: xi). Attending to the embodiment experiences of young mothers in schools exposes how the bodies of young mothers, physically and discursively exceed boundaries of school policy and case law (Pillow, 1997b, 2004). This point is more fully discussed later; for now, keep in mind that attention to embodiment helps policy studies see the enactment and production of power through experiences and discourses about the body.

Alongside feminism and embodiment, I turn to Michel Foucault's (1981, 1984) reformulation of Nietzsche's genealogy as a detailed and meticulous methodology – a 'history of the present' – that allows specific tracings of power through the body. Foucault's deconstructive approach does not look for a single, unified Truth narrative of human conditions, but rather traces techniques, discourses, knowledges and practices of power that inform and regulate systems and subjectivities. As Grosz (1994) states: 'Foucault is concerned with the material, corporeal costs of historical events and transformations, their investments in and reliance on systems of power' (p. 145). These 'costs' provide insight into what Foucault terms 'bio-power' – that is the lived, embodied effects of nation-state investments. Although greatly simplified, for the purposes of this chapter we can say that genealogy provides the policy analyst a way to approach policy with a focus always upon tracing complex movements of power and bodies, by attending to the discourses, techniques, practices and investments embedded in policy and by 'incessantly question(ing) the conditions under which policy is produced' (Pillow, 2004: 9).

A focus on the 'conditions under which policy is produced' shifts lens of analysis from the subject of policy to how policy is produced and enacted. It is not the young mother who is the target of evaluation – looking for explanations and theories that explain her sexual, cultural, social-psychological behaviour – rather feminist genealogy promotes an analysis that 'is not simply resistant but is meticulous in its search for the discursive strategies of power as they are camouflaged in the assumptive discourses and practices of policy theory, implementation, and evaluation' (Pillow, 2004: 9). Feminist genealogy opens questions of:

- Why this policy and why now?
- In whose interest?
- For whose needs?
- What is being contained or produced?
- What ideologies, constructions and discourses are proliferated?
- What is visible and what is made absent in these constructions?

In summary, feminist genealogy as a methodological and analytical lens provides:

- an intricate, historical tracing of power through discourses, texts and structures;
- an embodied narrative of this tracing; and
- a lens through which to shift and rethink policy studies.

A 'dearth of data'

Before looking at Title IX, it is necessary to consider the 'body politic' surrounding teen pregnancy in the US. This section provides a brief overview of how teen pregnancy has been defined as a problem and the lack of research on teen pregnancy as an educational issue.

In its review, *Title IX at 40*, The National Women's Law Center (NWLC, 2012) concluded that the promise and protection of equal opportunity under Title IX is 'far from being fulfilled when it comes to pregnant and parenting students' (p. 55). Key impediments to equal educational opportunity for young mothers are attributed to lack of awareness of Title IX's protection of pregnant/parenting students coupled with school practices and attitudes that create barriers to young mothers attending and completing school (Erdmans, 2012; Luttrell, 2003; Pillow, 2004). Despite evidence indicating practices of discrimination toward the female pregnant/ mothering student, legal scholar Michelle Gough (2011) notes: 'Title IX's prohibition of gender discrimination in the context of parenting and pregnant students has often been left out of the discussion and therefore the understanding, of the implementation of Title IX Regulations' (pp. 211–212). NWLC's 2012 publication, *A pregnancy test for schools*, echoes the lack of attention to Title IX's explicit protection against discrimination for pregnant and parenting students explaining that a 'dearth of data' makes it impossible to track pregnant/parenting students and thus difficult to identify discriminatory policies and practices through case law.

Although teen pregnancy is commonly negatively linked to school completion and earning capacity, policy discussions at the intersections of social welfare and education occur as if Title IX does not exist. Why are the educational rights of young mothers ignored when education is seen as vital to her economic future? Research indicates that shifting constructions of who the teen mother is and what she deserves has deeply influenced education policy development, implementation and practice (Pillow, 2004). The discursive, political and historical constructions of the young unwed mother has shifted from the 1972 Title IX subject, the young white girl who becomes pregnant and is deserving of treatment, to the racialized teen mother who is culturally deficit and a drain on society (Pillow, 2004).

The young mother has become an unsympathetic, racialized urban problem; a policy subject approached with deficit thinking. This shift has influenced which young mothers are viewed as educational subjects part of an educational policy agenda and which are not. Correspondingly, as teen pregnancy is constructed as a racialized/cultural deficit, a 'constructed and highly politicized silence' (Pillow, 2006: 60) surrounding education and young mothers has been established, limiting attention and research.

Title IX and pregnancy: review of case law

Before considering the role of case law in the construction of equal education opportunity for young mothers, it is useful to look at what Title IX says about the pregnant/parenting student.

> [A] recipient [of federal funding] shall not discriminate against any student, or exclude any student from its education program or activity, including any class or extracurricular activity, on the basis of such student's pregnancy, childbirth, false pregnancy, termination of pregnancy or recovery therefrom, unless the student requests voluntarily to participate in a separate portion of the program.
>
> *(106.40,b)*

A recipient which operates a portion of its education program or activity separately for pregnant students, admittance to which is completely voluntary on the part of the student as provided in paragraph (b)(1) of this section shall ensure that the instructional program in the separate program is comparable to that offered to non-pregnant students.

(104.40,3)

A recipient shall treat pregnancy, childbirth, false pregnancy, termination of pregnancy and recovery therefrom in the same manner and under the same policies as any other temporary disability with respect to any medical . . . In the case of the a recipient which does not maintain a leave policy for its students, . . . a recipient shall treat pregnancy, childbirth, false pregnancy, termination of pregnancy, and recovery therefrom as a justification for a leave of absence for so long a period of time as deemed medically necessary by the student's physician, at the conclusion of which the student shall be reinstated to the status she held when the leave began.

(106.40,5)

The implications of Title IX seem clear. Education institutions receiving federal funding should not: limit pregnant/parenting students from participation in class and extracurricular activities; force pregnant students into separate programs and if a separate program is chosen, the curriculum should be comparable; and leave of absences should be granted as needed with no retribution. Feminist law scholars like Deborah Brake (1994: 215–216), however, note the potentially conflicting demands of Title IX:

By including both accommodation rights, independent of how other students are treated, and comparative rights, treating pregnant students as well as other temporarily disabled students, Title IX straddles the equal treatment/special treatment divide that has characterized so much of the discourse surrounding discrimination law's treatment. Feminists have often struggled with whether to analyze pregnancy under a special treatment model, requiring extra accommodation of pregnancy, or an equal treatment model, requiring pregnancy to be treated as well (or as badly) as some comparable condition.

The 'equal treatment/special treatment divide' is prevalent in schools. Lacking case law determining state or district policy, individual schools determine how to treat pregnant/parenting students based upon beliefs about teen pregnancy (Pillow, 2004). This has led to uneven and disparate treatment of pregnant/parenting students (Pillow, 2004). While Brake (1994) suggests that Title IX's straddling of the equal/special divide is beneficial because each has flaws and thus Title IX 'mitigates the downsides of both', Michelle Gough (2011) argues 'coupling equal treatment requirements with accommodation has presented schools with unclear and challenging legal requirements' (p. 215). Gough articulates a problematic inherent in

Title IX litigation, the expectation that each pregnant/parenting student can pursue equal education opportunity under distinctly unequal conditions, however Gough moves away from critique when she reasons that 'failures to implement the regulations are less an issue of vagueness and/or complexities in the requirements and more an issue of lack of awareness' (pp. 215–216).

Although Gough acknowledges 'the number of Title IX cases addressing the rights of pregnant and parenting students is disproportionately small to the number of students that research indicates are having their rights violated in schools' (p. 218), she argues an update of case law will inform policy and practice. It should be noted her article provides evidence of the lack of attention in this area as: 'not since Brake's 1994 articles has any of the literature provided a thorough, updated review of the case law on point' (p. 219). Over a 40-year period, Gough found and reviewed 18 cases related to Title IX and pregnant/parenting students. She identi-fies cases according to the equal/special or in her terms 'accommodation/equal protection' divide, with five cases falling under accommodation and 13 under equal protection (p. 218). The 'accommodation' cases raised questions around childcare, paternal leave from athletics, and 'accommodations for coursework and/or class structure' (p. 218). It is important to note that all five of these cases involve post-high school, community college or university student claims.

Of the 13 'equal treatment' cases, eight directly involved school practice and treatment. Four cases involved high school pregnant/parenting students (all female) rejected for membership in the National Honor Society (NHS); one addressed admissions; two addressed hostile treatment at university; and one expulsion of a pregnant student from a private university.

The rulings on the above accommodation and equal treatment cases are varied and for the non-legal expert can seem confusing. For example, NHS cases have variously been decided in favor of the pregnant/mothering student based upon a judgment that NHS was discriminating against the female pregnant student, while three other NHS cases determined the female student 'was dismissed because of premarital sexual activity and not because of gender discrimination' (Gough, 2011: 230). NHS membership is primarily based upon grade-point-average, but can also consider 'character'. Pregnancy, which only girls experience, provides evidence of unmarried sex relations and yet 'immoral character' based on pregnancy is not gender discrimination?

Such determinations are confounding and have kept cases of discrimination from going forward; if pregnant/mothering students who are eligible for NHS are not 'good' subjects under the law, how could the young mother with a poor school record ever prove discrimination? While Gough states, 'it should be noted generally more than half of the cases were decided in favor of students' (p. 247), she finds trends including a 'failure to assert Title IX' and linking 'pregnancy and character' (p. 248). Title IX has not been effective at encouraging schools to implement the language of Title IX to the fullest extent nor has Title IX been able to separate entrenched social beliefs about teen mothers from the educational rights of these students.

Despite this, Gough argues there is progress when 'filing or threatening to file a case in which a district can reasonably expect to be found to have violated a rights law . . . has the potential to shift behavior without lengthy and costly litigation' (p. 253). She bases this on actions taken by New York City (NYC) school district between 2002–2007. In response to three complaints of hostile treatment and unequal education brought by young mothers and investigation by the New York Civil Liberties Union, NYC closed its separate 'P-schools' in 2007, which served 323 pregnant/mothering students. Superintendent Cami Anderson utilized the language of Title IX to explain the closure: 'It's a separate but unequal program . . . The girls get pushed out of their original high schools, they don't come to class and they don't gain ground in terms of credits' (Gough, 2011: 255).

Although Gough presents this as an example of potential effectiveness of Title IX, she fails to acknowledge that in reaction to fear of litigation, NYC did close the 'P schools' but failed to put any plans in place to provide equal education to pregnant/parenting students. In essence, young mothers are left on their own to navigate the NYC school system and attempt to find adequate, much less equal, education placements.

Feminist genealogy as a tool of intervention and analysis

In an arena of policy studies, that seems obviously all about gender, race and sexuality yet at the same time is characterized by discourses that silence and ignore these constructs, teen pregnancy as an educational policy issue is in need of a feminist genealogy approach that will pay attention to the structures, discourses and lived experiences of the pregnant and parenting/mothering body as an educational subject.

Gough's analysis demonstrates that over a forty-year time period there has been little to no movement on education policy and practice for young parents, specifically young mothers in high school. Despite Gough's attempt to read a line of possibility through the cases she reviews, she concludes, as have other scholars, that 'lack of knowledge' and 'marginalization' of young parents in schools remain key issues limiting pregnant and parenting students equal education opportunity (p. 258). Gough offers three recommendations to improve

> fulfillment of the Title IX law: first, increase awareness of existing case law and effective use of litigation as a strategy for improving enforcement; second impose law and education requirements for teachers and administrators; and third, increase regulation by the Office for Civil Rights.
>
> *(pp. 217–218)*

How can these recommendations be actualized? What insights can feminist genealogy contribute to 'effective use of litigation' and 'increased regulation'? As Gough (2011) states 'the presence of a coherent, consistent, and predictable body of case law goes a long way toward aligning action by otherwise recalcitrant groups, and persons' (p. 253). Until we have case law guiding educational policy and practice for pregnant/parenting students it is obvious that the mere presence of Title IX will not accomplish social and educational reform.

Is the 40-year gap in educational policy and case law under Title IX because we do not know how to educate young mothers? Do we really not have strategies and practices to increase attendance and graduation? Feminist genealogy as policy studies methodology reveals absences under Title IX as not simply gaps, but strategic, systemic patterns of power linked to social constructions of young parents (Pillow, 2006). Let's consider examples of how feminist genealogy provides intricate tracings of power; calls for an embodied narrative of this tracing; and provides a lens through which to shift and rethink policy studies and challenges terms of 'equality.'

In the summer of 2013, NYC ran a media campaign barely disguised as a 'shame campaign' (Durkin, 2013). The advertisements, displayed in bus stops and subway cars throughout the city, depicted clearly racialized (brown, bi-racial, black) babies crying or in distress as they appeal to their mothers: 'Honestly, Mom, chances are he won't stay with you. What happens to me?'; 'Got a good job? I cost thousands of dollars each year.'; and 'I'm twice as likely not to graduate highschool because you had me as a teen.' Feminist genealogy's insistence upon tracing of power yields a mapping of key discourses regulating knowledge, policy and practice. In this way, feminist genealogy considers the impact of the above ads not only on teens but also more keenly on the social discursive climate surrounding and shaping educational policy and practice about and toward pregnant/parenting students.

According to the advertisements, the young mother is a girl who is brown or black (or has sex with brown or black males) and is clearly a girl who is not thinking, is not responsible and based on her mistake and irresponsibility will now cost society a bundle while at the same time her actions have forever limited the future outcome of her child. It does not matter that the advertisements are not based upon evidence; what matters is how the advertisements portray and encourage the public to think about young mothers.

Feminist genealogy forefronts that tracing social constructions matters in policy and identifies what is both present and absent in discourses, but what can feminist genealogy offer to the problems of gender/sex equity policy and case law under Title IX? In other words, how can feminist genealogy – a poststructural analytics based upon tracings and multiplicities – be useful to the seemingly linear arenas of litigation and regulation under Title IX? This is a problematic I cannot pretend to have figured out – and as I conclude, feminist genealogy may disrupt a turn to Title IX – but I have found feminist genealogy useful as an interruptive tool of analysis. As noted, through feminist genealogy, it is the policy process – discourses, text and enactment – that is put under scrutiny. Feminist genealogy identifies discourses and surrounding policy and practices and identifies constraints, limitations and at times conflicting goals of messages surrounding young mothers. The same deep analysis can be applied to the arenas of litigation and regulation, which often operate as truth regimes.

What if these regimes are questioned; if productions of truths are traced and re-told? What if the terms of litigation and regulation are shifted?

In an example, let's consider what is invested in the phrasing 'equal treatment' under Title IX. A school may decide to take an 'equal treatment' approach to the pregnant/parenting student, applying school attendance policy without special treatment. From the school's point of view, it is operating in a fair and neutral manner – it is treating pregnant/parenting students like any other student. However, feminist genealogy would encourage investigation into why and how 'equal treatment' discourses and practices were put into place within a school and what investments/truths are governing this approach. Is 'equal treatment' enacted through discourses and beliefs that pregnant/parenting students deserve to be treated equally or because these students do *not* deserve any extra considerations? This distinction becomes key to implementation and regulation of policy – is equal treatment operating out of equality or deficit frameworks? How is 'equal treatment' being monitored and regulated? What does it look like?

Existing data on young mother's experiences demonstrate that such policies are not neutral and actively work against students attempting to return to and complete high school. Pregnant/mothering students may miss multiple days of school due to pregnancy related health concerns and after birth due to their child's illness or doctor appointments. If 'special treatment' is not applied to these absences, if young mothers are penalized for such absences, they accrue delinquent marks, fall behind on school work, and by school policy can be given non-passing grades or removed from school.

Additionally, young mothers are caught in dualistic and competing messages from social work caseworkers and schools. If they remain home for the first month after birth in order to recover and bond with their child as recommended by caseworkers, they are putting themselves at risk of being delinquent in school attendance. If they attend child parenting classes and baby check-ups as required by social welfare, they are at risk of building up school absences. If they access state-funded childcare, they are limited to the hours and training requirements of that care, which often conflict with a tradition high school day.

While these examples may seem obvious to the reader, traditional policy analysis, litigation and regulation under Title IX does not take into account the myriad demands and parcelling of identities young parents face. Is the young mother a subject of social welfare reform or an education subject? When is the young mother a mother and when is she a student? And how is 'equal treatment' defined, measured and regulated across these identities?

Feminist genealogy provides the tools and analytic lens to trace patterns across such questions, identifying the myriad of expectations, interventions into, and monitoring of young mothers lives. In this way, feminist genealogy can aid in pointing out discrepancies in discourses and practices of 'equal treatment' under case law and regulation and ideological investments enacted through educational policy and practice. Key to this tracing is working through and from an embodiment of young mothers – what are young mother's experiences in schools, how do they define and experience 'equal treatment', and how are technologies of power working through embodiment?

An embodied mapping of experience and power can visually demonstrate contradictory demands placed upon pregnant/parenting youth and demonstrate how discourses and practices of 'equal treatment' can delimit pregnant/parenting students' access to equal education opportunity. Once conflicting demands/investments are made visible, there is opportunity to rethink policies and practices to support pregnant/parenting students in educational access and attainment. Sometimes, simply altering attendance policies can help a young mother remain in a high school program, however as feminist genealogy helps us see, even simple alterations in policy are embedded in truth regimes and discourses about teen pregnancy and the young mother – who she is and what she deserves and needs as a student.

In further example, as discussed above, sex equity has become defined through gender-neutral discourses. In this way, Title IX seemingly allows attention to gendered bodies while at the same time gender-neutrality masks and limits attention to specificity of the female pregnant/mothering student. Feminist genealogy interrupts the litigation and regulation mask of gender-neutrality by focusing attention on the specificity of young mother's gender and racialized embodied experiences in order to make visible how she is defined and treated as an educational subject, in discourse, policy and practice.

By attending to tracings of power surrounding a policy issue; examining what is invested in policy discourse and practice; and thinking/tracing through the body, feminist genealogy allows gaps to be made visible and investments in gaps and productions addressed. Feminist genealogy encourages a detailed attentiveness to power enacted through the bodies of pregnant/parenting students by gathering data on: the environment of schools including social climate and curriculum, attendance/placement data, and interviews with young parents analyzed alongside public discourses and perceptions about teen sexuality and pregnancy and exiting policy texts (Pillow, 2004).

It will take this level of detailed data collection and analysis to rethink truth regimes in regulation and litigation efforts. Gough raises issues that require concerted effort to achieve and this will not occur until educators and researchers identify and see pregnancy as an equal education issue. However, traditional models of analysis will keep current policy practice in re-loop. Policy and regulation cannot remain static across a condition – pregnancy and parenting – that is anything but statics. What equality looks like for a pregnant student may be different from what equality looks like for mothering or parenting student. Until policy can account for this fluidity, schools remain stagnant in their approaches toward young mothers.

While feminist genealogy does not provide policy answers, it can provide a unique 'history of the present' that reveals lines of power and underlying investments in constructions of young parents as social problems and education subjects. Utilizing these revealing's – placing contradictory discourses back onto themselves, such as what is actualized and embodied through 'equal treatment' – can aid in reconstructing policies and practices that impact pregnant/parenting students' access to education.

Feminist genealogy is not a panacea for Title IX regulation and litigation and indeed narrow constructions of equality in litigation may create new truth regimes that are as problematic as the one before it. The task of feminist genealogy therefore is never ending; there will always be pathways of power to trace, identify and bring to a 'history of the present' while we attempt to move toward present day policies and practices that keep questions of 'equality' and 'equity' in play. For young mothers and pregnant/parenting students, this means keeping questions of 'equality' in play and developing policy and regulation that interrogate deficit constructions of young mothers and account for the necessity to develop shifting definitions of education equality for young parents across pregnancy and mothering/parenting.

References

Anzaldúa, G. (1987). *Borderlands/la frontera: The new mestiza*. San Francisco, CA: Aunt Lute Foundation.

Arvin, M., Tuck, E. and Morrill, A. (2013). Decolonizing feminism: Challenging connections between settler colonialism and heteropatriarchy. *Feminist Formations, 25*(1), 8–34.

Brake, D. (1994). Legal challenges to the educational barriers facing pregnant and parenting adolescents. *Clearinghouse Review*, 141–155.

Dillard, C. (2000). The substance of things hoped for, the evidence of things not seen: Examining an endarkened feminist epistemology in educational research and leadership. *International Journal of Qualitative Studies in Education, 13*, 661–681.

Durkin, E. (2013). Shame Campaign: NYC ad campaign on teen pregnancy marshals crying babies. *New York Daily News*, 4 March 2013. www.nydailynews.com/new-york/new-ad-campaign-teen-pregnancy-article-1.1278589.

Erdmans, M. P. (2012). Title IX and the school experiences of pregnant and mothering students. *Humanity & Society, 36*(1), 50–75.

Foucault, M. (1981). *The history of sexuality: An introduction*. Harmondsworth, UK: Penguin.

Foucault, M. (1984). Nietzsche, genealogy, history. *The Foucault reader*. P. Rabinow (Ed.). London: Peregrine.

Gough, M. (2011). Parenting and pregnant students: An evaluation of the implementation of the 'other' Title IX. *Michigan Journal of Gender & Law, 17*, 211–269.

Grosz, E. (1994). *Volatile Bodes/Toward a corporeal feminism*. Bloomington, IN: Indiana University Press.

Grosz, E. (1995). *Space, time, and perversion*. London: Routledge.

Lorde, A. (1984). *Sister outsider and other essays*. Boston, MA: Crossing Press.

Luttrell, W. (2003). *Pregnant bodies, fertile minds: Gender, race and the schooling of pregnant teens*. New York: Routledge.

Mason, M. A. and Younger, J. (2013). *Title IX and pregnancy discrimination in higher education: The new frontier*. Manuscript submitted for publication. www.law.berkeley.edu/files/bccj/Title_IX_Law_Review_Article_Final_5.29-3-5.pdf.

Mazur, A. G. (2002). *Theorizing feminist policy*. New York: Oxford University Press.

Moraga, C. and Anzaldúa, G. (1981). *This bridge called my back: Writing by radical women of color*. Boston, MA: Kitchen Table Press.

National Coalition for Women and Girls in Education (NCWGE). (2012). *Title IX at 40: Working to ensure gender equity in education*. Washington, DC: NCWGE. www.ncwge.org/pregnant.html.

National Women's Law Center. (2012). *A pregnancy test for schools/the impact of education laws on pregnant and parenting students.* www.nwlc.org/reports-overview/pregnancy-test-schools-impact-education-laws-pregnant-and-parenting-students.

Pillow, W. S. (1997a). Decentering silences/troubling irony: Teen pregnancy's challenge to policy analysis. In C. Marshall (Ed.), *Feminist critical policy analysis I: A primary and secondary schooling perspective* (pp. 134–152). London: Falmer.

Pillow, W. S. (1997b). Exposed methodology: The body as a deconstructive practice. *International Journal of Qualitative Studies in Education, 10,* 349–363.

Pillow, W. S. (2003). 'Bodies are dangerous': Using feminist genealogy as policy studies methodology. *Journal of Educational Policy, 18,* 145–160.

Pillow, W. S. (2004). *Unfit subjects: Educational policy and the teen mother.* New York: Routledge.

Pillow, W. S. (2006). Teen pregnancy and education politics of knowledge, research, and practice. *Educational Policy, 20*(1), 59–84.

Pillow, W. S. (2007). Searching for Sacajawea: Whitened reproductions and endarkened representations. *Hypatia, 22*(2), 1–19.

Pillow, W. S. (2012). Sacajawea: Witnessing, remembrance and ignorance. *Power and Education, 4*(1), 45–56.

St. Pierre, E. and Pillow, W. S. (2000). Introduction/Inquiry among the ruins. In St. Pierre and Pillow (Eds.), *Working the ruins/Feminist poststructural theory and methods in education* (pp. 1–24). New York: Routledge.

12

GOVERNMENTALITY

Foucault's concept for our modern political reasoning

Kaspar Villadsen

Michel Foucault's concept 'governmentality' has achieved significant importance within the social sciences and humanities (for introductions to 'governmentality studies', see Dean, 1999; Bröckling et al., 2011; Walters, 2012). Foucault used governmentality to designate the modern rationality of political governance that emerged in eighteenth-century Europe, concerned with problems of managing a living population. Governmentality is distinct from previous political reasoning on sovereignty since it does not simply take a territory and legal subjects as its object, but the living population. The population was discovered as a 'complex reality' composed by inherent mechanisms of self-regulations and possible disturbances. These included patterns of illnesses, mortality, birth rates, migration, etc., which in aggregation began to be viewed as an independent reality. Governmentality is a set of reflections about how it is possible to govern the self-regulating mechanisms that are supposed to constitute the population.

Foucault also invented the concept in order to advance an analytical perspective that did not start by taking the state as a natural and pre-given entity. Neither should the state be viewed as a centre of power that principally exercised a repressive power, 'top-down' on society, through its juridical and police apparatuses. In Foucault's view, the state-centred theories of power that dominated the late 1970s, the time of his governmentality lectures, were troubled by analytical, empirical and political problems. Foucault sought in these lectures (2003, 2007, 2008) to 'decentre' the state, that is, to problematize the conception of the state as possessing a coherence and unity. He undertook this decentring by demonstrating how the state was born historically from a series of specific governmental strategies that still permeate it, particularly discipline, biopolitics and pastoral power. By tracing the advent of the modern state back to a plurality of distinct governmental practices which emerged from the sixteenth century and gradually began to saturate the social body, Foucault sought problematize the idea of the state as invariant and given once and for all – a kind of 'transcendent reality' (2007: 358). Instead, it became possible to view the state as a set of practices which are not orchestrated by a central agency, do not have functional necessity, and are not pervaded by a particular ideology.

As is often the case with Foucault's use of concepts, he mobilized an already existing concept that he reshaped and gave new significations. In fact, Foucault adopted the concept of governmentality from Roland Barthes who had used the term to designate a 'naturalized myth' that represented the state as an omnipotent and benevolent regulator of all social relations (Barthes, 1972: 129). Foucault had a similar interest in contesting 'over-evaluations' of the state as a centre of power, although he did not adopt Barthe's argument in its entirety. In his usage of governmentality, Foucault conveyed a scepticism against both the conception of the state as a 'cold monster' in which the state had come to be regarded as essentially a repressive force that limits our potentiality in the world, as well as the excessive fascination with the state which had turned the seizure of state power into the paramount political objective (Villadsen and Dean, 2012: 405). Hence, Foucault's articulation of the governmentality concept can be seen, in part, as an attempt to contest contemporary political ideologies which took extreme viewpoints, but which nevertheless shared the 'over-valuation of the state', the conception of the state as the ultimate centre of power. Foucault's asserted that the state is only a 'mythicized abstraction whose importance is much less than we think' (2007: 109).

Governmentality as an analytical perspective

One difficulty with Foucault's governmentality is that he did not employ the term as a concept in the traditional sense – that is, as a descriptor that represents a particular phenomena or a delimited part of reality. Rather, governmentality served as a category for guiding empirical investigations, and Foucault articulated the concept in different ways depending on the problem he was studying (Villadsen, 2010: 125).

First of all, governmentality serves as an analytical perspective that has paved the way for specific empirical analysis and it is arguably as such that the concept has had its greatest impact. As an analytical framework, governmentality gives guidelines for an analysis that generates a novel perspective on the state and political power. Governmentality harbours 'a cluster of concepts that can be used to enhance the think-ability and criticize-ability of past and present forms of governance' (Walter, 2012: 2). In its core, a governmentality analysis avoids reducing the exercise of power to the state apparatus or other institutions. Foucault wished to undertake an anti-institutional analytical move, similar to what he did in his study of the prison. There, Foucault went 'behind' the institution in order to mark out the dispersed points of origin for a series of practices, deliberations, and techniques that had made possible the birth of the modern prison:

> [J]ust as for the prison we tried to go behind penitentiary institutions in the strict sense to seek out the general economy of power, can we carry out the same reversal for the state? Is it possible to move outside? Is it possible to

place the modern state in a general technology of power that assured its mutations, development, and functioning? Can we talk of something like a 'governmentality' that would be to the state what techniques of segregation were to psychiatry, what techniques of discipline were to the penal system, and what biopolitics was to medical institutions?

(Foucault, 2007: 120)

The strategy of 'going behind' the institution should be applied to the state. If the state's immediate identity was the constitution and formal legality, Foucault would trace alternative trajectories in biopolitics and the Christian pastorate. He used the term biopolitics to describe the tendency that from the eighteenth century has turned man's biological existence into an object of political calculation and intervention. Biopolitics marked the historical moment where the biological life of man became an object of political calculation as it 'passed into knowledge's field of control and power's sphere of intervention' (Foucault, 1994: 142). This political interest for man-as-species reached a high point in the nineteenth century, where Foucault detects 'a certain tendency that leads to what might be termed State control of the biological' (Foucault, 2003: 240).

Biopolitics principally targets vital processes at the level of populations: birth rates, public health, living conditions, migration and more, but biopolitics may also involve interventions targeting environments and life styles influencing people's health and vitality.

Another related modality of power, which Foucault discovered as a major constitutive element in the formation of the modern state, was pastoral power. It is a form of power or leadership that cares for the individual subject in a continuous and individualizing manner, particularly by demanding that the individual reveals his or her inner thoughts and proclivities. In a nutshell, pastoral power is a governmental practice that is concerned with individuals' spiritual development, or, the relationship of self to the self. The secularized welfare state has not done completely away with this modality of power, since, says Foucault (1982: 782), pastoral power has proliferated and become integrated in welfare institutions like social work, psychiatry, schooling and nursing. With this trajectory in mind, it becomes understandable why the modern state is not indifferent to our subjectivity (Foucault, 1982: 783), but displays a tendency to exercise forms of government irreducible to the legal codes and constitutions, intervening in individuals' life styles, and in the formation of subjectivity.

Foucault believed that discussions of state power centred on constitutions, formal legality and repressive instruments of power were reductive and insufficient. He sought to expand the framework by turning to practices – that is, by describing the practices of knowledge production and the procedures of division that state institutions relied upon and crystallized (2007: 120). As a set of guidelines for analysis, governmentality involves tracing the strategies for handling practical problems of government and the corollary production of knowledge. In brief, governmentality 'explores the conditions of possibility for the modern state'

(Walters, 2012: 12). The state becomes, on this view, nothing more than the 'accumulated effect' of series of practices.

Governmentalization as a historical process

Foucault (2007) also employed governmentality to describe a historical process which he called 'the governmentalization of the state', a movement encompassing a series of events and lineages in the formation of the modern state (p. 109). Of particular importance is, as mentioned, the discovery in the eighteenth century of 'the population' as the principal object of political calculation and regulation. Foucault (2007) gave emphasis to the novel idea that the living population possesses intrinsic mechanisms and self-generating orders, a 'naturalness of society' (p. 349) that governors must take into account. This discovery constituted, in Foucault's view, a crucial event in modern political thought. As a result, the ultimate justification for political governance transfigured from the idea that the sovereign/state had its own finality to securing a living population (Foucault, 1988: 160–61). Whereas previous political reasoning had centred on the sovereign and his place in a God-given cosmological order, liberal philosophers and economists inserted the empirical-natural reality as the target for, and the limit upon, political governance. A break in the self-referentiality of sovereign rule was hereby taking place. The exercise of political sovereignty would no longer have as its main object to guarantee the prince's sovereign rule over a territory but became about securing a 'complex of men and things' (Foucault, 2007: 96). The transcendence of sovereign territorial rule was superseded by the immanent reality of transactions and production discovered by political economists.

Modern political rationality that foregrounded the secular wellbeing of the population did not, however, break completely with religious motives and institutions. The passage to governmentality implies rather, observed Foucault, a re-articulation of the pastoral idea of continuous shepherdship with the purpose of salvation, only now in terms of ensuring well-being, happiness and protection against accidents in this world (Foucault, 1982: 784). At the same time, the advent of the modern state in the seventeenth and eighteenth century implied a perhaps surprising proliferation of pastoral guidance of consciousness, emblematically represented by the confession. In its secularized versions (practiced by judges, psychiatrists, social workers, etc.) the confession works by inciting the subject to produce a particular truth about his or her inner self. This unveiling of inner truth is to be integrated into the self-government of the subject, fostering a reflexive relationship to the self. The Christian pastorate did not envision a human being completely determined by an almighty God but invoked an individual free will to choose the ways of God. Similarly, the subject of modern government is not a passive, subordinated or controlled subject; instead the premise is a free individual who makes reflexive choices as to which principles to pursue in his or her self-government. Governmentality, in other words, would make the freedom of the governed and the harnessing of their capacities a fundamental and indispensable prerequisite for the exercise of government (Foucault, 2007: 353).

The pastoral technology offered a practice of government which exceeded sovereign or juridical power; it was care-oriented, continuous, directed at living beings and required each individual to produce a singular truth about him or herself. This power is fundamentally different from sovereign rule over a territory inasmuch as it operates by guiding, leading, conducting men and women, inducing self-reflection and conscience in the subjects (Walters, 2012: 24–25). Foucault asserted that the modern state is by no means indifferent towards who we are, the subjectivity of citizens. This is the case, he explains, since the welfare state has integrated an old technology of power used to shape individual subjectivity: Generalized therapeutic practice. The state is, in brief, 'a modern matrix of individualization or a new form of pastoral power' (Foucault, 1982: 783). Exercising juridical sovereignty and governing the lives of individuals are two distinct forms of power fused in the modern welfare state.

One must be careful not to read Foucault's analysis of governmentality as attesting to a subtle variant of social control that invades the most intimate relations and controls individuals' consciousness. The integration of the pastoral model of power rather implied a new reversibility in the relations of power. Insofar that governmentalization placed individuals' self-relation at the centre of political governance it is not possible to separate the individual's self-conduct (ethical practice) from the government of the state (political practice). The exercise of government should take into account and model itself upon 'the rational behavior of those who are governed' (Foucault, 2008: 312). Political authorities must acknowledge that they govern free agents who have their own aspirations, strategies and identities that need to be taken into account and aligned with. In this context, power cannot be one-directional or unifying, illustrated by Foucault's general view that power is reversible, immanent to micro-relations where it finds both support and multiple points of resistance (Foucault, 1994: 92–102). Governmentality hence operates with an immanent ontology of power in which power is defined by those singular points, through which it passes (Deleuze, 1988). These premises reflect Foucault's dictum: power does not originate from a power-holder, but fluctuates directly in social relations.

The above points about modern power can inspire studies of contemporary policy initiatives to reform educational institutions. Miller and Rose (1990) seminal work took inspiration from Foucault's injunction to study the interplay between governing the state or a policy sector and the government of professionals. They argued that authorities in advanced liberal societies seek to 'govern at a distance' by means of technologies that seek to align personal conduct with political objectives (Rose and Miller, 1992). Foregrounding technologies for governing 'at a distance' is pertinent insofar as educational reforms do not simply happen through legal regulation, but also by transforming the space of professionals' conduct. This may include instituting new educational objectives, quality indicators, benchmarks and reward systems, in order to influence the conduct of both managers and staff in educational institutions. During the last 25 years, we have witnessed political aspirations, often termed 'New Public Management', to breach the discretionary enclosure of the teaching profession (along with other welfare professions). The implementation of governmental instruments, like the above mentioned, has challenged the traditional prerogatives of teachers and their discretion over the internal working of the educational system. Taking a govern- mentality approach would help interrogate how, in the present context, reforming institutions crucially involves targeting the subjectivity of experts. At the same time, the approach would recognize that implementing reforms is never frictionless, but a rather open-ended process. Professionals may resist, negotiate or circumvent governmental power with reference to 'true knowledge' of learning, their professional judgment, or the need for institutional autonomy.

Regimes of veridiction: civil society and the market

In his 1979 lectures, Foucault discussed a key theme in political philosophy and the social sciences, namely 'civil society' (Foucault, 2008). Foucault was acutely aware that, in modern, political thought, civil society has an absolutely key role as the legitimizing principle for political regulation. He spent considerable time examin- ing how the problem of governing civil society or managing a population was deliberated within neo-liberal thinking. The reason for this focus was Foucault's contention that issues of population management fundamentally took shape within 'this governmental regime called liberalism' (2008: 22). He stated that the aim of the 1979 lectures was to study the way in which the 'specific problems of life and population' since the end of the eighteenth century have been 'constantly haunted by the question of liberalism' (2008: 324).

The birth of biopolitics can be read as a study of how various schools of liberal thinking rendered the market a source of truth production, a 'regime of verifica- tion' for the exercise of government (Foucault, 2008: 43 ff.). The key political significance of liberal political economics is that it gives the political gaze a par- ticular direction, since it points to the site where government will have to look to find the principle of truth of its own governmental practice. Foucault undertook detailed analysis of two major camps in twentieth-century neoliberalism. First, he traced how a new governmentality appeared within German Ordo-liberalism of the 1930–1940s, advocating that society should be governed for the market and not vice versa. Second, the neoliberal framework was developed in a different variant by the American neoliberalism of the 1960–1970s, which promoted an expansion of economic analysis and management to vast areas of social life, illus- trated in 'human capital' theory. It has often been suggested that Foucault in these lectures offered a critical presaging of what hegemonic market rationality would imply, once all aspects of human existence from education to punishment were subjected to cost–benefit calculation. A biopolitical government of life could henceforth merge with expansive market rationality.

An immediate implication from these observations would be to critically examine educational policies that invoke a discourse on 'national competitiveness in a globalized world' as an uncontestable a priori. Such a discourse may underpin appeals to students for exerting their educational choices as an 'investment' and the corollary demand for establishing flexible and competitive education services, 'the creation of a "milieu" in which enterprising individuals might better flourish' (Weiskopf and Munro, 2012: 698). Governmental attempts to transform education into 'markets' might invoke assumptions about the self-regulating capacities of the market system. This rationality is also evident in appeals to education professionals to transform the terms of their calculation from, schematically speaking, learning to production.

Multiple governmental technologies

Recent Foucault scholarship has demonstrated that Foucault made considerable efforts to avoid the impression that governmentality is a coherent epochal and internally consistent regime. Indeed, rather than a uniform break, the departure from the religious–cosmological continuum opened a space for multiple and at times contradictory rationalities of government. Collier observes that in the late 1970s, Foucault departed from his analysis of 'disciplinary society' marked by systematicity, functional coherence and a totalizing reach. Instead, he would pursue a 'topological' approach that unveiled a more complex terrain of multiple, heterogeneous configurations of power (Collier, 2009: 79–80). Evidently, Foucault (2003: 45) also struggled to challenge the idea of a unified and centralized state by highlighting the co-existence and interplay between different governmental rationalities of power:

> We should not be looking for some sort of sovereignty from which powers spring, but showing how the various operators of domination support one another, relate to one another, at how they converge and reinforce one another in some cases, and negate or strive to annul one another in other cases.

In the beginning of the 1978 lectures, Foucault introduced 'three major technologies of power', i.e. 'law', 'discipline' and 'security' (Foucault, 2007: 5–24). Reading seventeenth- and eighteenth-century texts on issues of how to regulate the cities, Foucault demonstrated that these co-existing technologies construct particular problems and solutions from within their own rationality. These issues included crimes, epidemics, the prices of grain and the planning of public space. In brief, *the legal technology* effectuates 'a binary division between the permitted and the prohibited, and a coupling, comprising the code, between a type of prohibited action and a type of punishment' (2007: 5). Within the framework of *discipline,* 'a series of adjacent, detective, medical, and psychological techniques appear which fall within the domain of surveillance, diagnosis, and the possible transformation of individuals' (2007: 5). *The technology of security* 'establishes an average considered as optimal on the one hand, and, on the other, a bandwidth of the acceptable that must not be exceeded' (2007: 6). Security is a rationality that recognizes that human reality is not amenable to planning and regulation that would completely eliminate the undesired. Rather, security has the more limited ambition of facilitating and optimizing the processes already inherent in this reality, 'minimizing what is risky and inconvenient, like theft and disease, while knowing that they will never be completely suppressed' (2007: 19).

Foucault described reverberations and frictions between these co-existing technologies in terms of their construction of governmental objects. The examples that Foucault gave in 1978 demonstrate how mundane problems of theft, the layout of towns, or the regulation of grain production were visualized and reflected upon from fundamentally divergent viewpoints (2007: 6–24). Different technologies may target the same problem, for instance, a specific crime, from within each of their limited optics, ascribing to it fundamentally divergent meanings, reasons and effects. Foucault's topology of power harbours several analytical potentials. Educational institutions, and other learning settings, could be viewed as 'over-determined' by the technologies of law, discipline and security. In case of such over-determination, issues of what is viewed as competence, qualifications and learning become indeterminate and open to recurring contestation.

A brief comparison of discipline and security may help demonstrating this point. The governmental rationality of security is not to prescribe the actions, movements, etc., of individuals in detail. Rather the principal task is 'to create a milieu, in which selves are allowed to unfold their potentials and entrepreneurial creativity within a specific frame' (Weiskopf and Munro, 2012: 696). Whereas discipline operates on the basis of fixed norms, for instance a defined curriculum and learning plan, security foregrounds differential modes of treatment of individuals, seeking to incorporate even deviances and resistance as potential resources (Ibid: 699). Instead of the enclosures of 'the disciplinary school', security regulation demands the adaptability to ever changing norms and seeks to create spaces of autonomy for entrepreneurial entities. The goals of 'organizational learning' and 'continuous learning' are emblematic for security. It can turn out that pursuing such goals are at odds with the formal regulations and functional divisions in many organizations. A potential of analysis, then, is to consider how policy initiatives based on a security rationality, which promote flexibility, diversity and entrepreneurial choice, contradict both legal and disciplinary rationalities which rely upon a binary and more rigid schematic. It might also be explored whether teachers and students are addressed as objects of discipline, law or security in educational contexts, and whether oscillations and tensions occur between these distinct forms of subjectivation.

Government of self

It is clear that Foucault wished to detach the problem of power from the central state and from prohibitive juridical and police regulation. This strategy of detachment is evident in the ways that Foucault rendered the terms 'government' and 'governmentality'. In 1978, he defined governmentality in a general and widely applicable manner, as 'the way in which one conducts the conduct of men' (Foucault, 2007: 186). First, this definition highlights that government is principally about guidance (not command or denial), influencing forms of self-government, structuring the field of possible actions of free subjects. Second, government is not an activity restricted to state authorities but can occur in multifarious contexts. Thus, governmentality is 'a framework for analysis that begins with the observation that governance is a very widespread phenomenon, in no way confined to the sphere of the state' (Walters, 2012: 11). We can thus examine the rationality at stake in a whole range of contexts where individuals act upon themselves or upon others in order to influence conduct.

We noted that Foucault in describing the emergence of modern governmentality linked the individual's capacity for self-governance to forms of political govern-ance. In the late seminar, *Technologies of the self*, Foucault transposed the question of the interconnection between self-government and integrating individuals into the social-political order back to the days of Greco-Roman philosophy and Christian philosophy (Foucault, 1988). He discussed how these two cultures conceived of 'government' understood in its broadest sense. Government would be the contact point connecting how individuals were influenced or dominated by others to how they conducted themselves. Departing from his earlier approach, Foucault then focused on the means by which the individual acted upon himself. He termed the latter 'technologies of the self' that 'permit individuals to effect by their own means or with the help of others a certain number of operations on their own bodies and souls, thoughts, conduct and way of being' (Foucault, 1988: 18).

Self-technologies played a key role in Foucault's interrogation of how the individual has acted upon himself back in history. In his analysis, Foucault contrasted the Greco-Roman philosophy in the first two centuries AD of the Roman Empire with Christian principles from the fourth and fifth centuries of the late Roman Empire. A significant difference between the two is that whereas the key principle for the ancient Greeks was 'take care of yourself', the later Christian tradition emphasized 'know yourself'. Foucault detected a 'profound transformation in the moral principles of Western Society' (Foucault, 1988: 22) by which the maxim of caring for oneself became subdued under the quest for knowing oneself, and Christian morality brought self-renouncement and an inclination to see 'taking care of oneself' as immoral. An examination of stoic techniques for self-inspection showed that these were not about discovering faults and excavating guilt but about remembering rules of action and acquiring mastery of oneself through particular practices. Christianity, by contrast, had another conception of subjectivity and self-decipherment, since most of the time the self was something that had to be renounced in order to prepare for another reality (Ibid: 35). In the choice between self-care versus self-renunciation, the goal of self-mastery versus disclosure of sins, and the exercise a good worldly life versus preparing for the extra-worldly, Foucault's sympa-thy for the Greek tradition is quite evident. The deep excavation of 'inner truths' to be renounced, stand in contrast with actively shaping subjectivity through practices.

Analytical implications

Foucault's framework offers ample possibilities for giving analytical attention to the connections between practices of government and practices of the self. Hence, we might study interconnections between the government of populations, nations or organizations and the government of subjectivity, or the self. A pertinent case is practices of educational counselling. In recent years, we have seen the promotion of techniques for establishing dialogues between school representatives and pupils and parents in an equalizing, non-tutelary fashion. This emergence of dialogue technology is identifiable across a range of welfare institutions, following the critique of bureaucracy and expertise. While dialogue technologies demand that professionals speak less and allow the subordinate or service recipients to speak, they nevertheless require a careful regulation (Karlsen and Villadsen, 2008). This is evident in the use of 'balance schemes', motivational models, or event 'contracts' regarding school children's learning. Dialogue technology vividly displays the paradox of governing individuals' self-government – it promises to deliver free, 'authentic' statements, but requires a meticulous pre-regulation of the conversational space. How this paradox is attempted and resolved in novel education technologies is an issue for future research.

The governmentality approach has further implications for studies of educational policies and programs. The analysis cannot conclude with central government, that is with law and implementation, but must extent to the modes of organizing knowledge and disciplining individuals that state authorities may co-opt and employ. This calls for an attention to the specific modalities of knowledge that become mobilized for governing educational practices, recognizing that these knowledges often do not arise in the state apparatus, but outside of it. In times of reforms for quality improvements of education at all levels, 'performance management' would be a pertinent object of critical analysis. A governmentality perspective would emphasize that performance management should not be viewed, fundamentally, as the instrument of central state administrations to control institutions and determine behaviour. Rather, it seeks to shape a space of conduct within which teachers and managers may choose forms of self-conduct that contribute to meeting quality standards (Triantafillou, 2012: 64). Following Foucault's non-institutional approach would imply 'going behind' the immediate educational programs and reforms to mark up the broader, historically deep-seated rationalities that made them possible. We have seen that for Foucault it is a matter of establishing the conditions of emergence for specific institutions, rather than focusing strictly on the institution, as if it were a naturally given, distinct entity (Deleuze, 1988: 116). Before hastily criticizing specific institutions' reforms, one should excavate their governmentality, that is, the diverse deliberations, theories and techniques of governing that they crystallize.

When analyzing educational policies we can find inspiration in the 'major technologies of power' – law, discipline and security – that Foucault discovered, considering to which extent their rationalities resonate in the specific programs under scrutiny. Are the objects to be governed construed as legal entities?, as human capacities and institutions to be disciplined?, or, as self-governing agents to be secured? The security rationality is certainly identifiable in recent 'interactive policymaking' that renders public administrations as facilitators, aims at activating the self-governing capacities of the governed entities, and foregrounds the risks involved in governmental intervention.

In terms of the selection of specific texts, or an 'archive', for analysis, Foucault gave emphasis to the minor, 'gray' sciences which had a low epistemological threshold like psychology, psychiatry and criminology. Although these sciences have significant power effects by way of their close interconnectedness with institutions like prisons, asylums and clinics they had been neglected by Marxist theorists in their attempt to gain status as 'objective' science. For our purposes, professional knowledge such as accountancy, HRM, coaching and organizational psychology can be expected to be particularly important in informing educational reforms and practices. Hence, the governmentality approach foregrounds political-administrative texts that directly inform the exercise of power. One must examine how concepts, theories and assumptions from different scientific-administrative domains are mobilized in educational policy.

Our reading of policy texts can be guided by Foucault's principles of discourse analysis (see Chapter 5). Indeed, Rose and Miller suggested that political rationalities could be analyzed in the same way as scientific discursive formations (1992). Eschewing hermeneutic and phenomenological approaches, the analysis proceeds by observing statements as pure discursive events. This non-reductionist approach to statements does not look for any subjective intentionality or pervasive ideology to explain them. Rather, it seeks to establish vertical connections, placing the text or statements in a network of other texts, statements, books, etc., that it articulates. One might examine whether there is a common a priori shared by modalities of knowledge that claim to be distinct, e.g. pedagogy and economics. This does not permit easy, ready-made demarcations of the textual archive, like 'only texts about higher education' or 'text from the last 15 years'. Pursuing Foucault's approach implies reading more broadly, perhaps including non-professional literature, obscure and marginal texts, images and architecture – all which can be analyzed in terms of the governmentality they express.

A governmentality approach does not preclude the use of other qualitative methods than textual analysis, such as ethnographic observations. Foucault's work has had quite a resonance within ethnographic studies and anthropology (e.g. Hill, 2009; Hoffmann and Villadsen, 2013). It is beyond this chapter to discuss in detail the strategy of combining Foucault with these research traditions (Marston and McDonald (2006) offer a collection of governmentality studies using qualitative methods). I briefly note that governmentality and ethnography are broadly reconcilable despite their different intellectual origins and methodologies. They both attempt to 'de-naturalize' and 'de-universalize' institutionalized truisms; they both work with a 'decentred subject' shaped through social practices; and they both bracket the question of true/false in order to examine the social effects of truth claims. Furthermore, governmentality writers and ethnographers alike address practices and rationalities aiming for a 'thick' description that avoids pre-given and reductionist interpretations.

Integrating ethnographic methods with governmentality studies allows investigating in greater detail the power struggles played out around discursive categories in specific social and organizational settings. It becomes possible to view discursive categories as unstable, since they are practiced, negotiated, twisted and, perhaps, circumvented. Helpful in this regard is Hacking's formulation of 'looping effects' which was to account for the dynamic reverberations between classifications and practices (Hacking, 2004: 279). The loop occurs since humans are capable of reacting to the way they are being classified and hereby might alter their behaviour and how they see themselves. This may cause classifications to be modified, since those individuals classified have changed. There is, then, a dynamic circuit where reactions and modes of conduct feed back into discursive and institutional systems. A full integration of the governmentality framework with qualitative field studies would require both genealogical work in the archive and extensive ethnographic research. However, careful specification of the study object is a viable pathway to span these two poles in investigating 'lived and practiced governmentality'.

References

Barthes, R. (1972). *Mythologies*. New York: The Noonday Press.

Bröckling, U., Krasmann, S. and Lemke, T. (Eds.) (2011). *Governmentality: Current issues and future challenges*. New York: Routledge.

Collier, S. (2009). Topologies of power: Foucault's analysis of political government beyond 'governmentality'. *Theory, Culture & Society, 26*(6), 78–108.

Dean, M. (1999). *Governmentality: Power and rule in modern society*. London: Sage Publications.

Deleuze, G. (1988). *Foucault*. Minneapolis, MN: University of Minnesota Press.

Foucault, M. (1982). The subject and power. *Critical Inquiry, 8*(4), 777–795.

Foucault, M. (1988). *Technologies of the self*. Amherst, MA: The University of Massachussetts Press.

Foucault, M. (1994). *The will to knowledge: The history of sexuality, volume 1*. London: Penguin.

Foucault, M. (2003). *Society must be defended: Lectures at the Collège de France, 1975–76*. New York: Picador.

Foucault, M. (2007). *Security, territory, population: Lectures at the college de France 1977–78*. London: Palgrave Macmillan.

Foucault, M. (2008). *The birth of biopolitics: Lectures at the Collège de France 1978–1979*. London: Palgrave.

Hacking, I. (2004). Between Michel Foucault and Erving Goffman: Between discourse in the abstract and face-to-face interaction. *Economy and Society, 33*(3), 277–302.

Hill, M. (2009). Ways of seeing: Using ethnography and Foucault's 'toolkit' to view assessment practices differently. *Qualitative Research, 9*(3), 309–330.

Hoffmann Pii, K. and Villadsen, K. (2013). Protect the patient from whom? When patients contest governmentality and seek more expert guidance. *Social Theory & Health, 11*(1), 19–39.

Karlsen, M. P. and Villadsen, K. (2008). Who should do the talking: The proliferation of dialogue as governmental technology. *Culture and Organization, 14*, 345–363.

Marston, G. and McDonald, C. (Eds.) (2006). *Analysing social policy: A governmental approach*. Cheltenham, UK: Edward Elgar.

Miller, P. and Rose, N. (1990). Governing economic life. *Economy and society, 19*(1), 1–31.

Rose, N. and Miller, P. (1992). Political power beyond the state: Problematic of government. *British Journal of Sociology, 43*(2), 173–205.

Triantafillou, P. (2012). *New forms of governing: A Foucauldian inspired analysis*. London: Palgrave Macmillan.

Villadsen, K. (2010). Governmentality. In M. Tadajewski, P. Maclaran, E. Persons and M. Parker (Eds.), *Key concepts in critical management studies*. London: Sage Publications.

Villadsen, K. and Dean, M. (2012). Statephobia, civil society, and a certain vitalism. *Constellations: A Journal of Critical and Democratic Theory, 19*(3), 401–420.

Walters, W. (2012). *Governmentality: Critical encounters*. Abingdon, UK: Routledge.

Weiskopf, R. and Munro, I. (2012). Management of human capital: Discipline, security and controlled circulation in HRM. *Organization, 19*, 685–702.

13

TAKING A 'MATERIAL TURN' IN EDUCATION POLICY RESEARCH?

Stephen Heimans

> Language has been granted too much power. The linguistic turn, the semiotic turn, the interpretative turn, the cultural turn: it seems that at every turn lately every 'thing' – even materiality – is turned into a matter of language or some other form of cultural representation. Language matters. Discourse matters. Culture matters. There is an important sense in which the only thing that does not seem to matter anymore is matter.
>
> *(Barad, 2003: 801)*

Karen Barad's influential 'agential realism' (Barad, 2007) focuses scholarly attention on to matter – and how it comes to 'matter', in both senses of the word. Her feminist, post-humanist philosophical work (Barad, 1998, 2007) is being widely taken up across many disciplines (see Alberti and Marshall, 2009; Edwards, 2012; Hanson, 2007; Hultman and Lenz Taguchi, 2010; Rouse, 2004; Udén, 2009). Barad contests the power that language, representation and related research practices have had. This aligns with Latour's (2011) suggestion that,

> we are usually in the habit of asking questions either about language or about ontology, a habit that is obviously the consequence of the bifurcation we want to put to an end by learning to count on all fingers instead of just two or three.
>
> *(p. 309)*

For Barad however, the focus, or the reason for engaging with matter, is that 'mattering and its possibilities and impossibilities for justice are integral parts of the universe in its becoming; an invitation to live justly is written into the very matter of being' (Barad, 2007: xi). Barad engages with quantum physics, and feminist and

Foucauldian scholarship – reading key insights from these distinct fields 'through one another' – as she puts it, to develop a thorough and convincing 'diffractive methodology' (with Donna Haraway foundations). While Barad's work is important there is a plethora of other scholarly activity that might help constitute a material turn. For example, Jane Bennett in *Vibrant matter: The political ecology of things* (2009) poses a question for herself, asking:

> How would political responses to public problems change were we to take seriously the vitality of (nonhuman) bodies? By 'vitality' I mean the capacity of things . . . not only to impede or block the will and designs of humans but also to act as quasi agents or forces with trajectories, propensities or tendencies of their own.
>
> *(p. viii)*

Bennett's work focuses on the capacity and politics of 'things'. Bennett draws on, and wants to extend, the work of Rancière (1999) to theorise what 'political' might mean here. She takes Rancière's dissensual politics involving human bodies (and their capacities) and applies these to the powers of non-human 'actants' (after Latour). This use of Rancière's version of politics indicates the post-critical aspect of the material turn where there is a shift in attention away from the Marxist interest in structures and dialectics, and research practices that can reveal the 'hidden' conditions that 'position' 'actors', to an interest in emergence, affect and immanence – to 'pursue a materialism in the tradition of Democritus–Epicurus–Spinoza–Diderot–Deleuze more than Hegel–Marx–Adorno' as Bennett (2009: xiii) puts it.

A material turn moves from the analysis of words for what they can reveal about the world, to the entanglements of words and matter – and how bodies (of all kinds) materialise and have effects. The focus is on 'more than human only' located and related potentialities. The 'post' human is a key interest for a turn to the material. With respect to education policy for example, Fenwick and Edwards (2011: 720) claim:

> policy actors therefore are not merely human, but are precarious assemblages, which methodologically point to different units of analysis in research. Contrary to the humanist view, no one thing can be identified as a cause or source of force. Policy actors are assemblages – moving in a web of relations with other assemblages – of variously distributed human and nonhuman materials that can collectively generate power, and that can extend themselves across space and time to generate action at a distance.

The rest of this chapter concerns the 'material turn' and researching education policy. A diverse range of resources that might have some traction for education policy research is overviewed. This diversity occurs through the kind of wide reading that St Pierre (2014) invites researchers to do in the post-qualitative, new materialist mode, where paradigmatic ways of doing qualitative research are

undone and new ways have to be invented along with whatever the research concerns are. So, discussing a 'turn' does not indicate a homogeneity that is actually
absent from the diversity of practices that might appear to be summarily subsumed
within its apparently smooth arc. With these limits in mind, this chapter nonetheless
seeks to highlight some of the emerging features of a material turn and then discusses
how this turn might be taken up in education policy research.

Taking a 'material turn'?

The basic categories that hold together ways of doing research (like data, theory,
methodology, researcher, the empirical, analysis, explanation) are reconfigured in
the material turn.

The kaleidoscope of emerging feminist (Barad, 2007)/post-critical (Hytten,
2004)/post-qualitative (Lather and St Pierre, 2013; St Pierre, 2011)/post-human
(Braidotti, 2013)/ontologically political (Singh, Heimans, and Glasswell, 2014)/
activist (Giardina and Denzin, 2011)/non-representational (Thrift, 2008), performing (Denzin, 2013) experimental (Whatmore and Landström, 2011), new
materialist (Dolphijn and van der Tuin, 2012) research practices indicate (though
does not prescribe or limit) the plethora of directions a 'material' turn might lead
toward.

At a minimum these directions bring into question the validity of the boundaries that hold the rationality of inquiry and its epistemological ends, and putative
virtues, separate from ontology, or performative effects (Law and Urry, 2004).
Likewise other boundaries are undone. Distinctions, for example, between the
discursive, the affective, the body, nature, culture, space, time, separated-out ethics,
critique and its normative desiring 'other' – these are subject to erasure or inter-
mingling. Naturecultures/spacetimes/ethico-onto-epistemologies (Barad, 2007),
multiverses and cosmopolitics (Stengers, 2010), are examples where pre-arranged
categories are 'undone'.

Taking a material turn does not involve leaving behind a will to disrupt, interrupt, intervene in, or otherwise upset, the rationalised perversities/realities/power,
and related effects, of prevailing intersecting racist, sexist, hetero-, class, able-ist,
othering normativities. Rather, it offers possibilities for research to enact new (un)
doings. It engages in what Lather (2010) calls 'policy from the side of the messy'.
Process philosophical underpinnings from Whitehead and Deleuze are potentially
formative, as are realist orientations (see for example speculative realism (Bryant,
Srnicek, and Harman, 2011), and (as suggested already) agential realism (Barad,
2007)), a concern for the way that matter, post-humanly, matters (Barad, 2007;
Bennett, 2009) and a desire to 'follow the actant' ANT (Latour, 2005). Barad
(2007: 42–43) summarises the extent of the subversion envisioned here:

> What is needed is a deeper understanding of the ontological dimensions of
> scientific practice . . . Is reality an amorphous blob that is structured by human
> discourses and interactions? Or does it have some complicated, irregular shape

that is differently sampled by varying frameworks that happen to 'fit' in local regions like coincident segments of interlocking puzzle pieces? Or is the geometry fractal, so that it is impossible for theories to match reality even locally? . . . And if we don't ask these questions, what will be the consequences? As Donna Haraway reminds us, 'What counts as an object is precisely what world history turns out to be about' (1988: 588). I seek some way of trying to understand the nature of nature and the interplay of the material and the discursive, the natural and the cultural, in scientific and other social practices . . . [s]ince there is good reason to question the traditional Western philosophical belief that ontology and epistemology are distinct concerns.

Seeking to undo inherent *a priori* distinctions – between the human and its 'others' and their potentials to act is an aspect of a material turn. Challenging anthropocentric educational assumptions is important to education policy research. This challenge aligns with Barad's (2007) focus on indeterminacy (which engages questions of ontology), and the implications of the ways in which relations determine which phenomena emerge, what is excluded in the process, and how these (phenomena and processual exclusions) come to matter. However, taking the human out of an assumed centre for/ of educational planning and action does not preclude human consequences or concerns but seeks to open up what it means to be and 'do' human – to transgress the assumptions and preclusions that coalescing definitions of humanity invoke. Currently, this is especially important in education policy work that is inf(l)ected by neo-liberal ideas, where the assumed proclivities of a presupposed *homo economicus* (rational, choosing, self-interested, male, white, heterosexual) figure in the emergence of which, and how, bodies come to matter through policy (and) in education.

Barad's (2007) indeterminacy is underwritten by a methodology derived through diffraction, which works against the representationist logics of reflection and one to one correspondences between the word and the world, that are either, easily assumed (in a straightforward realist sense), or to be revealed in their falsity, in a relativist sense.

Haraway notes that '[reflexivity or reflection] invites the illusion of essential, fixed position, while [diffraction] trains us to more subtle vision' (1992). Diffraction entails 'the processing of small but consequential differences,' and 'the processing of differences . . . is about ways of life' (ibid.) . . . I argue that a diffractive methodology is respectful of the entanglement of ideas and other materials in ways that reflexive methodologies are not. In particular, what is needed is a method attuned to the entanglement of the apparatuses of production, one that enables genealogical analyses of how boundaries are produced rather than presuming sets of well-worn binaries in advance.

(*Barad, 2007: 29–30*)

Barad reads the work of Haraway, Bohr (quantum physicist) and Foucault 'through one another'. This is her method of placing diverse ideas into the service of building a case for what she calls agential realism. This version of realism insists on an ethico-onto-epistemology (being responsible *a priori* for the 'other' in Levinasian sense, and for what emerges through practices – both in terms of knowledge and the 'world'), using a diffractive methodology (as above), and *intra*activity (where phenomena emerge through relations – as opposed to the more usual interactivity where entities pre-exist relations). She argues that, 'in contrast to the usual "interaction" – which assumes that there are separate individual agencies that precede their interaction – the notion of intra-action recognizes that distinct agencies do not precede, but rather emerge through, their intra-action' (Barad, 2007: 33). In this intra-action, the entanglement of the apparatuses of production, that Barad (2007) discusses in the quote above, is central. One aspect of this, Barad (2007) argues, following Niels Bohr's work in quantum physics, is that theories are themselves specific material configurations. This is an important point. Theories are not merely abstractions from the 'stuff' of the world with which scholars might make some further sense. They emerge through specific material arrangements that rely on and force bodies of all kinds, and the boundaries that they enact, to be taken seriously.

The point is that seeming immaterial entities (theory), that might be employed free of their derivational contexts, are inherently material. Related to this, and of equal consequence is the respect that Barad suggests should be paid to the material entanglement of ideas. This leads to forcing a 'slowing down' (following Stengers, 2005a) in the rationality of quick interpretations or words that become explanations and findings and evidence for some other use (for example to base policy development on). The power of the 'revealing researcher' is enervated. An analysis of some(one) else's 'other' or externalisable conditions is problematised. As Lather (2014) highlights (drawing on the work of Jeffrey Nealon (2008) in *Foucault beyond Foucault*), the alternative (that is being discussed in this chapter) is to track 'slow mutations, accretions, and accumulations' (Nealon, 2008: 38). There is a 'flattened' ontology (DeLanda, 2004) implied in this, where research and its objects get 'caught up in' one another, where there is an un-decidability about engagements between what research might do and what comes next as a result. These generate non-representational outcomes, neither attempting to represent reality nor its lack of foundation (in which ever way this is revealed). Instead relying on the idea that the world does not yet exist; as Bryant (2011: 278) puts it:

> The thesis that the world does not exist is crucial to flat ontology so as to avoid surreptitiously treating as collected that which is not collected. What the inexistence of the world teaches is that worlds are a work, that meshes must be produced, and that they cannot be said to exist in advance.

So research is not attempting to show what 'is' or what 'ought' to be (Stengers, 2005a), but rather it is enacting what comes to matter. The relations between the human and 'things' (taken to be what Latour (2005) calls 'matters of concern') extend or call into question boundaries on which pre-existing (human) 'sense' is based. In spite of this seeming flux and undecidability, there is an ethical underpinning that is evidenced in a close attention to the entanglements of ideas and the bodies they normalise/(re)materialise (including research bodies – of knowledge, new entities, researcher dispositions). These entanglements emerge from and reconstitute matter (Barad, 2007). Such enactments might be seen for example in work that is overtly performative (for example in arts-based research practice (Leavy, 2013)), and/or that attempt to engage with non-representationalist writing that performs to displace or upset the 'positions' or 'places' that authors and readers hold with respect to each other and the objects/subjects about which they write. These will push the boundaries of academic research publication possibilities where writing as a form of performative, enacted intervention challenges representationalist aims.

Taking a material turn in education policy research?

Taking a material turn when researching education policy opens the space to take an active interest in disrupting the production of 'easy' evidence that can straightforwardly be manipulated into a utilitarian framework for action by others (for example, policy makers and/or teachers). This is not to say that research should have no use. Rather the aim is to produce forms of 'policy knowledge' (Dumas and Anderson, 2014) that (as a minimum) respect the complexity of education institutions and intersections with research practices. Of course, such 'policy knowledge' can have different forms and recent examples of education policy enactment studies show this. On one hand, enactment might focus on how education policy enactment and research practices 'come to matter' in the materialist sense being described in this chapter (Heimans, 2012), or in contrast, critical education policy studies that also deal with enactment, do so from the point of view of *revealing* 'how schools do policy' (Ball, Maguire, and Braun, 2012). The conceptual and practical work undertaken in each of these instances of enactment studies is very different. For materialist studies enactment involves working 'in' the world and 'with' others. Critical education policy studies work 'on' policy, focusing, in terms of enactment, at the site where education policy is 'done'; that is, in schools or other education institutions. In spite of this however, it is important not to read such work as being mutually exclusive or engaged in a game of theoretical/methodological one-upmanship. This is especially so as attempts at materialist work arise out of the critical education policy studies *oeuvre* and seek to offer a diversity of directions that such policy research might take – broadening out and complexifying what counts as 'policy knowledge'.

To return to Barad (1998), she suggests that 'we are responsible for the world within which we live, not because it is an arbitrary construction of our choosing, but because it is sedimented out of particular practices which we have a role in shaping' (p. 102). This brings to attention the ontological politics (Mol, 2002) of research, focusing on what a research project wants to 'do'.

> As Mol and Messman (1996: 422) advise, when formulating a research or PhD project, we ought to consider not 'what we want to know', but 'what we want to do'. As Mol (2002: 151) puts it, 'veracity is not the point. Instead it is interference'.
>
> *(Bacchi, 2012: 152)*

But what education policy research can actually do, or interfere in – in what ways is such research ontological where research is somehow 'in', as opposed to 'on' education policy. There are at least three possible answers: (1) where the ontological politics (Singh et al., 2014) of research might be realised by conducting collaborative or participatory research (Maria Ozanira da Silva e, 2005) 'with' education policy makers and/or people who enact policy; (2) it might contribute to a 'percolation' of ideas from academic publication to research and/or education and/or policy practice (Lingard, 2010) (see also the excellent article on responding to the complexity of policy by producing policy knowledge for multiple audiences by Dumas and Anderson (2014)); (3) or aspects of both (1) and (2), as found in design-based approaches (see Anderson and Shattuck, 2012) to research that suggest a requirement for 'impact' both on practice and 'back' to the broader academic field. Researching *in* the world changes the diagonal of interest for researchers from revelation, understanding, interpretation, analysis, explanation and so on to interference, recognising that research enacts and performs the 'world'. Of course interference may include revelation, analysis and so on, the point is not to exclude *a priori* whatever research action might be necessary to the policy research focus, but to pay attention to, and complexify, the relations between whatever research 'is' and how this inter-, or more accurately, intra-acts, as Barad (2007) suggests, with its objects.

So, a material turn seeks to reinsert messy bodies (human and otherwise) into policy and research questions, and reformulate these around what 'comes to matter' (in both senses of the word) (Barad, 2007); the entanglements between the research 'apparatus' (theoretical, practical resources and tools used), the phenomena (in the case here – policy phenomena) and the reality that emerges in the process. Where 'entanglements are not a name for the interconnectedness of all being as one, but rather for specific material relations of the ongoing differentiating of the world' (Barad, 2011: 149).

But how might these specific material relations be enacted in education policy studies? As Nyberg (2009: 1182), in his organisational ethnography that draws on Barad's work argues, 'the move from "inter-actions" to "intra-actions" implies that the boundaries that define actors are fluid and temporal'. So, doing research in schools, for example, involves recognising the temporal fluidity of the boundaries that hold the materialities of schooling and research in place. What bodies matter? How? What 'teacher', 'student', 'classroom', 'researcher', 'observation', 'fieldwork' bodies are coming to matter in the relations between the 'agencies of observation' enacted (themselves a complex set of emerging, entangled, discursive materialities), and the school (is there a new name that might better describe the materialites of schooling perhaps?)? Fundamental questions have to be asked. What relations matter? Where are the boundaries, and what is excluded? Can you write this down without using any of the labels for categories one might expect? How does this act of writing itself materialise – and with what effects? How can intersecting policies (and their derivational governance/political/bureaucratic practices and provenance) and their bending into education practice be agentially 'cut' (Barad, 2007) with the observational agencies research is enacting? How long does research need to be engaged, to make a meaningful contribution? And who is this contribution for? Where do the exclusions that research can enact have their effects in what can come to matter? How is the responsibility for the 'other' manifest? How can research earn the right to participate (Whatmore, 2013), as opposed to assuming it? What 'things' are emerging/acting? What knowledge matters and in whose interests does this mattering manifest? What are the criteria for judging what counts here? What, which bodies, are at risk of not coming to matter? Why? What can/should research do about this? Answering these questions might offer a place to begin with taking a material turn in researching education policy.

Conclusion

There are of course no easy answers to these questions. And this lack of ease is a crucial aspect of recent discussion about 'new materialism' and the 'post-qualitative' turn. In a plenary on the 'post-qualitative' turn at the 2014 International Congress of Qualitative Inquiry, Bettie St Pierre (2014) argued that researchers ought to forget 'doing' qualitative research by the numbers that is based on any pre-existing set of theoretical or methodological resources/procedures; challenging us (researchers) to invent our methodology as we go along. Patti Lather (2014) gives us a related set of ideas to pursue:

> In Deleuzean terms, this is a molecular vision of the alternative, a plurality of fissions and margins, a system of deviances straining for communicability while protecting its marginality, registering in the local, enacting the future life of difference, and a way to dream and perhaps enact post-qualitative work. The question is: how might we move from what needs to be opposed to what can be imagined out of what is already happening, embedded in an immanence of doing?

If the concern for justice that Barad identifies provokes taking a material turn that undoes boundaries and cuts discursive-materialities and their related theoretical ambitions down to size, what can be imagined and done in a Latherian 'immanence of doing'? Perhaps, a material turn might lead to new 'practical landscapes' (Stengers, 2005b) that 'do more with less', concentrating resources on 'local' emergences where education and policy continue to 'fail' people. This goes against the idea of solutions being located elsewhere (for example, in [the material interests and logics of] expert knowledge), and that there is an underlying (implied) assumption of deficit with respect to those for whom solutions are to be found. The research task, on a theoretical and practical level, pays attention to the relations between epistemological and ontological processes and which (post-human) bodies come to matter as a result. Through these processes, whose outcomes are unforeseeable, conclusions are possible, in fact are required, but slow to be arrived at. As Stengers (2005a: 994) asks:

How can we present a proposal intended not to say what is, or ought to be, but to provoke a thought, a proposal that requires no other verification than the way in which it is able to 'slow down' reasoning and create an opportunity to arouse a slightly different awareness of the situations and problems mobilising us?

References

Alberti, B. and Marshall, Y. (2009). Animating archaeology: Local theories and conceptually open-ended methodologies. *Cambridge Archaeological Journal, 19*(3), 344–356.

Anderson, T. and Shattuck, J. (2012). Design-based research: A decade of progress in education research. *Educational Researcher, 41*(1), 16–25.

Bacchi, C. (2012). Strategic interventions and ontological politics: Research as political practice. In A. Bletsas and C. Beasley (Eds.), *Engaging with Carol Bacchi* (pp. 141–156). North Terrace, Australia: University of Adelaide Press.

Ball, S., Maguire, M. and Braun, A. (2012). *How schools do policy: Policy enactments in secondary schools*. New York: Routledge.

Barad, K. (1998). Getting real: Technoscientific practices and the materialization of reality. *Differences, 10*(2), 87.

Barad, K. (2003). Posthumanist performativity: Toward an understanding of how matter comes to matter. *Signs: Journal of Women in Culture and Society, 28*(3), 801–831.

Barad, K. (2007). *Meeting the universe halfway quantum physics and the entanglement of matter and meaning*. Durham, NC: Duke University Press.

Bennett, J. (2009). *Vibrant matter: A political ecology of things*. Durham, NC: Duke University Press.

Barad, K. (2011). Nature's queer performativity. *Qui Parle: Critical Humanities and Social Sciences, 19*(2). 121–158.

Braidotti, R. (2013). *The posthuman*: New York: John Wiley & Sons.

Bryant, L. R. (2011). *The democracy of objects*. Ann Arbor, MI: Open Humanities Press.

Bryant, L., Srnicek, N. and Harman, G. (2011). Towards a speculative philosophy. In L. Bryant, N. Srnicek and G. Harman (Eds.), *The speculative turn: Continental materialism and realism*. Melbourne: re.press.

DeLanda, M. (2004). *Intensive science and virtual philosophy*. London: Continuum.

Denzin, N. K. (2013). Performing methodologies. *Qualitative Social Work, 12*(4), 389–394.

Dolphijn, R. and van der Tuin, I. (2012). *New materialism: Interviews & cartographies*. Ann Arbor, MI: Open Humanities Press.

Dumas, M. J. and Anderson, G. (2014). Qualitative research as policy knowledge: Framing policy problems and transforming education from the ground up. *Education Policy Analysis Archives, 22*(11), 1–24.

Edwards, R. (2012). Theory matters: Representation and experimentation in education. *Educational Philosophy and Theory, 44*(5), 522–534.

Fenwick, T. and Edwards, R. (2011). Considering materiality in educational policy: Messy objects and multiple reals. *Educational Theory, 61*(6), 709–726.

Giardina, M. D. and Denzin, N. K. (2011). Acts of activism, politics of possibility: Toward a new performative cultural politics. *Cultural Studies ↔ Critical Methodologies, 11*(4), 319–327.

Hanson, J. (2007). Drag kinging: Embodied acts and acts of embodiment. *Body & Society, 13*(1), 61–106.

Heimans, S. (2012). Coming to matter 'in' practice: Enacting education policy. *Discourse: Studies in the Cultural Politics of Education, 33*(2), 313–326.

Hultman, K. and Lenz Taguchi, H. (2010). Challenging anthropocentric analysis of visual data: A relational materialist methodological approach to educational research. *International Journal of Qualitative Studies in Education, 23*(5), 525–542.

Hytten, K. (2004). Postcritical ethnography: Research as a pedagogical encounter. In G. W. Noblit, S. Y. Flores and E. G. Murillo (Eds.), *Postcritical ethnography: Reinscribing critique.* Cresskill, NJ: Hampton Press.

Lather, P. (2010). *Engaging science policy: From the side of the messy.* New York: Peter Lang.

Lather, P. (2014). *(Re)Thinking ontology in (post)qualitative research.* Paper presented at the International Congress of Qualitative Inquiry, University of Illinois, Urbana Champaign.

Lather, P. and St Pierre, E. (2013). Post-qualitative research. *International Journal of Qualitative Studies in Education, 26*(6), 629–633.

Latour, B. (2005). *Reassembling the social: An introduction to actor-network-theory.* Oxford, UK and New York: Oxford University Press.

Latour, B. (2011). Reflections on Etienne Souriau's les différents modes d'existence. In L. Bryant, N. Srnicek and G. Harman (Eds.), *The speculative turn: Continental materialism and realism* (pp. 304–333). Melbourne: re:press.

Law, J. and Urry, J. (2004). Enacting the social. *Economy and Society, 33*(3), 390–410.

Leavy, P. (2013). *Method meets art: Arts-based research practice.* New York: Guilford Publications.

Lingard, B. (2010). The impact of research on education policy: The relevance for doctoral students. In P. Thomson and M. Walker (Eds.), *The Routledge doctoral students' companion: Getting to grips with research in education and the social sciences* (pp. 377–389). New York: Routledge.

Maria Ozanira da Silva e, S. (2005). Reconstructing a participatory process in the production of knowledge: A concept and a practice. *International Journal of Action Research, 1,* 99–120.

Mol, A. (2002). *The body multiple: Ontology in medical practice.* Durham, NC: Duke University Press.

Nealon, J. T. (2008). *Foucault beyond Foucault: Power and its intensifications since 1984.* Stanford, CA: Stanford University Press.

Nyberg, D. (2009). Computers, customer service operatives and cyborgs: Intra-actions in call centres. *Organization Studies, 30*(11), 1181–1199.

Rancière, J. (1999). *Dis-agreement: Politics and philosophy.* Minneapolis, MN: University of Minnesota Press.

Rouse, J. (2004). Barad's feminist naturalism. *Hypatia, 19*(1), 142–161.

Singh, P., Heimans, S. and Glasswell, K. (2014). Policy enactment, context and performativity: Ontological politics and researching Australian National Partnership policies. *Journal of Education Policy, 29*(6), 826–844.

St Pierre, E. (2011). Post qualitative research: The critique and the coming after. In N. Denzin and Y. Lincoln (Eds.), *The Sage handbook of qualitative research* (pp. 611–626). Thousand Oaks, CA: Sage.

St Pierre, E. (2014). *Practices for the 'new' in the new empiricisms, the new materialisms, and post qualitative inquiry.* Paper presented at the International Congress of Qualitative Inquiry, University of Illinois, Urbana Champaign.

Stengers, I. (2005a). The cosmopolitical proposal. In B. Latour and P. Weibel (Eds.), *Making things public. Atmospheres of democracy* (pp. 994–1003). Massachusetts, MA: The MIT Press.

Stengers, I. (2005b). Introductory notes on an ecology of practices. *Cultural Studies Review, 11*(1), 183–196.

Stengers, I. (2010). *Cosmopolitics.* Minneapolis, MN: University of Minnesota Press.

Thrift, N. (2008). *Non-representational theory: Space, politics, affect.* Abingdon, UK and New York: Routledge.

Udén, M. (2009). A located realism: Recent development within feminist science studies and the present options for feminist engineering. *Women's Studies International Forum, 32*(3), 219–226.

Whatmore, S. (2013). Earthly powers and affective environments: An ontological politics of flood risk. *Theory, Culture & Society*. doi:10.1177/0263276413480949.

Whatmore, S. and Landström, C. (2011). Flood apprentices: An exercise in making things public. *Economy and Society, 40*(4), 582–610.

14

MOBILITIES PARADIGM AND POLICY RESEARCH IN EDUCATION

Fazal Rizvi

Since the early 1990s, much has been written about global mobility. Authors such as Appadurai (1996), Bauman (1998), Castells (2000) and Beck (2000) have shown how notions of mobility, movement and flows should now be treated as central to our understanding of the global processes that are re-constituting our communities, our social institutions and our lives. They have suggested that as we witness ever-increasing levels of mobility, facilitated not only by the revolutionary developments in communication and transport technologies but also by major shifts in the ways in which economic and political relations are structured, we need to re-think the contemporary processes of social and political formation, as well as approaches to social research. If this is so, then this must also apply to policy research in education, the main object of which is an analysis of the ways in which national governments prioritize educational funding, programs and practices. It is now abundantly clear that a range of globally mobile ideas and ideologies influences these priorities. If national systems of education are profoundly affected by the shifting dynamics of global mobilities, then clearly, so must our approaches to policy research in education.

Of all the recent social theorists who have written about global mobility and its implications for social research, John Urry (2007) is one of the most influential, and perhaps also the most radical. He suggests that in the face of multiple cross-national exchange, cross-cultural flows and global networks that now characterize the world, we need nothing less than to re-imagine sociology itself. He notes that 'the diverse mobilities of peoples, objects, images, information and wastes' have created 'complex interdependencies between, and social consequences of, these diverse mobilities' (Urry, 2007: 1). Yet, traditional sociology, he maintains, remains trapped within a nation-state-centric framework of discrete societies, misleadingly presupposing a world of stable and bounded national cultures and subjectivities that are reproduced endogenously. However, if social phenomena are 'on the move', then social descriptions and analyses can no longer afford to remain static, solid and sedentarist. He calls for a fundamental paradigm shift – a 'new mobilities paradigm' in which a concern with flows and movements of people, money, objects, information shifts to the centre stage of social research.

In this chapter, I want to discuss Urry's arguments regarding the theoretical significance of mobilities in understanding contemporary social processes; and consider some of the challenges that the mobilities paradigm poses for policy researchers in education. My argument is that while some of Urry's arguments may be a little exaggerated, the attention he draws to diverse mobilities that characterize contemporary social processes cannot be so easily dismissed. While his call for a 'sociology beyond societies' (Urry, 2000) may appear somewhat extravagant, I want to suggest that it can no longer be denied that global processes are reconstituting the nature of societies, making them subject to a whole range of new forces; and in so far as educational policy is both an expression of, and response to these processes, then new approaches to its understanding are clearly warranted.

Emerging forms of mobility

It is no longer possible to deny that educational ideas and ideologies move across national borders more rapidly and more decisively than they have ever done. They circulate globally, creating new modes and networks in the production and dissemination of educational knowledge. In recent years, this realization has led to wide-ranging discussions about the forms and extent of global policy convergence in educational policy around a neo-liberal social imaginary (Rizvi and Lingard, 2010). Authors such as Phillips and Ochs (2004) and Steiner-Khamsi and Waldow (2013) have examined the politics of 'policy borrowing'. Dale and Robertson (2013) have sought to understand the emerging grammar of the global circulation of policy ideas and ideologies. The grammar of mobilities is clearly evident in international aid and development policies in education (Ireton, 2013), and in the global politics of such programs as PISA (Grek, 2009). It is also evident in the demands that transnational corporations make of national governments to change their national policies in line with the human resource needs of these corporations, within the framework of the production processes that now span the globe (Dicken, 2011). Policy ideas have thus become globally mobile, along with shifts in global economic activity, reflected in emerging forms and practices of capital accumulation.

Not only have capital, finance, images, information and ideologies become more mobile, people have as well. Never before in history have as many people moved across national boundaries as they do now. People move for a whole host of reasons: for migration; as refugees; for trade and business; for employment opportunities; as tourists; to attend international conventions and conferences; and for education. There are more international migrants – both documented and undocumented – than ever before (Kennedy, 2010). Aware of the possibilities, potential migrants now have better sources of information, advice and support from government and non-government organizations alike. With the globalization of economic activity and trade, business executives are constantly on the move, as indeed are workers recruited and employed by transnational corporations (Rizvi, 2009). Many people, both professionally educated and those who are not, no longer hesitate, as they once did, to take employment opportunities abroad. International tourist numbers, as measured in terms of arrivals from another country, have grown exponentially. Despite enhanced possibilities of online communication, travelling to international conferences and conventions has become commonplace.

This unprecedented level of people mobility, in its various forms and modalities, is linked to the ways in which global economic and political systems now work. New international rules have had to be created to both facilitate and control flows of money, as well as of goods and services. Global cultural exchange is also shaped by global mobilities. For example, the movement of people is driven in part by consumerist desire and subjective awareness of global opportunities. This, in turn, is transforming social institutions, cultural practices and even people's sense of identity and belonging. Global mobility has transformed cities, such as London, creating urban conglomerates at the intersection of the global flows of finance and capital (Massey, 2007). Also affected are villages and smaller towns in the developing world whose economies are now dependent on remittances money (Orozco, 2013).

Education is deeply implicated in these changes. It has become a major driver of the global mobility of young people, re-shaping their desires and aspirations towards cosmopolitan experiences. The number of international students is now more than 2.2 million and is expected to more than double by 2025 (Cairns, 2014). Programs in student and faculty exchange have become commonplace. Demographically, the global mobility of students has transformed the character of campuses in many parts of the world, making them more diverse, creating new pressures for curriculum and pedagogic reform. Beyond physical travel, new communication technologies have enhanced the possibilities of 'virtual travel' across national borders through innovations in online education, such as Massive Online Open Courses (MOOCs) (Nanfito, 2014).

It is in the context of these and other unprecedented developments that Urry (2007) calls for a new mobilities paradigm. He notes that the increasing levels of people mobility have transformed both the places to which people gravitate and the places they leave, making them inextricably connected, not only culturally and economically but also politically. Mobilities are not only transforming the demographic composition of communities, they are also redefining the spaces in which social, economic and political exchanges take place. With economic and political systems becoming interconnected, new identities, practices and networks can now be forged out of long-distance cross-border connections among people. These developments, Urry concludes, pose major new challenges for the social sciences to which he considers the mobilities paradigm a response.

Mobilities paradigm

There is, of course, nothing new about the movement of people, ideas and capital, both within and across nations. Historically, people have always moved as migrants and refugees in search of jobs; security and other opportunities; for trade; as tourists interested in experiencing exotic locations and the cultural others; in search of new knowledge and; of course, as part of colonial conquests and indentured labour. Indeed, the contemporary architecture of international relations cannot be adequately understood without historical references to mobility, which include both long-established patterns of 'diasporization' of communities such as the Indians, Chinese and Jewish and colonial settlements that led to the formation of new nations such as the US and Australia. The movement of people created conditions in which flows of money, ideas and information became inevitable, through a range of complex processes.

However, while the contemporary dynamics of mobility is clearly continuous with some of these processes, it is now much more complex. Not only has the number of mobile people increased significantly over the past three decades, so has the way people think about and approach mobility. In the past, mobility was relatively permanent; now it is contingent and flexible, with new information and communication technologies enabling people to keep their options open and retain links with their countries of origin. As Aihwa Ong (1999) has argued, in an era of globalization, mobile individuals are able to develop a 'flexible' notion of citizenship, often designed to accumulate capital and power. In contemporary times, powerful incentives exist for individuals to pursue options that favour 'flexibility, mobility and repositioning in relation to markets, governments and cultural regimes' (Ong, 1999: 33).

Traditionally, discussions of mobility were largely couched in terms of various realist distinctions, such as between home and abroad, emigration and immigration, and push and pull factors. In the current era, such distinctions are becoming overwhelmed by technological innovations, as people are able not only to travel with greater regularity and ease than ever before but are also able to remain in touch with each other on a daily basis, using social media and communication technologies such as email and Skype. These changes have swept across frontiers, contributing to the declining capacity of the nation-states to maintain them. Beck (2000) has used the phrase 'place polygamy' to underscore the fact that some people are now able to live in more than one place at once, resulting in notions of citizenship that have become detached from a singular national origin. These people are able to have multiple senses of national and cultural belonging.

Emerging patterns of social interaction across national boundaries have transformed the spaces in which we now live and work, giving rise to 'the messiness of living and acting in the mediated world of today' (Morris, 1993: 39), both for those who are mobile but also for those who are not. Indeed, the lack of mobility of some cannot be adequately understood without comprehending the mobility of others. The spaces in which we live are created by complex inter-relationships between mobility and immobility. They are constituted by cross-border relationships, patterns of economic and political exchange, complex affiliations and cultural formations that potentially span the globe. They consist in multiple and complicated spaces in which identities, exchanges and societies are constantly crafted and re-negotiated (Rizvi, 2009).

Urry's call for the mobilities paradigm is based partly on recent theoretical insights associated with what has been called the 'spatial turn' in the social sciences (Warf and Arias, 2008). This describes the ways in which spaces are socially assembled and reassembled in changing configurations, often as a result of mobilities of various kinds – as well as the effects these mobilities have on identities, events and conceptions of sociality. As people, capital and things move, they form and reform space itself. For Urry, this line of argument goes back to the work of George Simmel (1997), who described the human will to connection, and the ways in which connections form the basis of the tempo and multiplicity of economic, political and social life. The topologies of social networks emerge out of these connections. In this way, mobilities give rise to complex systems that are neither perfectly ordered nor anarchic. They are dynamic and possess emergent properties. They develop over time, locking more and more aspects of their 'path-dependent' practices (Urry, 2007).

For Urry (2007), then, the recognition of the ubiquity of mobilities demands a new way of thinking about the social sciences. It has 'implications for most of the categories by which sociology and other social sciences have examined the character of social life', transforming 'many existing sociological controversies, such as the relative significance of social structure, on the one hand, and human agency, on the other' (p. 3). Urry (2007) insists that this disruption should not be viewed as merely an extra level or domain that 'can be "added" to existing sociological analyses that can carry on regardless' (p. 3). A fundamental transformation is needed in the ways in which we theorize the concepts of identity, structure, flows, ideology, performance, complexity and so on. Urry (2007: 18) further argues that a paradigm shift is needed because 'thinking through a mobilities "lens" provides a distinctive social science that is productive of different theories, methods, questions and solutions'.

Mobile methods

In an effort to develop new research approaches in the social sciences, Urry insists that the mobilities paradigm must make problematic two major set of extant theory. First, he suggests, we need to reject the *sedentarist* assumptions in much of traditional social sciences, with their inclination to treat 'as normal stability, meaning and place, and treats as abnormal distance, change and placelessness' (Sheller and Urry, 2006: 208). Such sedentarism, he argues, treats places or regions or nations as bounded, and as fundamental basis of human identity – and therefore fundamental units of social research. This leads to a form of methodological territorialism, which invites accounts that visualize and map human behaviour as explicable totally in territorial terms. It locates subjectivities, social networks and aspirations to modernity within territorially bounded spaces. In contrast, the mobilities paradigm, insists Urry, is based on a recognition that 'all places are tied into at least thin networks of connections that stretch beyond each such place and mean that nowhere can be an "island"' (Sheller and Urry, 2006: 209).

Second, Urry's critique of static social sciences departs from recent theories of post-national deterritorialization (for example, Tomlinson, 2000), which suggest that social life has increasingly become disconnected from nation-states. These theories suggest a shift from modernity seen as heavy and solid to an epoch in which speed of movement of people, money and images and information has become paramount, and in which freedom from moral ties to a particular location are celebrated. Bauman (2000) refers to this as 'liquid modernity'. Urry does not subscribe to such a normative view of mobility but underlines instead a set of new questions, theories and methodologies about the complexities of human relations. He suggests that the consequences of mobility are entirely contingent, and create 'zones of connectivity, centrality and empowerment in some cases, and of disconnection, social exclusion and inaudibility in other cases' (Sheller and Urry, 2006: 210). The new mobilities paradigm does not, he insists, rule out the possibility of mobilities, sometimes resulting in highly embedded and immobile outcomes.

The mobilities paradigm does not thus propose a 'romantic' reading of (perhaps cosmopolitan) mobility, but highlights instead the need to track the power of mobility in creating both movement and stasis (Sheller and Urry, 2006: 211). It asks how mobility of ideas, people and money is interpreted, enacted, managed and controlled, and how it both reflects and reinforces various forms and patterns of power. The point that Urry repeatedly emphasizes is that the lack and incapacity of movement cannot be adequately understood without an analysis of various modalities of mobility as well as the networks of relationships they create. Indeed, he points out, the 'acts of homing' (Brah, 1996) and 're-grounding' of immigrant communities (Ahmed et al., 2004), for example, demands an understanding of complex interrelations between travel and dwelling, home and away, and here and there. In this way, Sheller and Urry (2006: 212) conclude that:

> The new mobilities paradigm must be brought to bear not only on questions of globalization and deterritorialization of nation-states, identities and belonging, but more fundamentally on questions of what are the appropriate subjects and objects of social inquiry.

If 'mobile' processes lie at the heart of contemporary social experiences, then the key question for the social sciences is: how is research into such processes best conducted?

In his book, with Büscher and Witchger, Urry (2010) suggests that methods of social research themselves have to become mobile. He refers to them as 'mobile methods'. He suggests that researchers would benefit greatly if they track – sometimes physically travelling with their research objects – the various forms of intermittent movement of people, images, information and objects. In this way, Urry and his colleagues build on George Marcus's (1998) notion of 'multi-sited ethnography', which recommends investigations into chains, paths, threads and so on of human connectivities, in order to determine how various expressions of mobility intersect with each, and reflexively shape the orders of social, economic and political relations. By immersing themselves in multiple mobile, social and material realities, Urry suggests, researchers can gain an understanding of movement, not only in terms of how it is governed by rules but also how it gives rise to the emergence of new social structures, networks and practices.

Urry (2007: 40) highlights further the importance of observing people's bodily movements. It is possible to do this, while 'walking with' or travelling with people, 'as a form of sustained engagement with their world-view'. Through such 'co-present immersion', researchers are able to capture patterns of movement, in order to develop an understanding of how diverse mobilities constitute patterning of everyday life. Another way of capturing these patterns is through the keeping of time-space diaries in which research participants record what they are doing and where – and how and why they move during those periods (Urry, 2007: 40). Researchers can also 'explore the imaginative and virtual mobilities of people through analysing texting, websites, multi-user discussion groups, blogs, emails and list-servs' (Büscher and Urry, 2009). An analysis of texts produced in these various forms can elucidate the work of memory in social life, and how complex social networks are developed and maintained across places. This kind of empirical work will show, Urry insists, how the very constitution of places depends on mobilities across multiple tracks and territories.

Re-thinking policy research

Urry's insights have major implications for policy research in education, in a number of ways. To begin with, these insights undermine approaches to educational policy research that are fundamentally grounded in national structures and organizational practices. While educational policies continue to be made at national and sub-national levels, a focus on mobilities points to the importance of examining the ways in which policy ideas and information now circulate globally, and are interpreted and translated into local priorities and practices in a range of complex ways. National traditions of education still matter, but have to take into account ideas emanating from other systems of education. This can be shown, for example, in the case of South Africa, where, after transition to democratic governance in the mid-1990s, it imported consultants and ideas from Australia to promote reforms of the South African system of education around the concept of 'outcomes based education' (Mokhaba, 2010). These notions did not work, but indicated to policy researchers a wide variety of questions about how and why the South African Government felt it necessary to embrace notions of reform from elsewhere, and how their translation into the South African contexts proved highly problematic.

With rapid developments in transport, communication and information technologies, flows of ideas across national borders have never been greater, and are now mediated not only by the mobility of people but also in virtual spaces where these ideas can be exchanged. Over time, this leads to the creation of various international policy networks around particular sets of interests. With student mobility and exchange becoming a key feature of contemporary systems of education, ideas, information and ideologies now travel across and often beyond these networks. In circulating educational ideas, intergovernmental organizations (IGOs) such as the

World Bank and the OECD play a major role, often around a particular set of educational values and reform priorities. Indeed, it is not possible to understand the global popularity of neoliberal ideas in education without appreciating the ways in which their global circulation has been promoted by certain educational activists, IGOs and global corporations (Rizvi and Lingard, 2010). The mobilities paradigm thus highlights the importance of tracking educational policies and programs, beyond their national origins, in a wider set of policy networks.

In the circulation of policy ideas in education, the global media plays a major role. The media has become centrally important in the processes of policy production and dissemination. In a sense, these processes are now increasingly 'mediatized', with the policy texts carefully constructed, portrayed and distributed (Lingard and Rawolle, 2004). Indeed, the careful selection of language to promote policy ideas has now become central to the practices of educational governance. Appadurai (1996) has spoken of 'ideoscapes' to explain how ideas and information circulate throughout the world in a highly political manner. In education, the global concatenation of neoliberal ideas is evident in the processes of policy borrowing, modelling, transfer, diffusion, appropriation, mimicking and so on. There has emerged an almost universal language of education reform, couched in terms of the need to respond to the challenges of globalization. Indeed, a particular concept of educational effectiveness is now promoted globally, with the help of various international and regional agreements and settlements, such as the Washington Consensus and Bologna Accord, as well as technologies of benchmarking and tools for comparing educational performance.

Many of the traditional approaches to public policy research have focused on the content of policy – on the values that are articulated and allocated by the policy in a manner authorized by the state – and on the ways in which these policies are most efficiently and effectively implemented. The content of the policy is assumed to express the priorities of the state. Each state is thought to have its own set of policy preferences, developed within the confines of its own nationally-specific institutional structures. It is also assumed that the implementation of policy priorities involves a linear set of mechanisms – means to realize given ends. The mobilities paradigm problematizes this rationalist view of policy processes. It suggests instead greater complexity in the accounts of the ways in which policies are considered authoritative and the ways in which they are enacted. Indeed, policy processes increasingly transcend national borders, often involving comparative and benchmarking data that are generated by intergovernmental organizations. Policies travel in a range of diverse and uneven ways, and are taken up by states through multiple complex processes. The mobilities paradigm draws attention to the importance of the study of these processes, to appreciate how local priorities are often a product of travelling ideas, cutting across internal and external pressures and politics, in spaces that are transnational.

The mobilities paradigm thus builds on the idea that most communities around the world are constituted by complex transcultural exchange and transnational spatial awareness. Places can no longer be assumed to be internally homogeneous, bounded areas, subject to their own unique set of conditions. Instead they are better viewed as spaces forged out of transnational connectivities – constituted by cross-border relationships, connected patterns of economic, political and cultural relations, and complex affiliations and social formations that span the world (Vertovec, 2009). If education policy represents a response to these new transnational social conditions, then policy researchers in education face a range of new questions. How do we, for example, research spaces that do not have any clear boundaries and where social relations potentially span vast distances? How do we take into account the distribution and dynamics of power whose contours potentially involve the entire globe? How do we provide accounts of social meaning when these are not linked to any specific community? How do we study social inequalities when its causes do not necessarily reside within the community that is the object of our research? In other words, how do we address the conceptual difficulties that inevitably arise in research concerning mobile social phenomenon when the very construction of the 'social' cannot be easily defined?

Challenges of policy research

Educational research has many purposes: to provide an account of the role of education in the formation of personal and professional identities; to understand how people are encouraged to make meaning of their lives; to explain how educational institutions produce and reproduce patterns of inequality and power; to determine the nature of the deep structural barriers to the realization of educational objectives; and to discern the relationship between educational and social processes. The mobilities paradigm suggests that policy research in education is linked to these broader questions, with a specific interest in how the state addresses these issues within a set of spatial configurations. If this is so then the questions of how space is constituted in educational thinking, how its boundaries are drawn, and what effects such boundaries have, are central to policy research in education.

Of course, space is never constituted in a uniform and coherent manner. Not all spaces are transnationalized in the same way, or indeed, to the same extent. Some spaces – global cities such as Chicago and London – are transnationalized to a greater extent than isolated rural communities, for example. In this sense, transnationalization may be viewed as an on-going dynamic social process affected by the changing forms of connectivity between the global and the local, between a community's interior and its exterior. At a conceptual level, however, the notion of a transnational space would seem to undermine any meaningful distinction between the inside of a space and its outside, long regarded as central to policy research in education. If such traditional naturalistic distinctions as the inside and outside of a community or an organization cannot be easily maintained, then many new challenges emerge for policy research.

In recent years, numerous ethnographers have pointed out, for example, that in the emerging global context, both the ideas of 'ethno' and 'graphic' have become problematic. The relationship between ethnographers and the people they studied was already complex, but in a transnational context, new questions arise around such key terms as 'othering' and 'authorial control', leading to what Wittel (2001: 34) calls, a 'crisis in objectification'. With respect to the idea of 'ethno', a culture can no longer be treated as a coherent entity that has a unique form unaffected by its engagement with other cultures. Through enhanced mobility of capital, people and ideas, cultural contact has become a norm, leading anthropologists such as Clifford (1997) to suggest that human institutions are now constituted by displacement as much as by stasis.

Equally, the notion of 'the field', as a geographically defined research area, also becomes problematic, leading Gupta and Ferguson (1997) to suggest the need to redefine it, by 'decentring' it in ways that deny any clear-cut distinction between 'the here' and 'elsewhere'. If people, ideas and objects are increasingly mobile, then researchers have to engage these movements, and treat localities and institutions, such as schools, as products of circulation of meanings and identities. Research must become embedded self-consciously within a system of global networks, shifting its focus from single sites and local situations to become multi-sited and multi-local, responsive to networked realities. Most ethnographers in the field of education assume boundedness of their field and object of their inquiry. However, as Nespor (1997: xi) points out, 'by looking at schools as somehow separate from cities, politics, neighbourhoods, businesses and popular culture' educational researchers 'obscure how these are all inextricably connected to one another, how they jointly produce educational effects'. Once the realities of transnational space are recognized then the focus of research must shift to an understanding of transnational relationalities – on how different sites, institutions and identities are globally interconnected and are now jointly produced.

Global mobilities have thus transformed the social fields and objects of education. They require a new understanding of time and space, and of the relationalities between them. Traditionally, space and time have been interpreted against the assumptions of linearity, regularity and stasis. None of these assumptions can now be taken for granted. Urry (2003) has used recent developments in complexity theory to show how the social is in fact open-ended, uncertain, evolving and self-organizing, and how mobilities unsettle the assumption of social order, which has long been assumed to be the key problematic of educational research. In the functionalist tradition in particular, the central issue for social research was the question of how social order was secured and sustained. The problematics of transnational mobility have rendered this issue obsolete, because the criss-crossings of social formations have resulted in complex interconnections, with non-linear and unpredictable outcomes. This has meant that order and chaos are always intertwined.

These insights have major implications for education. Traditionally, nation-building has been one of the key tasks allocated to formal education. Each nation has been assumed to represent an apparently separate society, with its own ways of celebrating its nationalism. Education has played a major role in securing and sustained the presumed national order. But as Urry (2003: 107) points out, 'the development of global complexity means that each such banal nationalism increasingly circulates along the global informational and communicational channels and systems'. In the context of global mobility, nation-states now have to deal with not a fixed and clear-cut national population, but a complex cultural diversity characterized by a fluid and dynamic set of relationships. This has posed a range of new policy challenges for nation-states, caught between the need to keep social order, on the one hand, and to work with recognition of complex diversity on the other.

The challenges described above are not only conceptual and methodological, but also moral and political. If transnationalism describes new social formations that cut across national borders, leading to the emergence of certain kinds of relationship that are not only globally networked but also intensified, then how should educational policy respond to moral requirements in education that potentially span the globe? If pluralization and hybridization of cultures – with the idea of a geographically bounded object and field of educational research hard to sustain – then how should educational normativities be conceptualized, justified and promoted? If educational processes are constituted by new relationalities that are necessarily non-linear, complex, open-ended and evolving, then what are the ethical and political consequences of a shift in focus from order and stasis to uncertainty and dynamism? These are questions that Urry and his colleagues do not directly address. Yet they are central to any deliberation over educational aims and governance. Perhaps Urry's main contribution to social research then is that he has opened up a new range of questions in educational policy research that have yet to be fully explored.

References

Ahmed, S., Castaneda, C. and Fortie, A. (2004). *Uprooting/regrounding: Questions of home and migration*. London: Bloomsbury Academic.

Appadurai, A. (1996). *Modernity at large*. Minneapolis, MN: Minnesota University Press.

Bauman, Z. (1998). *Globalization: The human consequences*. Cambridge, UK: Polity Press.

Bauman, Z. (2000). *Liquid modernity*. Cambridge, UK: Polity Press.

Beck, U. (2000). *What is globalization?* Cambridge, UK: Polity Press.

Brah, A. (1996). *Cartographies of diaspora: Contesting identities*. London and New York: Routledge.

Büscher, M. and Urry, J. (2009). Mobile methods and the empirical. *European Journal of Social Theory*, *12*(1), 99–116.

Büscher, M., Urry, J. and Witchger, K. (Eds.) (2010). *Mobile methods*. London: Routledge.

Cairns, D. (2014). *Youth transitions: Youth student mobility and spatial reflexivity: Being mobile?* London: Palgrave MacMillan.

Castells, M. (2000). *The rise of the network society* (2nd edn). Oxford, UK: Blackwell.

Clifford, J. (1997). *Routes: Travel and translation in the late twentieth century*. Cambridge, MA: Harvard University Press.

Dale, R. and Robertson, S. (2013). Towards a critical grammar of educational policy movements. In G. Steiner-Khamsi and F. Waldon (Eds.), *World yearbook of education 2012: Policy borrowing and lending in education* (pp. 21–40). London: Routledge.

Dicken, P. (2011). *Global shifts: Mapping the changing contours of the world economy* (6th edn). New York: Guildford Press.

Grek, S. (2009). Governing by numbers: PISA 'effect' in Europe. *Journal of Education Policy*, *24*(1), 23–37.

Gupta, A. and Ferguson, J. (1997). *Culture, power and place: Explorations in critical anthropology.* Durham, NC: Duke University Press.

Ireton, B. (2013). *Britain's international aid policies: A history of DIFD and overseas aid.* London: Palgrave MacMillan.

Kennedy, P. T. (2010). *Local lives and global transformations: Towards world society.* London: Palgrave MacMillan.

Lingard, B. and Rawolle, S. (2004). Mediatizing education policy: The journalistic field, science policy and cross-field effects. *Journal of Education Policy, 19*(3), 361–380.

Marcus, G. (1998). *Ethnography through thick and thin.* Princeton, NJ: Princeton University Press.

Massey, D. (2007). *World city.* Cambridge, UK: Polity Press.

Mokhaba, B. (2010). *Policy objectives and implementation complexities: Outcome-based education in South Africa since 1994.* Cape Town: VDM Verlag Dr. Müller Press.

Morris, M. (1993). Introduction. In J. From and M. Morris (Eds.), *Australian cultural studies: A reader* (pp. 3–24). Sydney: Allen & Unwin.

Nanfito, M. (2014). *MOOCs: Opportunities, impact and challenges,* Creative Commons, (retrieved June 2014) www.amazon.com/MOOCs-Opportunities-Challenges-Colleges-Universities-ebook/dp/B00HBG8XNW.

Nespor, J. (1997). *Tangled up in school: Politics, space, bodies, and signs in the educational process.* Mahway, NJ: Lawrence Erlbaum.

Ong, A. (1999). *Flexible citizenships: The cultural logics of transnationality.* Durham, NC: Duke University Press.

Orozco, M. (2013). *Migrant remittances and development in the global economy.* New York: Lynn Rienner Publications.

Phillips, D. and Ochs, K. (2004). *Global policy borrowing: Historical perspectives.* London: Symposium Press.

Rizvi, F. (2009). Global mobility. In T. Popkewitz and F. Rizvi (Eds.), *Globalization and the study of education.* New York: Wiley Blackwell.

Rizvi, F. and Lingard, R. (2010). *Globalizing education policy.* London: Routledge.

Sheller, M. and Urry, J. (2006). The new mobilities paradigm. *Environment and Planning, 38,* 207–226.

Simmel, G. (1997). *Simmel on culture: Delected writings.* Thousand Oaks, CA: Sage.

Steiner-Khamsi, G. and Waldon, F. (2013). *World yearbook of education 2012: Policy borrowing and lending in education.* London: Routledge.

Tomlinson, J. (2000). *Globalization and culture.* Chicago IL: Chicago University Press.

Urry, J. (2000). *Sociology beyond societies: Mobilities for the twenty first century.* London: Routledge.

Urry, J. (2003). *Global complexity.* Cambridge, UK: Polity Press.

Urry, J. (2007). *Mobilities.* Cambridge, UK: Polity Press.

Vertovec, S. (2009). *Transnationalism.* London: Routledge.

Warf, B. and Arias, S. (Eds.) (2008). *The spatial turn: Interdisciplinary perspectives.* New York and London: Routledge.

Wittel, A. (2001). Towards a Network Sociality. *Theory, Culture & Society, 18,* 31–50.

15

A NARRATIVE APPROACH TO POLICY ANALYSIS

Peter Bansel

Intention

Whilst recognising that there are multiple and competing accounts of what narrative might be or mean (Jones and Macbeth, 2010), my specific purpose in this chapter is to articulate some of the theoretical and methodological possibilities for working with narrative as an approach to policy and its analysis. In so doing, I foreground the narrative character of policy; give an account of narrative and policy as technologies of government through which subject/citizens are constituted and regulated; emphasise the extent to which particular policy narratives are imbricated in larger ensembles of ambitions, mentalities, technologies and practices of government; and signal the possibilities and politics of generating alternative (policy) narratives. This narrative approach to policy analysis is animated by Mol's (1999) ontological politics; a politics that foregrounds relations between the real, the conditions of possibility we live with and the political.

In giving this particular account of a narrative approach to policy analysis, I draw on an ensemble of theories: Foucault's (1978–1979) theorisation of governmentality, discourse and subjectification; Ricoeur's (1984, 1985, 1988) theorisation of temporality, narrative and identity; Massey's (2005) theorisation of space and narrative; and Roe (1994) and Stone's (2002) theorisation of a narrative approach to policy analysis. I work these multiple theories together in order to give an account of a narrative approach to policy analysis in which narrative is more than story, more than linguistic, and more than representation or interpretation. Rather, I give an account of narrative as a temporal and spatial technology of government through which subject/citizens and socio-political worlds are constituted and regulated.

Narrative, governmentality, discourse and subjectification

Foucault (1978–1979) identifies three technologies of governmentality: diplomatic/military, economic and policy. Policy, as a technology of government, constitutes and regulates conduct through a biopolitics that entails state intervention in the everyday lives of citizens. As Butler (2004) points out, technologies of government operate at the level of everyday practices in order to establish and regulate what constitutes 'the normal'. These norms not only constitute the regulatory practices that order subjects, but also produce the very subjects they govern. What comes to be taken as 'the normal' (subject) is an artefact of relations of power and technologies, rationalities and ambitions of government that are coordinated, materialised, embodied and enacted through the technology of narrative.

Narrative is also a technology through which normative discourses and discursive practices are coordinated. Here, I emphasise an iteration of discourse as a body of constitutive and regulatory statements and practices (Foucault, 1991, 2002); and of discourse analysis as an investigation of how those statements are produced (and enacted) in different historical periods and in different spaces (in nation–states, institutions, schools, homes and so on). The identification of discursive practices (enactments of discourse) and discursive formations (the aggregation of multiple discourses) inform analyses of particular institutions and the ways in which orders of truth, or what is accepted as 'reality', are established. Discourse, as an ensemble of multiple statements and practices, meanings and actions, is, I suggest, ascribed coherence, continuity and endurance through the organising technology of narrative.

Narrative is a technology through which multiple discourses are organised and given coherence and continuity in the form of temporally unfolding sequences, trajectories or plots. Ricoeur (1984, 1985, 1988) refers to this temporal organisation as emplotment, as the organisation of multiple discourses into an intelligible whole in the form of a narrative. Emplotment, as the temporal organisation of discourses, is not primarily involved with the ordering of events, but with the ordering of actions or practices. These plots – or emplotted actions – are codified and regulated by historically specific practices of narration constituted through specific temporal and spatial practices and technologies of government. That is, multiple discourses cannot simply be 'stuck together'; they must be related in some way, and emplotment is the practice through which these relationships are established and stabilised. Further, the coordination and endurance of these relationships is a narrative accomplishment. Given this account of the relationship between discourse and narrative, narrative analysis opens a space for investigating the ways in which policy narratives are relational ensembles of discursive resources and practices located within particular historico-political contexts. Importantly, these resources and practices are neither monolithic nor stable, but multiple, mobile, diffuse, contradictory and historically variable. Given that these constitutive technologies and practices, along with the subjects and worlds they constitute, change over time and space, then an address to temporality and spatiality is critical to a narrative approach to policy analysis.

Narrative, temporality, spatiality and politics

Policies address particular programmatic ambitions or problem/solutions targeted at particular subject/citizens who are required to act in particular ways to achieve desired policy ends. These subject/citizens and their actions are shaped by historically specific practices of government. The temporality of policy as a technology of government refers not only to the specific moment of its enactment, but also to its expression as a narrative; an expression that establishes a present context, antecedent conditions and a possible or desired future shaped by present (in)action. In establishing a constitutive relation between policy as technology of government, narrative and the constitution of the subject/citizen, I draw on Ricoeur's (1988) account of narrative, temporality and identity as the 'refiguration of temporal experience' (p. 3). This refiguration involves a 'threefold mimetic relation between the order of narrative, the order of action and the order of life' (Ricoeur, 1988: 3); or as Mol (1999) suggests, a relation between the real, the conditions of possibility we live with and the political.

- Mimesis (1), prefiguration, refers to the normative practices of government through which the intelligibility and recognition of subjects is constituted and regulated; and constituted and regulated through narrativisations of what is normal, permissible, acceptable and possible (and what is not). I emphasise a reading of prefiguration as temporal and spatial socio-political conditions of narratability that include discourses, discursive fields, discursive practices and subject positions within discourse.
- Mimesis (2), configuration, refers to the emplotment or ordering of discourses, events, experiences, performances and subjects, through which relations between and among them are coordinated into intelligible and coherent narratives.
- Mimesis (3), refiguration, refers to the performative embodiment of these narratives in and as the life of a narrating (and narratable) subject. In this way technologies of government (policies, for example) are refigured in and as the life of the subject.

Working with Ricoeur's account of narrative as a mimetic relation, policy is understood as a constitutive and regulatory technology of government, and this technology is understood as composed of prefigurations of what it is possible to think, say, be or do in any given time and space. These prefigurations are coordinated and expressed in and as policy narratives through acts of configuration and emplotment, and the subject/citizen is a refiguration of these normative narratives (as technologies of government). The subject/citizen so constituted is, for Ricoeur (1984, 1985, 1988), a 'narrative identity'.

Narrative, as the refiguration of the ambitions of government in and as a subject, is a 'strategy of persuasion' aimed at imposing a vision of the world 'that is never ethically neutral, but that rather implicitly or explicitly induces a new evaluation of the world' – and of the subject (Ricoeur, 1988: 249). Policy, as narrative, is thus an interested and persuasive technology through which practice, experience, knowledge, meaning and expectation are materialised in the performative embodiments of authorised (or de/ and un/authorised) subjects. This mimetic relationship between the orders of narrative, action and life, foregrounds the technologies, practices and relations of power through which the polity, the subject/citizen, and the politics of every day life are authored and authorised. This politics of authorisation is a refiguration of the conditions of possibility and intelligibility emergent in any particular time and space.

Space, for Massey (2005: 71), is a realm in which distinct temporalities are brought into new configurations: it is 'the realm of the configuration' of narratives. Narrative is 'about interaction and *the process of the constitution of* identities' and entities (Massey, 2005: 71). For Massey, the terms 'trajectory' and 'story' signal the operation of time, movement and change on entities as spatialised relations. Importantly, spatiality involves recognising 'the existence of trajectories which have at least some degree of autonomy from each other and cannot simply be aligned into one linear story'. Here, 'story' is not something told, nor an interpreted history, but the history, change or movement of 'things themselves' (Massey, 2005: 12).

Space, in Massey's account, does not exist prior to identities/entities and their relations, but is the product of interrelations constituted through interactions, and these relations, practices and interactions, and the entities/identities they create, are political. This politics emphasises the 'relational constructedness of things' (Massey, 2005: 10) − including things called political subjectivities and political constituencies (that is, subject/citizens and polities). This is a politics that responds to a relational understanding of the world. Further, understanding space as relational and always in process, (that is, never a closed system), suggests a politics that insists on the openness of the future. This openness resists the 'inexorability which so frequently characterises the grand narratives of modernity' (Massey, 2005: 11): progress, development, modernisation and the succession of modes of production and economic management, all of which suppose that the general directions of history, including the future, are known and predictable. Arguing for a future that is radically open is critical to conceptualisations of a politics that can make a difference, and to resistance of policy narratives that suggest the future can be entirely known and predicted in advance of its arrival.

Narrative, policy and analysis

The account of narrative, politics and policy that I have given thus far, informs my reading of Narrative Policy Analysis (Roe, 1994; Stone, 2002) as an analytic that addresses both the production of policy narratives, and opportunities for the generation of counter narratives as a strategic political intervention into the space of policy. A narrative approach to policy analysis focuses on the centrality of narratives in understanding policy issues, problems and definitions. It foregrounds the ways in which particular 'stories of influence', or policy narratives, come to dominate the policy process, and the extent to which meaning is contextual and negotiated differently in different times and spaces. Policy narratives convey meaning and suggest action, and in so doing objectify a course of action as if independent from a specific author or narrator. In this way policy affects a transcendence that simultaneously authorises (gives authority to) and de-authorises (elides the human author of) truth accounts of the world-as-it-is and the world-as-it-must-become.

Importantly, the narrative form lays out both how a proposed program or policy will operate and what changes it will bring about. It provides an explanation of which particular course of action is necessary and why it is desirable. And yet, this narrative of problems and solutions is often articulated without identifying how the policy problem was defined in the first instance. Whilst policy problems and solutions may be contested and ambiguous, they are stabilised as narratives of causes and effects through rationalities that emphasise their truth, transparency and necessity. These problem–solution narratives emphasise their empirical (and apparently incontestable) foundations as justifications for particular regulatory practices and interventions. These empirical justifications for particular practices become stabilised as facts, taken for granted realities/truths and common sense narratives. Roe (1994) emphasises the extent to which the assumptions that inform particular policy narratives may be resistant to change or modification even in the presence of contradictory empirical data. Indeed, Radaelli (1999) emphasises that the stability and authority of policy narratives, and the management of contradictions, often depends on their narrative character.

In emphasising heterogeneity over homogeneity, Stone (2002) foregrounds the extent to which any (apparently) singular policy narrative is imbricated in a multitude of other policy narratives through which the ambitions of government are materialised. Given that meaning is negotiated differently in particular times and spaces, there cannot be any single coherent policy, nor any single coherent meaning that can be implemented uniformly by different policy actors in different times and spaces. Rather, policy narratives are political technologies through which multiple and diffuse discourses, discursive practices and subject positions within discourse are brought together as (if) a singular, stable and authoritative narrative. The apparent objectivity, necessity or inevitability of a policy narrative is, in part, a function of the conventions of narrative and practices of narration through which it is articulated.

Acts of policy analysis that generate alternative policy narratives are contingent upon an understanding of policy as heterogeneous and unstable, and constituted through multiple practices of negotiation, contestation, agreement, compliance and resistance. Given that this authority is in need of constant maintenance, there are strategic opportunities for de-stabilising existing authority, establishing different narratives and generating different accounts and practices. This articulation of different narratives is political – it generates different ontological accounts of the social world and the citizen/subject. These differences emphasise the transience of otherwise apparently intransigent policy narratives, and create multiple and different worlds of practice – that is, different ontologies. The ontological politics I'm proposing here is one in which these differences are opened up as spaces for reappraisal and intervention through the generation of alternative narratives. Such a politics: intervenes in the processes, practices and relations of power through which policies have been materialised as narratives; and identifies what patterns of materiality and conditions of narratability support or contest their continued narrativisation, embodiment and enactment. This involves articulation of the heterogeneity, temporality and spatiality of narratives as socio-political technologies, and resists homogenous universalised accounts of policy as having the same meaning, and the same effects, here, there and everywhere.

In what follows, I identify four interconnected tactics or strategies for applying some of my ideas on a narrative approach to policy in an analysis of the Australian Labor Government's (2009) Higher Education agenda for the period 2009–2025 (an especially ambitious timetable considering the radical reforms proposed by the conservative government elected in 2013). These strategies aim to:

- examine the intersections among multiple heterogeneous policy narratives and resist the idea that a policy is a singular object of study;
- consider how policy narratives constitute particular social groups and individuals as problems in themselves;
- temporalise and spatialise particular policy discourses as narrative; and,
- reflect on the possibilities for generating new narratives.

Emphasising the heterogeneity of education policy

The narrative approach to policy analysis that I give here is not so much concerned with the deconstruction or discourse analysis of a single policy, but rather, with the ways in which any apparently single policy is constituted from an ensemble of multiple technologies and practices that are temporalised, spatialised and coordinated as narrative. As Rizvi and Lingard (2010) note, 'Critical policy analysis in an era of globalization requires that we recognize the relationality and interconnectivity of policy developments' (p. 69). I have argued that relationality and interconnectivity are critical to the development of an ontological politics and to an understanding of policy as narrative. Any apparently single policy (document or enactment) is situated within multiple heterogeneous ensembles of technologies, practices and ambitions of government that are connected across multiple temporalities and spatialities (local, national and global). This ensemble constitutes the every day worlds of practice through which subjectivities are constituted, regulated and made intelligible through narrative and practices of narration. These narratives also constitute particular subjects as problematic and in need of intervention; subjects who are simultaneously the 'cause' of the problem and the locus of its solution.

In 2009, the Australian Labor Government released a policy (Transforming Australia's Higher Education System 2009) aimed at increasing participation in Higher Education (40 per cent of 25–34 year olds to have an undergraduate degree by 2025, 20 per cent of these to be low Socio Economic Status (SES) students by 2020). This policy ambition specifically targets those young people who are currently underrepresented: 'those students disadvantaged by the circumstances of their birth'. Three specific taxonomies of young people are identified: Indigenous, those who live in regional and remote areas of Australia and low SES students.

In Australia, as in many nations whose economies and policies are regulated by international governing bodies (such as the OECD), education policies mandate pedagogical and financial interventions to improve the schooling outcomes for low

SES students. In education policy, low SES is often code for students from poor/ working class families, racial and religious minorities, and individuals and groups who do not embody the idealised, normative, social, cultural and economic identity articulated in the imaginary of education policy and politics. Within this framing, low SES students, their families and communities are constituted as a category of persons whose deficits are the target of equity policies, pedagogies and interventions that aim to develop the capacities, dispositions, values and aspirations needed to become 'other than low SES' (and other than working class). Further, this construction of the low SES subject elides heterogeneity: the singular self-same low SES student or community is a policy fiction. Rather, the diverse intersections of geography, race, ethnicity, religion, gender, sexuality (and so on), through which SES is constituted are necessarily elided. Similarly, multiple axes of discrimination are occluded by oversimplifications of low aspiration or poor preparation as barriers to participation in Higher Education. So, discourses of underrepresentation, equity, access, class, age and so on, are brought together in a narrative that produces a simultaneously singular and universal account of the low SES subject; and this subject is constituted as the locus of heterogeneous social and economic problems and solutions. Low SES subjects are also articulated as particular sorts of subjects across a range of policies, documents, research papers, statistical models, university outreach programmes (and so on). These are narrative technologies through which specific programmatic ambitions, rationalities and technologies of government constitute and regulate low SES subjects, along with narratives about them. Further, Higher Education is identified as a specific space of intervention; a space in which the temporalised problem/solution of future economic benefit, both individual and national, is located.

> Higher education is integral to achieving the Government's vision of a stronger and fairer Australia. It fuels economic development, productivity and high skilled jobs and supports Australia's role as a middle power and leader in the region.
>
> *(Transforming Australia's Higher Education System, 2009: 5)*

> Education is the key to an individual's social mobility and to a nation's economic prosperity. It enables individuals to achieve their full intellectual potential and widen their life choices; it also enables the nation to develop its intellectual capital and thereby achieve a highly skilled labour force. A university degree increases a person's social standing and job opportunities . . . People from low socio-economic status (LSES) backgrounds . . . have a right to share equitably in the economic benefits that higher education can provide.
>
> *(Devlin, 2004: 5)*

> Higher education confers significant personal benefit on individuals in terms of personal development, social standing, career possibilities and lifetime earnings. But it is also important for national and community development in producing a more equitable, cohesive and economically successful society.

> For the individuals and the nation, Australia must do all it can to ensure all
> those who can benefit from higher education are able to do so.
>
> *(Universities Australia, 2008: 1)*

In these accounts, the benefits of participation in Higher Education for low SES
students are constituted through the coordination of multiple discourses as a
narrative of progress. I suggest that there is a co-constitutive semiotic and material
relation/interconnection among these policy narratives that not only connects
multiple narratives and subjects, but also materialises socio-political narrative
configurations of discourses in which

education = economy = opportunity = individual prosperity = GDP =
global competitiveness = equity = social justice = citizenship = democracy =
freedom = capitalism.

Recalcitrant low SES subjects (those articulated as having low ambition and not
inclined to go to university) are thus narrated as a national economic problem (and
burden).

The constitution of particular policy subjects as problems in themselves

Policies that emphasise access and equity for low SES youth simultaneously constitute those young people, and their families, as problems in themselves. Education
is proposed as the solution to a problem that is not entirely individual, nor entirely
educational. Government ambitions for improved educational outcomes for students are also ambitions for the constitution and governance of a particular
iteration of citizen, society and nation. This nation-building project has in more
recent times become embedded in the concept of a 'knowledge economy'. In a
'knowledge economy' the pedagogic is conflated with the economic, and individual 'improvement' as a knowledge project is conflated with national improvement
as an economic project. Low SES students, and their perceived deficits in achievement and ambition, are inimical to national efficiency, productivity and competition
in global markets, and so become targets for intervention and reform.

   Educational policies and interventions targeting low SES subjects are invariably
located in social justice and equity frameworks. These frameworks are, in turn,
embedded in the economic ambitions of government and the nation-state. This
policy relationship works to fuse the social with the economic by conflating: class,
race and poverty with poor educational outcomes; school performance with labour
market participation; the aspirations and productivity of individuals with the ambitions of the nation; and personal and national prosperity with international
competitiveness in a global knowledge economy. In these ways, the pedagogical
project of improving the educational outcomes of students from low SES backgrounds is imbricated in a larger social, economic and political narrative project of
improving the global competitiveness of the nation.

The subject of educational policy is also imbricated in a pedagogical project of class, race and nation building assigned to students, education institutions and teachers. This assignation is an act of epistemological enclosure, as it limits the locus of intervention to narrowly defined pedagogical practices, curricula and performance benchmarks, and ignores the social practices and relations through which knowledges and identities are unequally made and lived within and against the ambitions of government. Low SES subjects (and their families and communities) are narrated as the problematic product of their histories (intergenerational poverty, welfare dependence, lack of ambition), whose identities and future lives must be refigured to align with the ambitions of government. What is at issue here (among many things) is the temporal refiguration of the future desired by government as the desired future of the low SES subject.

Temporalising and spatialising educational policy

At the same time as policy narratives articulate desired subjects and futures in local spaces, they are typically de-personalised, de-temporalised and de-spatialised as disinterested and transparent accounts of the ways things are and must be. Countering this, I locate the education policy narratives through which ambitions for increased participation in Higher Education by low SES subjects are configured, in the spatio-temporal technologies of neoliberalism. As Rizvi and Lingard (2010) argue, neoliberalism has become the global social imaginary in the late twentieth and early twenty-first centuries, involving a complex mix of empirical, cognitive and affective aspects that exceeds the confines of pure rationality.

Importantly, the rationality and intelligibility of education policy narratives are co-implicated in narratives of the economy and the market. 'Redefining social and ethical life in accordance with economic criteria and expectations, neoliberalism holds that human freedom is best achieved through the operation of markets' (Dean, 2009: 51). Market logic, as Connell (2003) points out, functions as a meta-policy governing all areas of public life. Increasingly, the rationalities, technologies and ambitions of neoliberalism are configured, and refigured, as matters of economics. This is a technology of economisation (Caliskan and Callon, 2009) through which 'society' is refigured as 'economy', the social refigured as the economic, and the subject refigured as an economic agent. Policy, as a narrative technology of government, co-ordinates the multiple heterogeneous elements/entities through which this economisation prefigures the conditions of possibility and intelligibility through which socio-political life is constituted. Narrative is, in this sense, a socio-technical/socio-political apparatus through which what comes to matter is always a matter of the economy.

In this context, 'what passes as policy', is 'the attempt to expand the reach of markets, or to create markets where they did not exist before' (Connell, 2003: 46). As seen in the iterations of educational policy addressed earlier in this chapter, there is a conflation of education policy and economic policy that is explicitly directed towards labour market participation in a competitive global knowledge economy/market. However, it is not clear to what extent the expansion of low SES participation in higher education will indeed translate into more equitable labour markets, especially in the context of contracting full-time employment, poor graduate employment opportunities, increased casualisation of labour and contract work and underemployment. Further, hierarchical stratification and competition between Higher Education institutions and courses may simply translate into the continued hierarchical stratification of degrees and graduates and their labour market opportunities.

In considering the influence and reach of neoliberalism, Ball (2006) points out how neoliberalism has shifted the very grounds of what it is possible to think. Its impact 'has been discursive, that is it has facilitated a discursive reworking of the parameters of political possibility and acceptability' (p. 39). This involves, I suggest, the prefiguration of conditions of intelligibility and narratability, the configuration of practices of narration, and the refiguration of embodied subjects. These acts of prefiguration, configuration and refiguration normalise and embed neoliberal rationalities, ambitions, assumptions and worldviews in the embodied narratives and narrative practices of subject/citizens. They constitute and regulate what is legitimate (or even possible) to think, say, do, imagine, anticipate and desire in the service of neoliberal ambitions of prosperity – which results in the unequal distribution of wealth rather than equity.

> To retain its dominant position neoliberalism . . . has to offer something to the people whose lives it shapes. It has to structure their expectations and desires so that it feels right, like the way things just are. It can't say directly, 'Hey, you guys go work really hard so that rich people can get even richer.'
>
> *(Dean, 2009: 50)*

What counter-narratives of in/equity might we tell, and how might we tell them?

Reflecting on possibilities for new narratives

Since policy narratives typically occlude the diverse and multiple relations, technologies and ambitions through which socio-political realties and subjectivities are constituted, a strategy for analysis and intervention is to make visible that which has been occluded. Education policy narratives that assume a homogeneous low SES subject, and that increased participation by low SES subjects in Higher Education will (inevitably) produce subject/citizens with equal ambitions, aspirations, capacities, opportunities and outcomes, are opened to critique, contestation and revision through the generation of alternative narratives. These alternative narratives will give accounts of heterogeneous and contradictory subjects, relations and ambitions that destabilise the normative assumptions made in particular policy narratives and problems. For Touraine (2001), the point of identifying and analysing a problem is to resist becoming 'caught up in the logic of the crisis they helped to reveal' (p. 114). Here (some of) the logic to be avoided includes un-problematised accounts of: Low SES subjects, families and communities; equity, access and the promises of modernity and capitalism; and the inevitability, necessity and domination of the international knowledge economy, of the market and the enterprise model of commerce refigured as (the ambition of) the subject/citizen.

In refiguring policy as narrative, and policy narratives as technologies of government, I have given an account of a narrative approach to education policy analysis that augments practices of deconstruction and discourse analysis by emphasising the coordination of multiple discourses and practices in and as narratives. This de-emphasises the ways in which policy is assumed to confer meaning onto socio-political reality and experience, and emphasises an account of policy as a socio-political narrative technology through which realities and subject/citizens are prefigured, configured and refigured.

This narrative approach to policy analysis foregrounds the extent to which the ambitions of government – such as equity, social justice, prosperity and wellbeing – can be refigured through the generation of alternative narratives; narratives that emphasise multiple different dilemmas, ambitions, causes, effects and solutions. Further, if policy problems and solutions are configured through the temporal organisation of relations among entities/identities as narrative, they can be configured differently: that is, they can be refigured. This works towards opening space for refiguring the narrative 'if we don't follow these steps now, undesirable things will happen'. This is a space in which different narratives of the real, the conditions of possibility we live with and the political might be given. This is the work of the education policy analyst.

References

Ball, S. (2006). *Education policy and social class*. London and New York: Routledge.

Butler, J. (2004). *Undoing gender*. New York and London: Routledge.

Caliskan, K. and Callon, M. (2009). Economization part 1: Shifting attention from the economy to processes of economization. *Economy and Society*, *38*(3), 369–398.

Commonwealth of Australia. (2009). Transforming Australia's Higher Education System, Commonwealth of Australia. www.innovation.gov.au/highereducation/Documents/TransformingAusHigherED.pdf.

Connell, R. W. (2003). Working-class families and the new secondary education. *Australian Journal of Education*, *47*(3), 237–252.

Dean, M. M. (2009). *Governmentality: Power and rule in modern society*. Thousand Oaks, CA: Sage.

Devlin, Y. (2004). A review of the participation of students from low socio-economic background at the University of New South Wales. www.adcet.edu.au/EdEquity/View.aspx?id=5234.

Foucault, M. (1978–1979). The birth of biopolitics: Lectures at the College de France 1978–1979. In M. Senellart (2008) (Ed.), *Michel Foucault, the birth of biopolitics: Lectures at the College de France 1978–1979*. Basingstoke, UK and New York: Palgrave Macmillan.

Foucault, M. (1991). *Discipline and punish: The birth of the prison*, (trans A. Sheridan). London: Penguin.

Foucault, M. (2002). *The archaeology of knowledge*. London: Routledge.

Jones, M. D. and McBeth, M. K. (2010). A narrative policy framework: Clear enough to be wrong? *Policy Studies Journal*, *38*, 329–353.

Massey, D. (2005). *For space*. London: Sage.

Mol, A. (1999). Ontological politics: A word and some questions. In J. Law and J. Hassard (Eds.), *Actor Network Theory and after* (pp. 74–89). Oxford, UK: Blackwell.

Radaelli, C. M. (1999). Harmful tax competition in the EU: Policy narratives and advocacy coalitions. *Journal of Market Studies*, *37*, 661–682.

Ricoeur, P. (1984, 1985, 1988). *Time and narrative (Vols. 1, 2 and 3)*. Trans. K. Blamey and D. Pellaur. Chicago, IL and London: University of Chicago.

Rizvi, F. and Lingard, B. (2010). *Globalizing education policy*. London and New York: Routledge.

Roe, E. (1994). *Narrative policy analysis: Theory and practice*. Durham, NC: Duke University Press.

Stone, D. (2002). *Policy paradox: The art of political decision making* (3rd revised edition). New York: W. W. Norton.

Touraine, A. (2001). *Beyond neoliberalism*. London: Polity Press.

Universities Australia. (2008). Advancing Equity and Participation in Australian Higher Education (April). www.universitiesaustralia.edu.au.

16

QUEER THEORY, POLICY AND EDUCATION

Mary Lou Rasmussen and Christina Gowlett

Marcus Weaver-Hightower and Christine Skelton (2013), in the introduction to their book *Leaders in gender and education: Intellectual self-portraits*, point to shifts in the way that gender has been theorised in the field of education and some of the tensions that this has created, particularly mentioning the introduction of poststructuralist and postmodern turns in gender theories beginning in the mid-1980s and continuing today. Queer theory is part of this poststructuralist and postmodern turn which

> created rifts between feminists engaging in policy creation (an intrinsically normative activity) and those 'post-' positions deeply skeptical of engagement with policy and the state . . . In return, earlier feminists lament the withdrawal from activism and engagement with schools represented in mainly theoretical projects.
>
> *(Weaver-Hightower and Skelton, 2013: 8)*

We, therefore, see queer theory as relevant to those working on policy issues related to gender and sexuality in education because it can provide one mechanism by which people can challenge fixed ideas about identity and subjectivity when they underpin policy production.

There have also been some divisions within queer research in education and this also has implications for how the relationship between queer theory and policy in education is conceived. As Talburt and Rasmussen (2010: 1) indicate:

> Research hailing itself as queer theory has often tethered itself to subjects of gender and sexuality and to narratives of political progress. Despite many creative projects that interrogate pleasures of teaching and learning (McWilliam, 1999), imagine queer pedagogies (Britzman, 1995; Kumashiro,

2002; Luhmann, 1998), or rethink the implications of queer research (Haver, 1997; Honeychurch, 1996), queer theory has [often] been limited by researchers' imaginings of a need for a 'subject' of queer research and particular ideas of educational and political progress.

Our preference is for a queer theory that is not read as gay and lesbian studies. Rather, we see queer theory as of use 'for interrogations of all normative and non-normative acts, identities, desires, perceptions and possibilities' (Giffney, 2004: 73). There is a strong historic association of queer theorising with studies of gender and sexuality. We believe that this association, while important, has also constrained the possibility of conceptual ideas that may be associated with queer theory – performativity, intelligibility and misrecognition – from drifting into other areas of policy research and exposing the constraints embedded in everyday and 'common sense' practices and logics of thinking in schools, education and the policies that govern them.

Below we give a brief outline of queer theory and its relationship to the scholarship of Judith Butler and Michel Foucault, two key figures associated with this body of work. Our work commences with Butler, whose work *arguably* has been more influential in the production of queer research in education. Both theorists would baulk at the idea of being classified principally as queer theorists because of the essentialising tendencies associated with such a moniker. We also consider the significance of queer theory for education policy within the context of education policy related to studies of gender and sexuality, and also beyond this frame.

What is queer theory?

Teresa de Lauretis is credited with coining the term 'queer theory' in 1990 (1991). According to David Halperin (2003), a historian of sexuality, de Lauretis used the term to mark as problematic sexuality research that too often focused on the experiences of gay, white, middle class, men from the global north. Gloria Anzaldua (1991) also warns against the problems of using queer as an umbrella term that often erases class, ethnic and racial differences between people associated with the term. 'Queer' theory draws on the pejorative queer in order to draw attention to the labels people use to describe genders and sexualities in different historical and cultural contexts. Queer theorists perceive the categories that are used to describe gender and sexuality as powerful regulatory fictions. These categories, which are shaped by heteronormative religious, political, national and transnational institutions categorise groups of people privileging those who conform most closely to heteronorms (monogamous, married, fertile, white, middle class, heterosexual). Another key element in queer theory is a critique of essentialism. Diana Fuss (1989) describes essentialism as belief in a true essence or authentic self. The notion that one is born lesbian or straight is a form of essentialism. Essentialists believe they come to know who they are by coming to terms with themselves as straight or gay or lesbian or trans or intersex. In this sense, the search for a self is motivated by the desire to understand one's essence. Queer theorists critique the notion of an essential self.

Jasbir Puar (2006) also decisively illustrates how 'homonationalism' (the relationship between homosexuality and the trans/national state) works to construct 'heteronormativity as temporally and spatially stable, uninflected and transparent'. For Puar much queer theoretical work 'fails to theorize the class-, race- and gender-specific dimensions of heteronormativity' (2006: 71). This tendency to smooth over the differences between people is related to the notion of 'homonormativity'. Lisa Duggan (2004) in her book *The twilight of equality* developed the notion of homonormativity to denote queer politics that is anti-democratic and does not contest heteronormative assumptions or institutions. In this sense struggles for gay marriage, gays in the military, or even gay proms at high school may be seen as at odds with queer theory. Two other key figures associated with queer theory are Judith Butler and Michel Foucault.

Judith Butler and queer theory

Judith Butler draws on several key theorists including Michel Foucault, Jacques Derrida, Louis Althusser, J. L. Austin and Sigmund Freud. Her most famous text is *Gender trouble: Feminism and the subversion of identity* (1990/1999), the second edition of which provides a Preface in which Butler valuably reflects on the key arguments of this dense text as well as providing some interpretations of her own work.

For Butler sex (male, female), gender (masculine, feminine) and sexuality (lesbian, gay, bisexual, heterosexual) are not fixed, nor are they dependent upon one another. In this sense, sex, gender and sexuality are performative. This notion of performativity is likely Butler's key contribution to queer theorising. This concept perceives sex, gender and sexualities as conventions that are produced by processes of repetition over time. Gender norms may appear to be expressing what is natural, but for Butler this appearance of gender as timeless, essential or somehow natural conceals the production of norms about gender that are definitely not timeless, stable or natural.

Butler's contribution to queer theorising is significant because she prompts us to recognise the instability of identities. It is this instability that opens up possibilities for thinking about and doing gender, sex and sexualities differently, though Butler's later work also suggests the possibilities for this reworking are highly constrained. Butler's notion of performativity also makes it possible to see how struggles related to gender and sexual norms are not specifically related to individuals, but to techniques of power that endeavour to control or classify individuals through specific discourses. Consequently, we can see that discourses that might, for example, aim to be inclusive of boys in education, are not about one specific boy, but rather classify all boys as having specific educational requirements, because they are boys. In this manner, policies which may endeavour to be inclusive of boys who are seen to be disengaged at school, might also be read as specific techniques of power that essentialise boys in particular ways.

Butler is careful to distinguish the concept of performativity from notions of performance: 'while the latter presumes a subject, the former contests the very notion of the subject' (1993: 33). Performativity is usually associated with speech act theory and 'in this framework, a performative is that discursive practice that enacts or produces that which it names' (Butler, 1993: 13). This Butlerian rejection of performance is underpinned by the Foucaultian notion that 'power is not invested in a single divine subject' (Salih, 2002: 107). When power is not invested in the subject, then the subject may not simply adopt or reject constitutive labels. There is a recognition that some subjects are willingly labelled while others may 'not willingly embrace though will nonetheless be constituted' (Salih, 2002: 106–107) by the names they are assigned (Rasmussen and Harwood, 2003: 32).

In plainer terms, Butler helps us to see that it doesn't make sense to declare that you are 'gay' or 'gifted' unless there is some broader categorical understanding about what 'gayness' or 'giftedness' refers to as an identity category. Other 'regulatory fictions' can also be examined using a Butlerian analysis. For instance, normative categorisations of Indigenous peoples continue to change according to (often racist) systems of classification devised by colonial powers. Looking back at the construction of categories over time it is possible to see 'regulatory fictions' that rationalise and reinforce discrimination. *Importantly, this process of looking back at the history of identity categories is not motivated by the search for the origins of identity.*

Michel Foucault and queer theory

Michel Foucault (1926–1984), a French philosopher and historian of ideas, is integrally associated with queer theory. Foucault's notion of discourse is a critical concept in queer theory. In the *History of sexuality,* Vol. 1 (1978/1990), Foucault demonstrates how discourses (speech acts) form us as objects, and they are also how we come to know ourselves as gendered and sexual subjects. Discourse is not something over which individuals have control because we are constructed as men and women, boys and girls, straight and queer, black and white, through competing figures of speech that precede us, surround us, and have a future with, or without us. In this way, discourse operates as a form of disciplinary power (which is different to the power of the state or *sovereign power*). In a piece entitled 'Critical perspectives on race and schooling' David Gillborn and Deborah Youdell (2009) elaborate on this notion of disciplinary power and its relationship to the racialisation of subjects in education. They argue the Foucaultian notion 'of discourse and its productive force is a central concept for thinking about race not as biologically or culturally fixed but as the *product* of prevailing discourses that *make* race and ethnicity [appear] as *if* they were biologically or culturally fixed' (pp. 180–181).

For Foucault, an act such as coming out as gay or lesbian might be classified as a 'truth effect' or a practice of disciplinary power. Coming out, for instance, is frequently understood as a therapeutic discourse, a public embrace of gayness that conventionally evidences the freedom of the gay subject because it enables them to speak the truth about themselves. But utilising a Foucaultian understanding of discourse it is possible to question the logic of coming out. Coming out only makes sense within a discursive framework in which we understand sexual desire as something innate. In this way of seeing, certain types of sexual subjects come to understand themselves as gay or lesbian. But, following Foucault, it is possible to read the act of coming out as principally the confirmation of a fable, produced by expert knowledges about the psyche and sexuality, which continue to evolve over time. For Foucault, the process of coming out is located within the regulatory frameworks that continuously classify sexual acts and identities as moral and immoral, legal and illegal, abhorrent and worthy of tolerance.

In this conception of discourse the stories we tell about sexuality and gender are discontinuous and contradictory and are therefore fluid and capable of change, as well as being susceptible to challenge. Even while discourse related to sexuality and gender may be characterised as 'truth effects,' this is not to say that these discourses are not powerful. Education policies can also be understood as powerful discourses that are discontinuous and contradictory. An example of this discontinuity relates to the employment of teachers in Australia. Gay male sex was only decriminalised in Victoria in 1980 and this process of decriminalisation has necessarily changed laws related to the employment of teachers who are openly gay (Marshall, 2014). It is now recognised that public schools cannot discriminate against teachers on the basis of their sexual or gender identity. However, most Australian states continue to allow religious exemptions that permit discrimination on the basis of sexuality and marital status in employment of teachers (Evans and Ujvari, 2009). Some religious schools are also asking teachers to sign lifestyle agreements that require teachers to reflect school values in their private lives (Maddox, 2014) – teachers who are living with partners but are not married, or who are single and pregnant may be construed as having contradicted a school's lifestyle agreement. In thinking about educational policy, one might ask if it is contradictory to have educational policies that simultaneously mandate that teachers and students may not be discriminated against on the basis of sexual and gender identity, but concurrently allow for religious exemptions in hiring in a proportion of Australian private schools, that also receive government funding. We tell this story about law and associated education policy not with a view to determining which discourse is right on the question of sexuality, but rather in attempt to illustrate the instability of discourse.

In *Wounds and reinscriptions: Schools, sexualities and performative subjects* an ethnographic study of boys, homophobia and different types of masculinity in school contexts, Deborah Youdell (2004) draws on the work of Butler and Foucault to highlight the limits of equal rights and antidiscrimination-based policies and interventions. She does this by using an ethnographic approach to examine how 'identity categories, including those of gender and sexuality, constitute subjects. These categorical names are central to the performative interpellation of the subject who is unintelligible, if not unimaginable, without these' (p. 481). In order to exist as a boy you need to be hailed as a boy, but there are many ways to be hailed as a boy and the fag discourse is a powerful way by which boys are hailed as gendered and sexual subjects. While Youdell's research was published in 2004, more recent research also reports on and further complicates young men's use of the fag discourse (see C. J Pascoe's *Dude, you're a fag* (2011)). Using educational ethnography Pascoe (2011) and Youdell illustrate how day-to-day practices constitute students as particular types of subjects (fags) in ways that are both injurious and part of friendship discourses. Either way, such language is not easily regulated by policy reform (2004). Youdell (2004) helps us understand how such everyday performatives – 'Dude, you're a fag' – are important for grasping the limits of policy reform and to why 'social justice policies and programmes have not shifted radically, in the ways hoped for, the inequalities with which they have been concerned' (p. 490).

Thinking about policy with Foucault and Butler, it is possible to perceive policy as a form of disciplinary power – exercising power over students, teachers and schools and operating to incite particular bodily citations, expert knowledges and regulatory practices. Education policy is thus one of the 'regulatory fictions' by which schools, students and educational institutions come into being within and outside the field of education. Education policies that fail to apprehend the significance of norms and deficit-based discourses in framing people's access to, everyday experiences of, and desires for education – inadvertently contribute to people's disengagement and can limit how they might imagine their own and others' educational futures.

Miscrecognition, precarity and gender

The fag discourse, referred to above, might also be understood as part of the politics of misrecognition. This notion of recognition relates to the absence or refusal of recognition and it is central to the politics of recognition (Schippers, 2014: 24). For instance, recognising, or misrecognising students as gay, trans, gifted or special needs will put into play a chain of events that will influence students' own sense of themselves (processes of subjectivation and identification), it may also shape how others perceive them (parents, peers, future employers) and thereby shape the futures they imagine for themselves and their aspirations. This is why recognition and misrecognition have been, and continue to be, considered crucial concepts in queer theory.

In *The political philosophy of Judith Butler* Birgit Schippers (2014: 25) writes that Butler's contribution to debates about recognition and misrecognition pertains particularly to the attention she pays to how recognition relates to corporeality (the significance of body morphology and sexual difference which she defines in *Undoing gender* as 'the site where a question concerning the relation of the biological to the cultural is posed and reposed . . . but where it cannot, strictly speaking, be answered' (Butler, 2004: 186), and intersubjectivity (the processes whereby we come to understand ourselves as gendered and sexual subjects). Related to both of these is the question of liveability – how does the way in which our gender and sexuality is recognised (or fails to be recognised) influence our capacity to engage in work, education and relationships? How does it influence our sense of ourselves (psyche), our bodies (somatics), and our relations to others (social)? Do school uniform policies, for instance, enable young people to become intelligible as a gendered subject in a manner that reflects their body morphology? Is it possible for students and teachers whose bodies are perceived as non-normative to engage in different educational contexts – so questions of recognition are also relevant to people with disabilities and to students who are pregnant and parenting. Does the misrecognition of their morphology limit their access to different educational contexts?

In the context of this text's focus on education policy, it is worthwhile thinking about how misrecognition in education can play a role in designating certain subjects as precarious. Judith Butler draws on the notion of *precarity* to describe 'a politically induced condition in which certain populations suffer from failing social and economic networks of support and become differentially exposed to injury, violence, and death' (2009: ii). To our minds, it is imperative that education policy also attends to questions related to populations of students who are differentially exposed to injury, violence and death. One contemporary international example of precarity in education relates to the right of girls to attend school. This right is under assault in places like Nigeria, Afghanistan and Pakistan (Shah, 2014).

For Butler (2009: ii), such manifestations of precarity can be

> directly linked with gender norms, since we know that those who do not live their genders in intelligible ways are at heightened risk for harassment and violence. Gender norms have everything to do with how and in what way we can appear in public space; how and in what way the public and private are distinguished, and how that distinction is instrumentalised in the service of sexual politics . . . who will fail to be protected by the law . . . on the job, or in the home [or at school]. So these norms are not only instances of power; and they do not only reflect broader relations of power; they are one way that power operates.

Following on from this, it is important to question how it might be possible to devise policy which publicly supports young women who wish to attend school – especially in contexts where such a decision may place them and their families at risk.

Young people who are exploring their sexual and gender identifications within the context of the school may also be constituted as precarious subjects. They may strive to become intelligible as lesbian, gay, bisexual and transgendered subjects while also recognising the risks associated with gender and sexual-based violence within school contexts. It is therefore important to consider those school practices and policies that reinscribe specific gender and sexual identities while erasing others from view.

For example, unisex bathrooms are rarely at the forefront of struggles for equality in schools, yet for some students access to such facilities within the school can provide respite from frequent harassment in sex-specific toilets and change rooms.

Thus, the implementation of such policies might be critical in enabling people to engage in school. In these ways we can draw on Butler's writing to construct alternative practices and policies which disrupt essentialist understandings of sexual and gender identity, recognise and combat precarity, while simultaneously apprehending some of the material requirements necessary to live as a trans student or teacher within the secondary school context.

What's the relevance of 'queer(y)ing' for education policy beyond the study of sexuality and gender?

Applying queer conceptual ideas can be thought of as a methodological approach to doing research, and in this sense, has profound utility for the area of policy analysis. The act of using queer theory – 'queer(y)ing' – is a mode of inquiry that interrogates borders and boundaries (Gowlett, 2014: 407). It unsettles and un-anchors ontological and epistemological claims often thought to be natural and common sense, and it does so without the intention of reinstating another hegemonic norm. Queer(y)ing can also be a form of political critique since it draws upon confounding examples that disrupt the logic of 'common sense' thinking at play (Britzman, 1995: 157). It is consequently concerned with questioning the social order and in Atkinson and DePalma's (2007: 67) words, 'keeping questions open when faced with the temptation of easy certainties'.

Queer(y)ing a dominant understanding of policy through a Butlerian prism would likely first involve an analysis of the normative understandings about it – what Butler (1990: 24) would call the 'rules of intelligibility' – in operation at the site and/or context being examined and then an analysis of either a disruption to those norms (hence questioning their utility) or the consequent positioning of people in relation to those norms. We offer two examples of what this may 'look like', with the two functioning in quite different ways.

For instance, Gowlett (2013) explores the dominant understandings seemingly associated with the application of new schooling accountability policies. 'New schooling accountabilities' being the most recent wave of managerial auditing policies sweeping across many western contexts. In this vein, she makes the argument that there are three dominant understandings (intelligibilities) in circulation. These are:

1 that they (new schooling accountabilities) make schooling test-focused;
2 that they narrow curricula; and
3 that they induce prescription 'from above' about the most appropriate methods for effective schooling, thus creating a formulaic and generic approach to 'best practice'.

She draws upon policy literature to make this claim. She does not discredit these norms, but suggests that policy researchers, by consistently focusing on the constraints, self-perpetuate this narrative. She then goes on to explore how one particular case study school is enacting policy accountability pressures quite differently – in a way that disrupts this monolithic representation. The case study school has a complicated relationship with these norms. It is able to rework the norms in a manner that fosters student inclusion and post-schooling opportunity by thinking differently about managing accountability pressures. This alternate thinking was driven by the school's initial unintelligibility since on regular testing measures, the school used to perform quite badly.

Instead of teaching to the test and narrowing curricula (as was, and often still is, the norm) the school uses student performance data to open up conversations about pedagogy and curriculum that feeds into discussions about student access to learning. It uses student grades to discredit the idea that the students are incapable, and instead uses data to show teachers what the students are good at, thus pushing the agenda to provide a more challenging learning environment for the students.

The importance of examining disruptions to the intelligible is thus an important political project. It creates alternative ontological possibilities where students may move from being seen as having little chance of thriving within school because of poor test scores, to a context in whereby the same data enables teachers to fashion curriculum in order to enhance learning outcomes. The unintelligibility of students' capacity, within the grid of Australia's National Assessment Program in Numeracy and Literacy (NAPLAN), drove the school to create policies and curricula that reworked norms about student performance. Foregrounding these disruptions can be considered a form of 'counter-politics', a term Youdell (2011: 15) uses to describe the 'everyday struggles and resistances enacted by students, teachers or others in the practices of their everyday lives'. Thinking otherwise, by embracing the counter-narratives, unsettles ideas that have seemingly become obvious and grants space to alternative and/or subjugated knowledges. The field of policy analysis already benefits from this way of engaging in political action.

Examining how people within educational settings are positioned in relation to policy intelligibilities is another way to invoke a queer(y)ing methodology. For example, Gowlett (2012) explores the enactment of Senior Education and Training (SET) plans at an outer-metropolitan school in Queensland, Australia. This policy was introduced across the State and serves to ensure that there is a formal process in place to help students select their senior schooling subjects. At the case study school Gowlett examined, teachers possessed quite deficit-based understandings about their students. For instance, one teacher involved in the counselling process made the following comment:

> I have tried my absolute best, and I've worked really hard to get them into direct entry to university. I write up special considerations. I believe I'm giving them an opportunity . . . I've got kids in with straight Ds simply based on their home environment, the abuse they've gone through or the lack of opportunities they've had. All sorts of limits. I've written up pretty persuasive stories as to why they should be given an opportunity. I can only do that. That's how I can help. That's how I'm trying to break through that generational

poverty. Otherwise, those kids wouldn't get in, they'd get a little job at Hungry Jacks or K-Mart, get themselves pregnant and have three kids by the time they're 21 and they would just continue generational poverty. I don't know what else we can do . . . I think we all do our best and I certainly persist and do what I can and give kids an opportunity to break out of generational poverty. It's just that mental culture . . . After all, mum has done alright hasn't she? They're all living on government assistance and their six kids and they're doing okay. That's all they know . . . The local community is the world – THE world. If you have to go into the city, I mean, oh God! It's like going to a foreign country for them.

These injurious assumptions, linked to gender and socio-economic status, were routinely used by teachers enacting the new state-based education policy related to SET plans. These assumptions are injurious because they form the contours of recognisable subjecthood and thus bring into being a constrained form of social existence for the students at the case study school. Butler's work encompasses the idea that language has an ontological effect. Language 'sustains the body, not by bringing it into being or feeding it in a literal way; rather, it is by being interpellated within the terms of language that a certain social existence of the body first becomes possible' (Butler, 1997: 5). This means that language, like that used by the teacher above, has the ability to injure because it defines the parameters of understanding about people's actions. By using Butlerian-inspired queer theory, Gowlett illustrates how students at the school are positioned by these preconceived ideas, and thus have their future pathway imaginings constrained as a result of them.

We draw upon these two examples to help illustrate the utility of queer theory in policy more generally. 'Queer(y)ing' (written as 'queer' with an insertion of a 'y' to pay homage to its origins in gender and sexualities research while also relating it to the act of raising questions) is a post-foundationalist way of doing research. In other words, it disrupts epistemological and ontological premises and is therefore *de*constructive in mindset. Importantly, it is not a version of deconstruction that aims to find an end result and/or put forward a new method of 'best practice'. On the contrary, queer(y)ing seeks to unsettle the social order and raises questions about who the social order stands to serve, who benefits from it, and how those not recognised within it are subsequently positioned. Cultural intelligibilities are everywhere and queer theory is a useful method of analysis for drawing attention to seemingly neutral normative expectations. Policies are made and enacted, but within them, there are particular logics of thinking that shape what we deem as normal and legitimate behaviour. Queer theory is consequently useful for analysing the boundaries of acceptability created by, in and through the enactment of policy. It is useful for exploring the way policy serves particular interests. Importantly, queer(y)ing can also highlight fissures and cracks in the dominant logic at play and by doing so, question the utility of what is deemed common sense.

A recurring analytic in education policy analysis has been the understanding of policy 'take up' in schools. Much attention has consequently been given to making sense of the various interpretations, translations and enactments of policy. According to Braun, Ball and Maguire (2011: 3), policy enactment is 'the creative process of interpretation and recontextualisation – that is, the translation of texts into action and the abstractions of policy ideas into contextualised practices'. Queer theory is a most suitable conceptual framework to be suturing into policy enactment literature since it delves deeply into sedimented knowledges and the creation of those knowledges in particular spaces and places. Importantly, queer theory also has the potential to explore the positioning of people in relation to the norms under investigation, thus encouraging an even deeper level of policy analysis.

Queer theory is useful for examining the complexity and messiness of policy. In this respect, it complements the existing body of policy literature exploring small-scale case studies to help generate broader understandings about policy implementation in schools (for example, Braun, Ball, Maguire and Hoskins, 2011; Thomson, Hall and Jones, 2010). Queer theory can draw attention to the idiosyncratic, which is too often side-lined, despite its importance.

Conclusion

The use of queer theory in education policy might prompt an interrogation of how policy operates as a form of disciplinary power. Disciplinary power can profoundly influence the way individuals conduct themselves and also the ways in which they might apprehend people and practices in their education contexts. Keeping this formation of disciplinary power in mind, one might ask – how does education policy play a part in fashioning different contours of recognisability related to diverse bodies, sexualities, genders? Education about inclusion is often focused elsewhere. Would having a policy that mandated schools, or teacher education faculties dedicated more/some time to discussions of issues related to bodies, sexualities and genders have desired effects? Is it possible to agree in advance what the desired effects of education policies related to bodies, sexualities and genders might be? In part, Rasmussen's *Becoming subjects* (2006), studies how policies related to peoples' understanding of sexualities and genders lead to quite radically different approaches to inclusion – from the production of Gay, Lesbian, Straight Education Networks – through to the repudiation of such networks because of their perceived essentialising tendencies. It is crucial that policy formation be informed by an understanding that while we might think we need a policy, we can never really predict what effects policy might have. This is all the more reason to continue to interrogate how expert knowledges and regulatory fictions are insinuated through all aspects of the policy process.

The use of queer theory in education policy analysis also provokes us to think about the cultural intelligibilities that policy incites. New policies are always emerging at both the system and school level, what normative ideas are embedded in them? Importantly, what normative ideas are entrenched in long-standing education policies and practices often deemed to be neutral and 'common sense'? For example, what normative intelligibilities underpin university pre-requisites? If certain subjects (like advanced mathematics) are so important to the completion of a degree, why is the content not integrated into the university degree in question? Are pre-requisites a disciplinary technique used by universities to shape senior secondary school curriculum offerings? We use this as an example because university pre-requisites are so embedded in the everyday workings of senior schooling and university entrance, and as such, are rarely questioned. What other education policies remain and operate as unquestioned? Furthermore, queer theory invites scholars to examine how intelligibilities are disrupted, fractured and reworked. Importantly, these three features of a queer(y)ing methodology are useful for thinking about policy relating to and extending beyond gender and sexualities research.

References

Anzaldúa, G. (1991). To(o) queer the writer: Loca, escrita y chicana. In B. Warland (Ed.), *In Versions: Writing by dykes, queers and lesbians*. Vancouver: Press Gang.

Atkinson, E. and DePalma, R. (2007). Exploring gender identity: Queering heteronormativity. *International Journal of Equity and Innovation in Early Childhood, 5*, 68–82.

Braun, A., Ball, S. J. and Maguire, M. (2011). Policy enactments in schools (introduction): Towards a toolbox for theory and research. *Discourse: Studies in the Cultural Politics of Education, 32*(4), 581–583.

Braun, A., Ball, S. J., Maguire, M. and Hoskins, K. (2011). Taking context seriously: Towards explaining policy enactments in the secondary school. *Discourse: Studies in the Cultural Politics of Education, 32*(4), 585–596.

Britzman, D. (1995). Is there a queer pedagogy? Or, stop reading straight? *Educational Theory, 45*(2), 151–165.

Butler, J. (1990). *Gender trouble: Feminism and the subversion of identity*. London: Routledge.

Butler, J. (1993). *Bodies that matter: On the discursive limits of 'sex'*. New York: Routledge.

Butler, J. (1997). *Excitable speech: A politics of the performative*. New York: Routledge.

Butler, J. (2004). *Undoing gender*. New York: Routledge.

Butler, J. (2009). Performativity, precarity and sexual politics. *AIBR: Revista de Antropología Iberoamericana, 4*(3), i–xii.

de Lauretis, T. (1991). Queer theory: Lesbian and gay sexualities. *Differences: A Journal of Feminist Cultural Studies, 3*(2), iii–xviii.

Duggan, L. (2004). *The twilight of equality: Neoliberalism, cultural politics and the attack on democracy*. Boston, MA: Beacon Press.

Evans, C. and Ujvari, L. (2009). Non-discrimination laws and religious schools in Australia. *Adelaide Law Review, 30*, 31–56.

Foucault, M. (1990). *The history of sexuality: An introduction, Volume 1*. New York: Vintage Books.

Fuss, D. (1989). *Essentially speaking: Feminism, nature and difference*. New York: Routledge.

Giffney, N. (2004). Denormatizing queer theory: More than (simply) lesbian and gay studies. *Feminist Theory, 5*, 73–74.

Gillborn, D. and Youdell, D. (2009). Critical perspectives on race and schooling. In James A. Banks (Ed.), *The Routledge international companion to multicultural education* (pp. 173–185). New York: Routledge.

Gowlett, C. (2012). Injurious assumptions: Butler, subjectification and gen(d)erational poverty. *International Journal of Inclusive Education, 16*(9), 885–900.

Gowlett, C. (2013). Queer(y)ing new schooling accountabilities through my school: Using Butlerian tools to think differently about policy performativity. *Educational Philosophy and Theory*. doi: 10.1080/00131857.2013.793926.

Gowlett, C. (2014). Queer(y)ing and recrafting agency: Moving away from a model of coercion versus escape. *Discourse: Studies in the Cultural Politics of Education, 35*(3), 405–418.

Halperin, D. (2003). The normalization of Queer Theory. *Journal of Homosexuality, 45*(no.2/3/4), 339–243.

Maddox, M. (2014). *Taking God to school: The end of egalitarian education?* Sydney: Allen & Unwin.

Marshall, D. (2014). Queer reparations: Dialogue and the queer past of schooling. *Discourse: Studies in the Cultural Politics of Education,* 35(3), 347–360.

Pascoe, C. J. (2011). *Dude, you're a fag: Masculinity and sexuality in high school* (2nd edn). Berkeley, CA: University of California Press.

Puar, J. (2006). Mapping US homonormativities. *Gender, Place and Culture, 13*(1), 67–88.

Rasmussen, M. (2006). *Becoming subjects: Sexualities and secondary schooling.* New York: Routledge.

Rasmussen, M. and Harwood, V. (2003). Performativity, youth and injurious speech. *Teaching Education, 14*(1), 25–36.

Salih, S. (2002). *Judith Butler.* London: Routledge.

Schippers, B. (2014). *The political philosophy of Judith Butler.* New York: Routledge.

Shah, B. (2014). Boko Haram beyond Nigeria: Girls' education under threat. *Aljazeera,* 3 June. www.aljazeera.com/indepth/opinion/2014/06/boko-haram-nigeria-education-20146363912922864.html.

Talburt, S. and Rasmussen, M. (2010). 'After-queer' tendencies in queer research. *International Journal of Qualitative Studies in Education, 23*(1), 1–14.

Thomson, P., Hall, C. and Jones, K. (2010). Maggie's day: A small scale analysis of English education policy. *Journal of Education Policy, 25*(5), 639–656.

Weaver-Hightower, M. B. and Skelton, C. (2013). *Leaders in gender and education: Intellectual self-portraits.* Rotterdam: Sense Publishers.

Youdell, D. (2004). Wounds and reinscriptions: Schools, sexualities and performative subjects. *Discourse: Studies in the Cultural Politics of Education, 25*(4), 477–493.

Youdell, D. (2011). *School trouble: Identity, power and politics in education.* London and New York: Routledge.

17

THINKING RHIZOMATICALLY

Using Deleuze in education policy contexts

Eileen Honan

In their collaborative work Deleuze and Guattari (1987) developed a conceptual understanding of knowledge as rhizomatic. This is a figuration that describes an interrelated and messy root system such as that found in grasses and tuberous plants, rather than the trunk, branch and roots system found in trees and shrubs. Even here in this brief description I have fallen into many of the linguistic traps that Deleuze and Guattari continually warn against. In their explication of rhizome in the introduction to *A thousand plateaus*, they insist that 'The rhizome is reducible neither to the One nor the multiple' (1987: 21). In other words, rhizome cannot be explained using binaries. They refuse binary thinking, and in doing so refuse to accept the 'either/or' comparative metaphors used; 'they refuse the domination of linguistic/literary/semiological models, which all seek some kind of hidden depth underneath a manifest surface' (Grosz, 1994: 198); they refuse linear and causal explanations of the connections and linkages between things.

This refusal of linguistic models is at the same time a call for more complexity in thinking about how language works, and a call to develop a more heterogeneous understanding of the relation between words and things, between the *signified* and the *signifier*.

> We have to break open words or sentences, too, and find what's uttered in them. And what can be uttered at a given period corresponds to its system of language and the inherent variations it's constantly undergoing, jumping from one homogeneous scheme to another (language is always unstable).
>
> *(Deleuze, 1995: 96)*

Rhizomatic ontology cannot be expressed in binary, cannot be captured using the traditional model of language that relies on stability of meaning, but can help think differently about the nature of texts, and the relation between text and reader.

In this chapter, the analytic methods associated with 'rhizo-textual analysis' (Honan, 2004, 2007) will be explicated. These methods draw on the ontology developed by Deleuze and Guattari to develop an understanding of texts themselves, and the readings of those texts, as rhizomatic. These understandings can help develop analyses of policy texts that disrupt common assumptions about the relations between teachers and policy.

Texts as rhizomes

> The ideal for a book would be to lay everything out on a plane of exteriority of this kind, on a single page, the same sheet: lived events, historical determinations, concepts, individuals, groups, social formations.
>
> *(Deleuze and Guattari, 1987: 9)*

The difficulty of writing rhizome is captured by Deleuze and Guattari themselves in their introduction to *A thousand plateaus*. Rhizomatic thinking and writing involves making ceaseless and on-going connections:

> Any point of a rhizome can be connected to anything other, and must be . . . A rhizome ceaselessly establishes connections between semiotic chains, organizations of power, and circumstances relative to the arts, social sciences, and social struggles.
>
> *(Deleuze and Guattari, 1987: 7)*

The ceaselessness of the connections, the movements across and through different organisations, the need for a different way of speaking and writing, the disruption of barriers between different semiotic systems require a different kind of text, a different kind of page. For some of those exploring texts as rhizomes, attention has been paid to the creation of multimodal texts, texts that include colour, image, and sound, as well as typography, the type of digital text that makes creative use of the affordances of digital technologies available in the twenty-first century (see for example, the blog hosted by the Education and Social Research Institute at Manchester Metropolitan University at http://museumofqualitativedata.info/). Others have paid attention to the way in which language is used in texts including the formatting and alignment on the page itself (see for example, Koro-Ljungberg, 2012). Other attempts to create rhizomatic texts within the conventional boundaries of an academic journal have made use of the online digital publication format (see Honan, 2014).

A Deleuzean understanding of how texts work requires a discursive analytic framework that takes account of texts as rhizomes. This requires asking different types of questions about the nature of the text and its relations to other things. As Grosz explains:

> It is thus no longer appropriate to ask what a text means, what it says, what is the structure of its interiority, how to interpret or decipher it. Instead, one

must ask what it does, how it connects with other things (including its reader, its author, its literary and nonliterary context).

(Grosz, 1994: 199)

This provides an analytic framework for understanding the relations between text and reader, between text and author, between text and other texts. Such an analytic framework that works rhizomatically itself also requires making ceaseless and on-going connections 'between semiotic chains, organizations of power, and circumstances relative to the arts, social sciences, and social struggles' (Deleuze and Guattari, 1987: 7).

Discourses as rhizome

Undertaking an analysis of texts that are rhizomatic requires an understanding of the possibilities for discourses to operate in rhizomatic ways, and here it is useful to think of Foucault's discursive formations (1972) and Deleuze's discussion of Foucault's work (1988). A formalist or structuralist approach to discourse analysis creates a typology, a categorisation that appears to suggest that discourses operate separately, hierarchically and linearly. Foucault provided an alternative understanding of discursive formations as:

> ways of constituting knowledge, together with the social practices, forms of subjectivity and power relations which inhere in such knowledges and relations between them.

(Weedon, 1987: 108)

In Deleuze's discussion of Foucault's work he draws attention to the multiplicity of statements: 'not only is each statement in this way inseparable from a multiplicity that is both "rare" and regular, but each statement is itself a multiplicity, not a structure or a system' (1988: 6) and that this understanding of multiplicity necessarily creates a topology of statements. Nothing is fixed or stable, meanings and interpretations bend and stretch, there are no fixed points, rather only lines, 'lines of variation' (Deleuze, 1988: 6).

Rhizomatic thinking and writing involves making ceaseless and on-going connections. Any point of a rhizome can be connected to anything other, and must be . . . A rhizome ceaselessly establishes connections. Mapping these connections can involve following 'lines of flight', another figuration used by Deleuze and Guattari. 'There are no points or positions in a rhizome, such as those found in a structure, tree, or root. There are only lines' (Deleuze and Guattari, 1987: 9). Following these lines of flight allows the possibility of creating new connections between quite different thoughts, ideas, pieces of data, discursive moments. These lines of flight move beyond and between, across and within those power relations as described by Foucault. Here Deleuze explored this Foucauldian understanding of power relations:

> Power-relations are the differential relations which determine particular fea-
> tures (affects). The actualization which stabilizes and stratifies them is an
> integration: an operation which consists of tracing 'a line of general force',
> linking, aligning and homogenizing particular features, placing them in series
> and making them converge.
>
> *(Deleuze, 1988: 75)*

Lines of flight move beyond the series, and following them involves finding the
moments of connections, and, to Deleuze, these couplings, 'bring things to life':

> One's always writing to bring things to life, to free life from where it's
> trapped, to trace lines of flight. The language for doing that can't be a
> homogeneous system, it's something unstable, always heterogeneous, in
> which style carves differences of potential between which things can pass,
> come to pass, a spark can flash and break out of language itself, to make us
> see and think what was lying in the shadow around the words, things we
> were hardly aware existed.
>
> *(Deleuze, 1995: 141)*

It is this spark, this illumination of the dark shadows, that a rhizo-textual analysis
can contribute to discourse analyses of policy texts, unveiling what has been
taken-for-granted, thinking differently about assumed relations, relations between
readers, texts, and writers.

Rhizo-textual analyses

A rhizo-textual analysis treats discourses as intersecting and overlapping, rather
than linear or operating on planes. Within and across any one text, discursive lines
can be mapped, following pathways, identifying intersections and connections,
finding the moments when an assemblage of discursive lines merge to make plausible and reasoned sense to the reader. Any one discursive pathway does not render
another (im)plausible. St Pierre (2000: 279) explains that this goes beyond the
layering of a palimpsest that relentlessly overwrites, but rather lines of flight are
always in the middle, in flux, 'disrupt[ing] dualisms with complementarity'.

Each discourse interweaves and interconnects with others forming a discursive
web or map. In keeping with Deleuze and Guattari, each text's complex web–map
also connects with other texts, so that forms of discourse taken up within one text
can be mapped across and into other texts. This kind of analysis reveals that there
are lines of flight that connect discourses to each other through linkages that are
commonalities and taken-for-granted assumptions that seem reasonable and
unquestionable. These discursive linkages are like the lumpy nodes that can appear
within a rhizomatic root system, or like the couplings that connect varied systems
of pipes in underground water systems and it is these linkages that can explain the
plausibility of seemingly contradictory discourses.

This ceaselessness of the connections between rhizomes shifts attention away from the construction, inner meaning, particular reading of any text towards a new careful attendance to the multiplicity of linkages that can be mapped between any text and other texts, other readings, other assemblages of meaning. A rhizo-textual analysis of the relation between texts and readers reveals a variety of 'scrupulous and plausible misreadings' (Spivak, 1996: 45). There is no one correct path to take through a rhizome, no one true way of reading rhizomatic texts. Elizabeth Grosz describes this understanding of texts as rhizomatic:

> A text is not a repository of knowledges or truths, the site for storage of information . . . so much as a process of scattering thoughts, scrambling terms, concepts and practices, forging linkages, becoming a form of action.
>
> *(1995: 126)*

Understanding texts as rhizomes, and the relation between texts and readers as rhizomatic, provides a new way of understanding how teachers work with and against and between policy texts. The (im)plausibilities of diverse, contradictory readings of texts is emphasised as the rhizo-analyst carefully maps the paths of meaning, the lines of flight, that readers take to forge linkages. There is an infinite array of mappings possible: no journey through, across, in and out of a rhizome is ever able to be duplicated exactly, no matter how hard we try to trace over our mappings. There are always offshoots, tangents, ways of linking particular rhizomes with other rhizomes. There is a ceaseless flow of connections between, across, and through rhizomes. A rhizo-textual analysis is not concerned with following traditional, scientifically rigorous channels of inquiry; rather it is a mapping of connections, of the fleshy tubers that are the rhizome. The mapping draws on various and often-contradictory work, ideas and concepts. Such 'disparate phenomena' can be drawn together to 'connect diverse fragments of data in ways that produced new linkages and revealed discontinuities' (Alvermann, 2000: 118).

The ideas of rhizome and their relations to texts and textual analyses have been taken up and used by educators in different ways. Indeed, Cumming (2014) points to the dangers inherent in thinking that these ideas, figurations or affects could be put together into some kind of analytic model. While each of us works with the idea of rhizome, and have taken it up in some analytic way, there is no one method applied, no set of rules to be followed.

For example, while Gardner (2014) believes that a text's semantic is located in the dynamic interplay of multiple lines of inquiry (p. 4), he moves beyond the text to undertake a rhizotextual analysis of identity and subjectivity. This line is also followed by Kevin Leander and his colleagues, who also believe that 'rhizoanalysis permits us to understand literacy performances in ways that more fully engage their affective intensities' (Leander and Rowe, 2006: 432). Leander and Rowe also draw on Hagood's (2004) understanding of rhizomatics as 'cartography' work. I have emphasised the 'textual' part of my methodological inquiries (Honan, 2004, 2007), while others such as Masny (2013: 341) focus on the possibilities involved in disrupting understandings about all kinds of data: 'Rhizoanalysis is an assemblage (participants, researchers, research assistants, research settings, etc.) that disrupts or deterritorialises in situ. Each time the composition of the assemblage differs'.

In the following section I provide some examples of the use of rhizotextual analytic strategies in particular relation to the policy texts.

Possible analytic strategies

Rather than seeing discourses operating within policy texts as separate, or layered, rhizotextual analyses uncover their connections through multiple and diverse threads and links. The term, 'provisional linkages' can be used to describe these connections between 'elements, fragments, flows, of disparate status and substance' (Grosz, 1994: 167). These provisional linkages are not 'localizable linkages between points and positions' (Deleuze and Guattari, 1987: 21) but connections between lines:

> The rhizome is made only of lines: lines of segmentarity and stratification as its dimensions, and the line of flight or deterritorialization as the maximum dimension after which the multiplicity undergoes metamorphosis, changes in nature.

Provisional linkages make connections between what seemed to be disparate 'lines of flight', and this enables an understanding of the different and multiple readings producing particular and multiple lines of meaning across and within the rhizome of texts. While at times these paths followed through the texts seemed to be contradictory and inconsistent, they always produce equally (im)plausible readings.

For example, one of the provisional linkages identified as operating in quite contradictory discourses within the English curriculum texts in Queensland, Australia (Honan, 2001) was that literacy is inherently power(ful). In the construction of the literate subject in the texts, literacy, or in particular knowing about and how to engage in certain literacy practices, becomes a rationality, a taken-for-granted truth about how power is exercised by individuals.

These provisional linkages also help with an understanding of the discursive connections across and between different texts. A rhizo-textual analysis follows the paths provided by provisional linkages, through and across the various discursive plateaus that are formed by disparate flows and fragments. Such an analysis does not stop at the pages' borders though, but maps the connections and linkages between and across one set of texts and those other texts that provide some kind of historical, social and economic contexts, as well as 'circles of convergence' (Deleuze and Guattari, 1987: 22).

For example, in discussing the teaching of literacy, some commentators present a linear historical view of the development of certain approaches (for example, Green, 1995; Lo Bianco and Freebody, 1997), in which each approach supplants and replaces what has come before. Rhizo-textual analytic strategies shed light on the multiple and ceaseless presence of the discourses used in these approaches

(Rowan and Honan, 2005). One does not render another invisible. Understanding texts as rhizomatic helps make sense of this layering – each discourse interweaves and interconnects with each other forming a discursive web.

Another analytic strategy, mapping, is associated with rhizomatic cartography (Hagood, 2004) and involves following pathways across and into other texts. Each text's complex web connects with other texts, so that forms of discourse taken up within one policy text can be mapped across and into other policy texts.

For example, the P-10 Queensland English Syllabus published in 1994 (Department of Education Queensland, 1994) and the Victorian Early Years Literacy Program (Victorian Department of Education, 1997) are two policy texts related to the teaching of literacy, developed at different times and in different states, and by different groups of curriculum writers, yet a skills-based or functional approach to the teaching of literacy is taken up in both sets of documents. In the Queensland Syllabus this discourse is called on to establish the value of literacy. The benefits of literacy are not only restricted to the advancement of individuals, but are seen to be of value to the 'nation as a whole'. Literate people are better people because they can take part in activities related to employment, further education and recreation (Department of Education Queensland, 1994: 2). There is an implicit assumption about the relationship between the social development of the individual and the economic development of the nation (Rose, 1999). Expressing ideas about individuals and their 'value' allows a relationship to be constructed between individual wellbeing and a 'better' society.

In a different policy space, at a different chronological moment, this same skills-based discourse is called on to explain the optimal conditions for literacy teaching in the early years of schooling (Victorian Department of Education, 1997). The discourses used to describe these conditions, including isolating the teaching of literacy as a discrete subject, and breaking down the subject into separate modes so that Reading and Writing are treated separately, can be mapped back, across, and through other time/space moments, even back to New South Wales in 1886 when Inspectors wrote reports calling for 'a full knowledge of our mother tongue including Reading, Writing, Grammar, Analysis of Sentences, and Composition' (quoted in Green and Hodgens, 1996: 213).

This mapping of discourses forms an assemblage – a conglomerate, a pulling together, of texts and language, of meanings and words, of times and spaces – so that the 'Formal elements (phonics, punctuation, sentence and paragraph structure)' (Reid, 1996: 151) of the English curriculum of 1941 is understood as reasonable, as meaningful, as curriculum-as-it-is-now, by teachers in 2014.

Another rhizo-textual analytic strategy useful in policy work interrogates the relations between teachers, their daily work, and the policy documents that appear to govern this work. For example, I analysed the various polices related to literacy and new technologies operating in one very specific context, that of primary school education in Queensland, Australia (Honan, 2010). By providing a specific list of policies impacting on one small group of teachers I hoped to illustrate the immediate and overwhelming affects of the proliferation of policy documents on teachers' work. As Stephen Ball (2008: 5) has pointed out: 'Policy discourses [. . .] organise their own specific rationalities, making particular sets of ideas obvious, common sense and "true"'. In the analysis, I attempted to make the familiar strange, by illuminating how the current contextual discourses make some ideas about the nature of teaching literacy using new technologies appear to be reasonable and true to the extent that other more useful strategies appear to be invisible to classroom teachers. The analysis of teachers' talk revealed the centrality of policy discourses in their work, or how these policies are 'inflected, mediated, resisted and misunderstood' (Ball, 2008: 7) by teachers. In their taking up of these discourses, in this case, about the logic of adopting a technical or operational approach to using new technologies, and the focus on the production of digital texts in their classrooms, the teachers in this study demonstrated both their agency and their submission to policy, their compliance with policy and their expert use and application of the policy in their classroom practice. The paradoxical and contradictory relations between submission and mastery, between text, reader, writer, between teachers and educational policy makers, between different teachers, are always between, in the middle, the 'intermezzo' (Deleuze and Guattari, 1987: 25). A rhizo-textual analysis can illuminate this middle space, can provide some insights into the moments where 'either/or' becomes 'and . . . and . . . and . . .' (Deleuze and Guattari, 1987: 25). Contemporary literacy teachers are situated within a complex and contradictory variety of discourses about the kinds of literacies they should engage with in their classrooms.

In one study (Honan, 2010), it was evident that teachers struggled with contradictory discourses related to teaching literacy and using new technologies. Again and again they reported that their attempts to engage with cultural or critical literacy practices when using ICTs in their classrooms were frustrated or stymied by factors as varied as resourcing, time allocations, parental attitudes, their own lack of skills or knowledge in using ICTs, and the actual physical space of a contemporary classroom. A rhizo-textual analysis of this talk drew on a particular view of teachers and their professionalism that prevented accepting these as excuses, or some evidence of their unwillingness to change. Rhizomatic thinking provided a view of agentic and professional teachers who were interested in changing their literacy teaching and methods for engaging with digital texts in their classrooms yet at the same time appeared to be unwilling. Understanding their relationship to policy discourses and understanding the conflicting and contrary nature of these positions allowed me to provide some account of the prevalence of particular discourses used in their talk, the connections between these discourses and those used in policy documents, and the apparent rationality associated with using these discourses, so that any other way of talking about literacy or using digital texts became impossible or unreasonable.

Part of the analysis involved mapping these discourses from the teachers' talk into other 'circulating texts' (Ball, 1994) such as policy documents, web pages about current departmental initiatives, and texts explaining professional development offered to teachers using ICTs. This analysis revealed the discursive connections between policy and practice, in that the discourses that are privileged within policy documents are those that are taken up and used by teachers as they talk about their work with digital texts. Tracing the lines of flight between the policy texts and the teachers' talk made visible the normative value associated with operational and technical work as well as the taken-for-granted importance of production work with digital texts.

Concluding thoughts

Policy writers, syllabus developers, even bureaucratic heads of department, assume teacher compliance, acceptance of and obedience to the policy texts that are introduced into their classrooms. This assumption of teacher compliance requires teachers to act upon policy texts where the relations are always/already uneven and disproportionate. However, undertaking a rhizo-textual analysis that reveals the connections between quite contradictory discourses as well as the paths that connect teachers' talk with curriculum and policy documents offers a more agentic reading of teachers' work. Thinking with Deleuze about how teachers work, and their relations with texts, and policy texts in particular, flattens out the hierarchies enveloped within binaries of compliance, subservience, competency and expertness. Teachers are (im)plausibly constituted as both expert and subservient, as professional and compliant.

Webb and Gulson describe a policy intension that 'extends approaches to micropolitical analyses of educational policy in order to demonstrate the ways that implementation folds affects into, and writes bodies with, policy' (2013: 64). The relationship between teacher and policy is described here as a fold, and 'In this spirit, policy asks subjects to face themselves differently' (p. 57).

Rhizo-textual analysis provides some possible ways to closely examine the ways in which teachers interact with policy texts, are folded and fold themselves within and with policy, drawing attention to the particular individual ways that teachers are constituted and constitute themselves as subjects in their daily lives. Rose (1999: 279–280) calls for an examination of such day-by-day work, which would draw attention to the 'minor politics' of the 'cramped spaces of the everyday'. While rhizo-textual analyses can contribute to an understanding of the complex theoretical work that teachers do in these 'little territories of the everyday' (Rose, 1999: 280), and the amazing intellectual and creative resources they bring to the teaching task, there are dangers inherent in expecting to find solutions or answers to research questions through undertaking this analytic work.

Rhizo-textual methods are not fixed in themselves. Indeed, thinking rhizomatically requires a movement away from Method, 'There is no methodological instrumentality to be unproblematically learned. In this methodology-to-come, we begin to do it differently wherever we are in our projects' (Lather, 2013: 635). What I have attempted to provide here is a possible explanation of how thinking rhizomatically can challenge and change the way we think about the relations between teachers and policy texts.

Recommendations for further readings

Alvermann, D. (2000). Researching libraries, literacies, and lives: A rhizoanalysis. In E. A. St Pierre and W. S. Pillow (Eds.), *Working the ruins: Feminist poststructural theory and methods in education* (pp. 114–129). New York: Routledge.

Coleman, R. and Ringrose, J. (Eds.) (2013). *Deleuze and research methodologies*. Edinburgh, UK: Edinburgh University Press.

Deleuze, G. and Guattari, F. (1987). *A thousand plateaus. Capitalism and schizophrenia*. London: The Athlone Press.

References

Alvermann, D. (2000). Researching libraries, literacies, and lives: A rhizoanalysis. In E. A. St Pierre and W. S. Pillow (Eds.), *Working the ruins: Feminist poststructural theory and methods in education* (pp. 114–129). New York: Routledge.

Ball, S. J. (1994). *Education reform: A critical and post-structural approach*. Buckingham, UK: Open University Press.

Ball, S. J. (2008). *The education debate*. Bristol, UK: The Policy Press.

Cumming, T. (2014). Challenges of 'thinking differently' with rhizoanalytic approaches: A reflexive account. *International Journal of Research & Method in Education*. doi: 10.1080/1743727X.2014.896892.

Deleuze, G. (1988). *Foucault*. London: The Athlone Press.

Deleuze, G. (1995). *Negotiations: 1972–1990*. New York: Columbia University Press.

Deleuze, G. and Guattari, F. (1987). *A thousand plateaus. Capitalism and schizophrenia*. London: The Athlone Press.

Department of Education Queensland. (1994). *English in Years 1 to 10 Queensland syllabus materials. English syllabus for Years 1 to 10*. Brisbane: State of Queensland.

Foucault, M. (1972). *The archaeology of knowledge*; and, *The discourse on language*; translated from the French by A. M. Sheridan Smith. New York: Vintage Books.

Gardner, P. (2014). Who am I? Compositions of the self: An autoethnographic, rhizotextual analysis of two poetic texts. *English in Education, 48*(3), 230–249. doi: 10.1111/eie.12032.

Green, B. (1995). Post-curriculum possibilities: English teaching, cultural politics, and the postmodern turn. *Journal of curriculum studies, 27*(4), 391–409.

Green, B. and Hodgens, J. (1996). Manners, morals, meanings: English teaching, language education and the subject of 'Grammar'. In B. Green and C. Beavis (Eds.), *Teaching the English subjects. Essays on English curriculum history and Australian schooling* (pp. 204–228). Geelong, Australia: Deakin University Press.

Grosz, E. (1994). A thousand tiny sexes: Feminism and rhizomatics. In C.V. Boundas and D. Olkowski (Eds.), *Gilles Deleuze and the theater of philosophy* (pp. 187–210). New York: Routledge.

Grosz, E. (1995). *Space, time and perversion*. Sydney: Allen & Unwin.

Hagood, M. C. (2004). A rhizomatic cartography of adolescents, popular culture, and constructions of self. In Leander, K. M. and Sheehy, M. (Eds.), *Spatializing literacy research and practice* (Vol. 15) (pp. 143–160). New York: Peter Lang.

Honan, E. (2001). (Im)plausibilities: A rhizo-textual analysis of the Queensland English Syllabus (unpublished doctoral thesis). Townsville, Australia: James Cook University.

Honan, E. (2004). (Im)plausibilities: A rhizo-textual analysis of policy texts and teachers' work. *Educational Philosophy and Theory, 36*(3), 267–281.

Honan, E. (2007). Writing a rhizome: An (im)plausible methodology. *International Journal of Qualitative Studies in Education, 20*(5), 531–546.

Honan, E. (2010). Mapping discourses in teachers' talk about using digital texts in class-rooms. *Discourse: Studies in the Cultural Politics of Education, 31*(2), 179–193.

Honan, E. (2014). Disrupting the habit of interviewing. *Reconceptualizing Educational Research Methodology, 5*(1). Available at: http://journals.hioa.no/index.php/rerm.

Koro-Ljungberg, M. (2012). Researchers of the world, create! *Qualitative Inquiry, 18*(9), 808–818.

Lather, P. (2013). Methodology-21: What do we do in the afterward? *International Journal of Qualitative Studies in Education, 26*(6), 634–645.

Leander, K. M. and Rowe, D. W. (2006). Mapping literacy spaces in motion: A rhizomatic analysis of a classroom literacy performance. *Reading Research Quarterly, 41*(4), 428–460.

Lo Bianco, J. and Freebody, P. (1997). *Australian literacies: Informing national policy on literacy education*. Belconnen, Austalia: Language Australia.

Masny, D. (2013). Rhizoanalytic pathways in qualitative research. *Qualitative Inquiry, 19*(5), 339–348.

Reid, J. (1996). Working out one's own salvation: Programming primary English teaching. In B. Green and C. Beavis (Eds.), *Teaching the English subjects. Essays on English curriculum history and Australian schooling*. Geelong, Australia: Deakin University Press.

Rose, N. S. (1999). *Powers of freedom: Reframing political thought*. Cambridge, UK: Cambridge University Press.

Rowan, L. and Honan, E. (2005). Literarily lost: The quest for quality literacy agendas in early childhood education. In N. Yelland (Ed.), *Critical issues in early childhood education* (pp. 197–223). Milton Keynes, UK: Open University Press.

Spivak, G. (1996). Explanation and culture Marginalia. In D. Landry and G. MacLean (Eds.), *The Spivak reader. Selected works of Gayatri Chakravorty Spivak*. New York: Routledge.

St Pierre, E. A. (2000). Nomadic inquiry in smooth spaces. In E. A. St Pierre and W. S. Pillow (Eds.), *Working the ruins: Feminist poststructural theory and methods in education* (pp. 258–283). New York and London: Routledge.

Victorian Department of Education. (1997). *Early years literacy program*. South Melbourne: Addison Wesley Longman.

Webb, T. P. and Gulson, K. N. (2013). Policy intensions and the folds of the self. *Educational Theory, 63*(1), 51–67.

Weedon, C. (1987). *Feminist practice and poststructuralist theory*. Oxford, UK: Blackwell.

18

RELATIONAL SPACE AND EDUCATION POLICY ANALYSIS

Kalervo N. Gulson

Just as none of us is outside or beyond geography, none of us is completely free from the struggle over geography.

(Said, 1993: 7)

It is very easy to argue that we should 'take space seriously'. Everybody says it these days. There has indeed, it is rumoured, been something called 'the spatial turn'. The rhetoric is everywhere; the content is more elusive.

(Massey, 1999: 11)

Education policy is a temporal intervention into the world. It focuses on the period of development, the timeline for and to implementation of policy; the years until review; and, enrolment data over multiple years and the resourcing implications for teaching that come with this sort of data. Policy further aims to create change over time such as having a three-year curricula review, a four-year teaching program, a five-year matriculation certificate, and so forth. In this chapter I foreground the notion that understanding policy through time is also about understanding the policy through space – that time and space are distinct from each other, but also necessary for understanding each other. For example, when you are travelling on a train you are not just moving through or over space. This movement 'is also temporal. It is a movement in/of (a production of) both space and time' (Massey, 2000: 226).

The premise of this chapter is while education policy is about when and how change happens it is also about *where* change happens. I will focus on the *where* of policy in order to understand how and why policy is made and enacted. This means asking:

- Why and how might we use various theories of space in educational policy research?
- When we use space in education policy analysis then what are we asking?

- Are we asking about the spatial features of policy, that is, a description?
- Or are we asking about the analytical outcomes of using space?
- We might further ask, therefore, what are some of the implications of using theories of space when space is the object of study and the analytic framework?

As Smith notes in relation to the 'spatial turn' in social theory – and more on this below – we do need to be able to articulate a rationale for our choice of theories.

> There is a crucial question of the extent to which this 'spatial turn' has been more than skin deep . . . Put most crudely, perhaps, why space? Why *should* our analysis of social difference and political possibility be rewritten in the language of space?
>
> *(Smith, 2004: 13)*

In this chapter, I am going to focus on the concept of relational space, drawing predominantly on the work of two geographers Doreen Massey, especially her later work (e.g. 2005), and Jonathan Murdoch. I will outline three features of relational space – interrelations, multiplicity and openness. I will then identify the ways relational space might inform ontological and methodological examinations of education policy.

Before continuing, I want to note that relational space corresponds with a critical policy studies approach to investigating and analysing education policy. Critical policy studies can provide ways of thinking differently about education policy, and have been characterised as a broad 'ensemble of approaches and perspectives' that aim to 'speak truth to power' (Orsini and Smith, 2007: 1). These approaches call attention to issues of power in relation to education policy, especially ideas of contestation and compromise, and posit policy as provisional and incomplete. I suggest a relational spatial analysis has a complementary function to critical policy studies, and that as such I propose that the use of relational space permits a focus on what policy spaces are made possible, and what are deferred or subjugated, and about how this occurs as a spatial politics.

'It's your only space; it's not your only space'[1]: relational space

It now appears common sense to recognise the intensification of spatialisation of contemporary life, and the multiple forms of communication networks and modes of mobility that are increasingly connecting and disconnecting individuals across the planet. As Shields notes:

> space and time are intrinsic to the intellectual ordering of our lives and our everyday notions of causality. When we turn to our daily speech, read the headlines of our newspapers or scan learned journals, we find an unexpected cornucopia of spatial references, elaborate expressions and elegant spatial

metaphors which position the term within our own knowledge as well as practice. 'Space' evidently plays an important role in knowledge and in knowing the world.

(Shields, 2006: 147)

While we have these quotidian notions of space and a recognition and experience of space in our lives, spatial analyses have been under-represented in the social sciences in deference to historical analysis (see Soja, 1996). It has, nonetheless, been possible to trace spatial approaches across a range of disciplines and fields, including linguistics, and a revitalisation of spatial disciplines such as geography (see Peters and Kessl, 2009). The revitalisation has been based on the primacy of space in understanding social relations. This turn was predicated on the idea that '[g]eography matters, not for the simplistic and overly used reason that everything happens in space, but because *where* things happen is critical to knowing *how* and *why* they happen' (Warf and Arias, 2009: 1).

Now, before going further, it is important to note the obvious point that there are many theories of space. In this chapter I am using what are broadly termed ideas of social space – what we might understand by the interactions of social relations and physical and metaphorical space. This could also be extended to constitute socio-spatial relations as cultural-spatial, economic-spatial and politico-spatial relations.

While I will be outlining a specific set of ideas about relational space, I think of these theories as open. As Thrift notes, with theory the 'main purpose is not to "represent" but to "resonate"' (Thrift, 1999: 304 cited in Murdoch, 2006: 16). Relational space is sometimes, but not exclusively, identified with poststructural geographies, and has some affinity with other socio-material approaches such as actor-network theory (ANT).

It is worth briefly noting approaches that contrast with or are distinct from relational space (see reading list at end of the chapter). The most common form of space critiqued by relational approaches is *abstract* space. This follows a Newtonian conception in which space is a discrete and autonomous container for action. What this means is that space does not constitute events or actions, it merely contains events and actions. Another type of space is relative space. This more active than abstract space, and is conceived as a plane with implications for distance and scale. Space is defined relative to the objects and processes being considered in space and time. There is no fixed relation for locating things so, for example, we can never categorically say that something is here and now without having reference to other objects (Jones, 2009). As we will see below, relative space has some resonance with ideas of relational space.

Relational space is the idea that space is something generated by interactions and interrelations, and that space generates interactions and interrelations. It is this mutually constitutive relationship that underlies what is called socio-spatiality, or the relationships between space and social relations. We can know about space as an object – we do it all the time through mapping using mathematical formulae: think of the map function on a smart phone; engineering that knows space such as bridge spans; and we know it through the reshaping of land and by living on land. What Shield (2006) argues is that we need to introduce verbs – so that '[w]e need to know about "spacing" and the spatializations that are accomplished through everyday activities, representations and rituals' (p. 149). This is the realm of relational space, where space is made from processes and practices that are both consensual and contested; with both creating space as a 'provisional accomplishment' – as something that can be different from the way it is now and here. As Thrift notes: 'Spaces can be stabilised in such a way that they act like political utterances, guiding subjects to particular conclusions' (Thrift, 2003: 2022 cited in Nayak, 2010: 2378).

At this stage, this necessarily means that space is about power relations in the creation of space as an accomplishment – for 'while multiple sets of relations may well co-exist, there is likely to be some competition between these relations over the composition of particular spaces and places' (Murdoch, 2006: 20). This necessitates examining how power is mediated at different times and in different spaces; an identification of the difference geography makes in understanding power (Allen, 2003). Massey has posited the notion of 'power-geometries' to conceptualise that 'not only is space utterly imbued with and a product of relations of power, but power itself has a geography. There are cartographies of power' (Massey, 2009: 18).

Relational space: interrelations, multiplicity, openness

Relational space is premised on three things:

1   that space is constituted by interrelations between people, and between people and the non-human (the physical world, the animal world – see the field of environmental humanities for the latter, and non-representational theory for the former);
2   that multiplicity is the norm rather than the exception when understanding space and spatial formations; and
3   that openness is the precondition and constitution for space as political.

I will go through each of these in turn, before identifying ways in which relational space can be applied in education policy analyses.

Interrelations

When we talk about interrelations we are assuming that space is not an empty container in which social life occurs, or where entities and processes interact. Rather, what is proposed is that space is produced by entities and processes that are relational – that combine through interaction, and it is the combination of materiality and representation that is crucial to interrelations. As Massey (2009: 17) notes: 'If there is to be a relation (or, indeed, a non-relation) there needs to be at least more than one thing to do the relating, or not'. There are clearly relationships between things in the world, such as entities and identities, and actions, but this becomes quite difficult to think about – do things have agency in the same way that humans do? If we think about the example of a building, for example, it can impact actions through the apportioning of memory or significance, but these are related to other forms of organisation. So, a heritage building precludes certain forms of change, but this remains across time until the building's status is changed. But would we say that this building has agency in the same sense as a human? Are we at risk of anthropomorphising relational space in this sense? Or does it not matter, in that we are working from the premise that we are dealing with social space? And if so, this might mean that agency is always constrained, depending on the type of power relations that are constituted and understood. What we need to focus on, then, is not 'locating power' but rather 'the task becomes one of understanding how sociospatial relations serve to constitute particular modalities of power, and how in turn these sustain distinct forms of spatial ordering (such as the local, global and so on)' (Bulkeley, 2013: 454).

One of the keys here is that we understand space as a situational and contingent outcome. Massey, following the work of Lefebvre (1991), has argued space as produced by social relations and space producing social relations. This requires refusing to accede a determining structure to space, and that we are committing to the unsettling idea of entities as contingent and provisional. We can see what this entails, when using the example of travelling in a car, on the train, walking – though this might be complicated by the idea of travelling 'online'. What Massey argues is that when you are moving, '[y]ou are not just travelling across space; you are altering it a little, moving it on, producing it' (Massey, 2000: 226). Think about how you might walk across a school playground, for example. As you walk you are moving across a physical entity, the concrete or grass. But as you move you are also impacting on how this space is produced. If you are moving with a ball in hand, and bouncing it on the ground, then you are creating this space as one of recreation, or enjoyment. But if you are a student and you are bouncing the ball it may be part of a pedagogical activity, or it may be on the part of the playground that is demarcated as 'out-of-bounds', then what you are dealing with is the interrelations between a transgressive activity, the ordering of that space through cartography, and the power relations that a school may be infused with through disciplinary policies. We can think of this example in more detail, concerning the ways in which some spaces seem to be fixed and ordered. At other times educational spaces are infused with multiple readings through the interaction of education policies with other kinds of policies. For example, the example of full-service or extended schools, in which a variety of social services are provided in a school, are intended to be one-stop shops that allow parents and students to access services that would otherwise require travelling (Cummings, Dyson and Todd, 2011). Interrelations here are both circumscribed and open, and the school is changed through this provision of services, when compared to other schools that are not full-service.

Relational space depends on the idea that, as Murdoch (2006: 23) asserts, 'spaces are made of complex sets of relations so that any spatial "solidity" must be seen as an accomplishment, something that has to be achieved in the face of flux and instability'. This can be understood through the example of classrooms in schools. Some seem to have permanence of function but this is always the act of work, of fixing its solidity. Policy operates as one mode of provisional spatial ordering, that paradoxically can be construed as the spatial relations of permanence (Jones, 2009). A classroom is a physical entity, but it is constantly being modified through the interrelations of students, teachers, administrators – classrooms are spaces that are defined through policies at the school level, and through discipline, safety and other policies, as spaces that are constantly rearticulated.

Multiplicity

The premise of multiplicity is to recognise plurality as a necessary condition of relational space, and space as the realm of concurrent and distinct heterogeneity (Massey, 2005). Massey suggests that:

> Without space as a dimension it would not be possible for there to be multiplicity (in the sense of the simultaneous coexistence of more than one thing). Equally, and as the mirror image of this, without multiplicity space itself could not exist (space is the product of relations within multiplicity). Space and multiplicity are mutually constitutive.
>
> *(Massey, 2009: 17)*

Multiplicity involves two key aspects. The first is, perhaps, an obvious one; that multiplicity requires 'an emphasis on the proliferation of diverse relations' (Anderson and Harrison, 2010: 15), and this emphasis on difference accords with the centrality of difference in poststructural theorising (Murdoch, 2006). 'Simultaneous coexistence' means that difference can result in two things: one, as distinctions between entities (e.g. people, schools) that can be assumed to be equivalent (e.g. School A student a, School A student b, School A student c, etc.). For example, we often know cities, not as coherent wholes, but through the idea of different parts of cities through connection to identities (e.g. multicultural cities in countries like Australia and Canada have the Italian quarter, the Greek quarter). What this points to, furthermore, is that difference refers to variations between groupings and invokes processes of comparison (Stagoll, 2010). While the city is being seen as having distinctions, it paradoxically depends on the fixing or essentialising of identity (i.e. that there is such a thing as a coherent Italian identity in a multicultural city). This illustrates that difference can be spatially stabilised, and that this stabilisation is the product of power relations.

This leads to the second aspect of multiplicity – that of the links between power and movement. This includes how multiple processes bring about spatial formations and how social groupings are affected by relational formations. Massey uses the idea of 'power-geometry' to explore this, positing that as relations meet in and make space:

different social groups and individuals are placed in very distinct ways in relation to these flows and interconnections. This point concerns not merely the issue of who moves and who doesn't, although that is an important element of it; it is also about power in relation to the flows and the movement. Different social groups have distinct relationships to this anyway differentiated mobility: some people are more in charge of it than others; some initiate flows and movement, others don't; some are more on the receiving end of it than others; some are effectively imprisoned by it.

(Massey, 1991: 25–26 cited in Murdoch, 2006: 22)

All relations, therefore, are situated, obviously, and as such multiplicity depends upon the contingency of proximity and distance (Allen, 2003). Multiplicity requires some sense of limitations – 'just because space is "relational" does not mean it is less restricting or confining' (Murdoch, 2006: 22).

Proximity and distance are not only about measurement, for 'distance – like difference – is not an absolute, fixed and given, but is set in motion and made meaningful through cultural practices' (Gregory, 2004: 18). An example we can use here is that of schools in an education market. School choice policies ostensibly make all schools equal as possible choices in the market – parents should be able to choose from different schools, and different schools should be able to compete equally in the market. As a meritocratic proposal, school choice ignores the historical, and for our purposes, geo-historical dimensions of choice. This notion of history is important, for as Massey notes, when we are talking about spaces we are not talking about merely the present space. All spaces then:

are all tales of the continued presence of 'the past' in the spatial surface of today. Yet surely the point is rather that the whole of the simultaneity that is 'the spatial surface of today' – even the mundane things, the modern things, the easily normally recognized things – consists of such moments, together, in their histories. This is no spatial surface it is a contemporaneity of trajectories.

(Massey, 2000: 228)

The spatial question we might start to ask about school choice as a policy example, is as follows: are all differences equal and are these differences marked out depending on where the schools are located? This can be illustrated through the example of Islamic schools in Sydney, Australia. In one case, a development application to establish a federal-government-funded Islamic school was rejected by the local government in an area of Sydney that is constituted, demographically, as dominantly White and Christian, especially compared to the rest of Sydney. In another case, a proposed Islamic school was rejected by local government in an area that was constituted, demographically, as non-White, with a relatively high proportion of residents who identified as Muslim. A simple explanation of these decisions on the basis of demographics fails to account for the rejection in both cases for difference and distance are different in each case. We need to map the connections between multiplicity and the cultural and political practices that are part of relational space. In both cases, these schools are marked out as an illegitimate difference in the school market, through connection to Islamophobia and notions of local manifestations about the 'Other' and global terrorism (see Al-Natour, 2010; Gulson and Webb, 2013).

Openness

The third aspect of relational space pertains to the idea of *openness*, as the necessary condition for politics. Space is central to the issue of 'living together'. That is, what space forces us to deal with is 'that most fundamental of sociopolitical questions: how are we going to live together? It is space as a dimension that offers up the challenge, the pleasure and the responsibility of the existence of "others", and of our relationship to them' (Massey, 2009: 18).

Space as interactional emphasises process.

> Space is always in a process of being made. It is always 'under construction'. It is never a fully connected and finalised thing . . . There are always relations which are still to be made, or unmade, or re-made. In this sense, space is a product of our on-going world. And in this sense it is also always open to the future. And, in consequence, it is always open also to the political. The production of space is a social and political task. If it is conceptualised in this manner, the dimension of space enters, necessarily, into the political (for if the future were not open there would be no possibility of changing it and thus no possibility of politics).
>
> *(Massey, 2009: 17)*

We can think, therefore, of the notions and examples above as the ways in which space and time are inexorably connected. One way to think this through as part of relational space is to deal with trajectories. In this way, then, things (us, policies, etc.) are about moving through space and time as a trajectory that interacts (not intersects as if this would mean passing over) without becoming intricately intermeshed. When trajectories interact then we are faced with the idea of fresh configurations, 'new stories will emerge, new trajectories set in motion' (Massey, 2000: 226). If we are dealing with space and time, then it not a matter of having some sort coherent narrative, in which space as messiness is layered over the top. Rather, what we are dealing with here is the idea that there is neither a singularity to time (history) nor to space:

> What the simultaneity of space really consists in, then, is absolutely not a surface, a continuous material landscape, but a momentary coexistence of trajectories, a configuration of a multiplicity of histories all in the process of being made. This is not a 'problem', unless of course you long for the order of the singular story and the legibility of the smoothness of a surface; rather, it is part of the delight, and the potential, of space.
>
> *(Massey, 2000: 229)*

This is openness as the entry point for politics. To bring the above two aspects together, space as interactional emphasises there are connections that have both been made and are yet to be made, and some that may never be accomplished.

> However, these are not the relations of a coherent, closed system within which, as they say, everything is (already) related to everything else. Space can never be that completed simultaneity in which all interconnections have been established and in which everywhere is already linked with everywhere else. A space, then, which is neither a container for always-already constituted identities nor a completed future of holism.
>
> *(Massey, 2005: 11–12)*

This, therefore, is not unfettered openness, for '[w]hile constructed, space is not infinitely malleable' (Thiem, 2007: 32). This simultaneous constraint and multiplicity reinforces why relational space is an approach with an affinity for, and contribution to make to, critical policy studies. In the last section of the chapter I will propose some possible implications of a relational approach to analyses of education policy.

Implications for analysing policy

What sorts of questions does a relational spatial approach lead us to ask? What sorts of questions are possible? When adopting a relational spatial approach to policy analysis I suggest there are two, among many, consequences to consider.

The first consequence is a re-articulation of the ontology of policy, that is, a spatial approach changes how you see policy. It forces us to ask, again, 'What is policy?', a question that is often side-lined in educational research but one that remains salient if we are to examine the politics of policy. Is policy always a form of spatial ordering? For example, in my work on the links between education policy and urban change, I have concluded that education policy repeatedly and insistently intervenes to make spaces (e.g. schools, cities), and create new racialisations (Gulson, 2007, 2011). When we look at studying education policy using ideas of relational space, this can mean taking an approach that sees policy as not only unfolding in designated spaces but also constitutes 'those spaces as part of the governing activity' (Dikeç, 2007: 280).

The second consequence is that examining education policy using a spatial approach is that it challenges the ideas of what defines the boundaries of the case. It also speaks to the ways in which these boundaries are created through particular spatial knowledge. In my work this has meant being attendant to the spatial politics inherent in educational policy changes, such as the ways that spatial measurement data like demographics are used to make claims about space that carry certain legitimacies in policy debates and political machinations (Gulson, 2007, 2011).

In reflecting on what a relational approach to space requires of us, I would contend that the ideas of interrelations, multiplicity and openness, require us to 'think through the specificity and performative efficacy of different relations and different relational configurations' (Anderson and Harrison, 2010: 45). As the notion of specificity indicates, a relational spatial analysis of policy is concerned with territorial and relational aspects of policy (McCann and Ward, 2013) – and this is a topic for another chapter.

Note

1 With thanks to They Might Be Giants 'Little birdhouse in your soul'.

Further reading

I have left a lot out of this chapter. For those interested in reading further the following might be of use:

Overviews of space and place

Crang, M. and Thrift, N. (Eds.) (2000). *Thinking space*. London: Routledge.
Hubbard, P. and Kitchin, R. (Eds.) (2011). *Key thinkers on space and place* (2nd edn). Thousand Oaks, CA: Sage.

Feminist and race geographies

Dwyer, C. and Bressey, C. (Eds.) (2008). *New geographies of race and racism*. Aldershot, UK: Ashgate Publishing.
Moss, P. and Falconer Al-Hindi, K. (Eds.) (2008). *Feminisms in geography: Rethinking space, place and knowledges*. New York: Rowman & Littlefield Publishers.

Relational spaces/Topological spaces

Shield, R. (2013). *Spatial questions: Cultural topologies and social spatialisations*. Thousand Oaks, CA: Sage.
Thrift, N. (2008). *Non-representational theory: Space | politics | affect*. New York: Routledge.

Power and space

Allen, J. (2003). *Lost geographies of power*. Oxford, UK: Blackwell.

Scale

Herod, A. (2011). *Scale*. London and New York: Routledge.

References

Allen, J. (2003). *Lost geographies of power*. Oxford, UK: Blackwell.
Al-Natour, R. J. (2010). Folk devils and the proposed Islamic school in Camden. *Continuum*, *24*(4), 573–585.

Anderson, B. and Harrison, P. (2010). The promise of non-representational theories. In B. Anderson and P. Harrison (Eds.), *Taking-place: Non-representational theories and geography* (pp. 1–36). Farnham, UK: Ashgate.

Bulkeley, H. (2013). Commentary 2: Making space for power? *Progress in Human Geography*, *37*(3), 454–456.

Cummings, C., Dyson, A. and Todd, L. (2011). *Beyond the school gates: Can full service and extended schools overcome disadvantage?* London: Routledge.

Dikeç, M. (2007). Space, governmentality, and the geographies of French urban policy. *European Urban and Regional Studies*, *14*(4), 277–289.

Gregory, D. (2004). *The colonial present.* Oxford, UK: Blackwell.

Gulson, K. N. (2007). Mobilizing space discourses: Politics and educational policy change. In K. N. Gulson and C. Symes (Eds.), *Spatial theories of education: Policy and geography matters* (pp. 37–55). New York: Routledge.

Gulson, K. N. (2011). *Education policy, space and the city: Markets and the (in)visibility of race.* New York: Routledge.

Gulson, K. N. and Webb: T. (2013). 'We had to hide we're Muslim': Ambient fear, Islamic schools and the geographies of race and religion. *Discourse: Studies in the Cultural Politics of Education*, *34*(4), 628–641.

Jones, M. (2009). Phase space: Geography, relational thinking, and beyond. *Progress in Human Geography*, *33*(4), 487–506.

Lefebvre, H. (1991). *The production of space.* Oxford, UK: Blackwell.

Massey, D. (1999). Negotiating disciplinary boundaries. *Current Sociology*, *47*(4), 5–12.

Massey, D. (2000). Travelling thoughts. In P. Gilroy, L. Grossberg and A. McRobbie (Eds.), *Without guarantees: In honour of Stuart Hall* (pp. 225–232). London: Verso.

Massey, D. (2005). *For space.* London: Sage Publications.

Massey, D. (2009). Concepts of space and power in theory and in political practice. *Documents d'Anàlisi Geogràfica*, *55*, 15–26.

McCann, E. and Ward, K. (2013). A multi-disciplinary approach to policy transfer research: Geographies, assemblages, mobilities and mutations. *Policy Studies*, *34*(1), 2–18.

Murdoch, J. (2006). *Post-structuralist geography: A guide to relational space.* London: Sage.

Nayak, A. (2010). Race, affect and emotion: Young people, racism, and graffiti in the postcolonial English suburbs. *Environment and Planning A*, *42*, 2370–2392.

Orsini, M. and Smith, M. (2007). Critical policy studies. In M. Orsini and M. Smith (Eds.), *Critical policy studies* (pp. 1–16). Vancouver: UBC Press.

Peters, M. A. and Kessl, F. (2009). Space, time, history: The reassertion of space in social theory. *Policy Futures in Education*, *7*(1), 20–30.

Said, E. (1993). *Culture and imperialism.* New York: Vintage Books.

Shields, R. (2006). Knowing space. *Theory, Culture & Society*, 23(2–3), 147–149.

Smith, N. (2004). Space and substance in geography. In P. Cloke, M. Crang and M. Goodwin (Eds.), *Envisioning human geographies* (pp. 11–29). London: Arnold.

Soja, E. W. (1996). *Thirdspace: Journeys to Los Angeles and other real-and-imagined places.* Cambridge, MA: Blackwell.

Stagoll, C. (2010). Difference. In A. Parr (Ed.), *The Deleuze dictionary.* Edinburgh, UK: Edinburgh University Press.

Thiem, C. H. (2007). The spatial politics of educational privatization: Re-reading the US homeschooling movement. In K. N. Gulson and C. Symes (Eds.), *Spatial theories of education: Policy and geography matters* (pp. 17–36). New York: Routledge.

Warf, B. and Arias, A. (2009). Introduction: The reinsertion of space in the humanities and social sciences. In B. Wark and S. Arias (Eds.), *The spatial turn: Interdisciplinary perspectives* (pp. 1–10). Abingdon, UK: Routledge.

INDEX

absent presence 55–6
abstract space 221
academics, and construction of policy cultures 36
access to education, pregnant/parenting students 144
accountability: new schooling accountability policies 202–3; of schools/teachers 129
accumulation, existence as 75
actants, human/non-human 90, 117, 118, 161
actor-network theory (ANT) 9, 87–96
Actor-network theory in education 94
actors, in actor-network theory (ANT) 90
affective performativity, of educational policy 105
affective shocks, in TALIS 104–7
affective turns 101–2
affectivities 102, 104, 107, 112–13
affect(s): concept of 99–107, 101; determinate 104, 107; and emotions 102, 103, 104, 112–13; and shame 104, 107; translation of 106
affirmation, ethics of 58
agency: congregational/distributive 117; and data 40; educational 126; sense of 53; sexual of children 116; of teachers 216; of things 223
agential realism 160, 164
Ahearne, J. 28–9, 32, 33, 36

alienating loss 76–7, 80
alienation, of mirror stage 76, 77
alterity, of everyday life 37
American neoliberalism 152
analysis: anti-institutional 148–9; critical/ethical issues 35; discourse 157, 210; feminist genealogy as tool for 141–5; of interview transcripts 52, 53; policy-product 69–70; rhizo-textual 209, 211–13, 216
analysts, complicity of 33, 34–5
analytical frameworks, governmentality as 148–50
analytical implications, of governmentality 155–8
analytic strategies, rhizotextual 213
Anderson, C. 141
'Another Place' art work 116–17
anthropocentric educational assumptions 163
antidiscrimination policies 199 *see also* discrimination
anti-institutional analysis 148–9
anti-Oedipal tradition, poststructural thought 67, 70
Anyon, J. 46
Anzaldua, G. 196
aporias 58–60
Appadurai, A. 178
application of policies 215
archaeology of knowledge, The 63

art, as mode of thought 42
art education assemblage 115, 118
ascending analysis, of power 69
assemblage ethnography 111
assemblage(s): and actor-network 88;
    affectivities as components of 112–13; art
    education 115, 118; blackout 117–18;
    childhood sexuality 115–16, 118;
    classroom 114; defined 117–18; economic
    116–17, 118; education 112, 118, 119; as
    ethnography 119; governmental 114; idea
    of 111–12; mapping of discourses as 214;
    pedagogic 114–15, 118; policy actors as
    161; rhizoanalysis as an 213; risk/safety
    116–17, 118; sexualization of children
    115–16, 118; youth service 113–14, 118
assemblage theory 9, 110–20
assessments, large-scale 46
assumptions: of policy narratives 187; of
    teacher compliance 216
Atkinson, E. and DePalma, R. 202
Australia: discrimination against teachers
    199; education system 78–80; Higher
    Education agenda of 188–90; Islamic
    schools 225; low Socio Economic Status
    (SES) students 188–90; National
    Assessment Program in Numeracy and
    Literacy (NAPLAN) 203; National
    Partnership Agreement for Low Socio-
    Economic Status Schools Communities
    66; National Partnerships programme 66;
    P-10 Queensland English Syllabus 214;
    Senior Education and Training (SET)
    plans 203; Victorian Early Years Literacy
    Program 214

Ball et al. 70
Ball, S. J. 4, 6, 21, 192, 215
Barad, K. 160–1, 163–4, 165
Barthes, R. 148
Bauman, Z. 176
Beck, U. 174
Becoming subjects 205
Bennett, J. 117–18, 161
Bigum, C. and Rowan, L. 96
biology, as performative 103
biopolitics 149, 152, 184
bio-power 137
blackout assemblage 117–18
Black Papers 129

Black Supplementary Schooling, Britain
    125–6
Blaise, M. 115–16, 118
bodies, problematic 136
Bohr, N. 164
Bourdieu, P. 8, 15–25
Bowie, M. 76
Bowker, G. C. and Star, S. L. 92
Bradley, A. 60
Brake, D. 139, 140
Braun et al. 205
Brinkmann, S. 7
Brown, S. D. 105
Brown, W. 5
Bryant, L. R. 164
Buchanan, I. 30
bureaucratic state field 21
Burkitt, I. 29–30
Burman, E. 59
Büscher et al. 176
Büscher, M. and Urry, J. 177
Bush, George W. 19
Butler, J. 3, 6, 64, 184, 196, 197–8, 201, 202,
    204

Callaghan, James 129
Callon, M. 87, 88, 90, 91
'Can the subaltern speak?' 125
capacity, of things 161
capital, and the state 21
capitalism: adaptive capabilities of 127, 128;
    in crisis 127–30; democratic compromise
    of 123; knowing 39, 48; neoliberal 128,
    131; and neoliberalism 114; new forms
    of 128; and policy reform 128–9
capital, forms of 19, 23
cartographic tracing 116
cartographies of power 222
case law, and Title IX and pregnancy
    138–41
case studies, actor-network theory (ANT)
    93
categories, construction of 198
centres of calculation, actor-networks as
    91
Certeau, M. de 8, 27–37
change: conservative movements for 127;
    resistance to 187
chaos, and philosophy/science 42, 43
character, and pregnancy 140

childhood sexuality assemblage 115–16, 118
Christian morality 155
circles of convergence 213
citizenship, flexible notion of 174
civil rights law, US 134
civil society, and political regulation 152–3
classroom: assemblage 114; logic of the 21
Clifford, J. 180
'closing the gap' framework 57
Colebrook, C. 31
Collier, S. 153
colour-blindness 55, 58
coming out 198–9
commensuration 39, 40, 43, 48
Common Core State Standards Initiative for Mathematics and English Language Arts 19
common sense narratives 187
communication technologies, and global mobility 173
community based education 126
comparative data, on school performance 24
comparisons, international 107
competitiveness of the nation 190
complexity theory 180
complicity, in cultural production 32, 33, 34–5
concepts, philosophy creating 42–3
congregational agency 117
Connell, R. W. 191
consensual views, as concepts/facts 48
conservative challenge, to education policy 129
construction of teen mothers 138
constructivist structuralism 23
continuous learning 154
control societies 39–40
controversies, as 'big things'/matters of fact 96
Copjec, J. 76
Council of Australian Governments 79
counter-narratives: of in/equity 192–3; as political action 203
counter-politics 203
counterpublics: black educational 129; and policy reform 126; subaltern 123–7, 131
creative violence 43
crises, and policy discourses 130

critical education policy 47, 165
critical issues, and analysis 35
critical policy analysis, and globalization 188
critical policy studies 5–6
critique 6, 7
cultural exchange, global 173
cultural intelligibilities 204, 205–6
cultural policy, work of Certeau 36
cultural practice(s): heterogeneity/alterity of everyday 37; incommensurability of 32; and multiplicity 226; policy as 28
cultural production, complicity in 32, 33, 34–5
cultural studies 103
culture(s): and everyday practices 28, 31; national and education policy 29; pluralization/hybridization of 181; polemological analysis of 33, 36; and policy 28, 29, 31, 36; and practice 27–8; strategies and tactics to formulate 31; via education 29; writing/practising 34–6
Cumming, T. 212

data: interview 54; production and usage 46–7; social 40, 48; testing 105; transgressive 52
Dean, M. M. 192
deconstruction 51–60
deficit-based understandings, of students 203–4
de Lauretis, T. 196
Deleuze, G. 102, 208–16
Deleuze, G. and Guattari, F. 8, 39–48, 88, 111, 112, 114, 116, 119–20, 208, 209, 210
Derrida, J. 8, 51–60
desire: capacity for 75–6; fantasmatic/sublime object-causes of 80; and interest 104; subjects of 74–5
determinate affects 104, 107
deterritorialization: art education assemblage 115; post-national 175–6; and reterritorialization of social formations 114
dialogue technologies, and welfare institutions 156
diasporization, of communities 174
difference, spatially stabilised 224
diffraction 163

diffractive methodology 106, 161, 163, 164
Dimitriadis, G. and Kimberlis, G. 58
disadvantage 55
disadvantaged students, Australia 188
disavowal, defensive strategies of 80
disciplinary power 198–9, 200, 205
disciplinary society 153
disciplinary technique, university pre-
    requisites as 206
disciplinary technologies, of institutions 65
discipline: and security 154; as technology
    of power 153, 156
Discipline and punish 65
discourse analysis of policy texts, and
    rhizo-textual analysis 211–13
discourse(s): analysis 157, 210, 211–13;
    concept of 71; contradictory 215; as
    disciplinary power 198; fag 200;
    Foucauldian analytic strategy 67–70;
    Foucault's notion of 63–5; mapping of
    214, 215; and narratives 184; national
    competitiveness 152–3; normalised/
    engrained as truth 135; policies as 30, 66,
    130, 199, 215; political of urgency/
    necessity 128; and queer theory 198;
    rational of private individuals 123; and
    regimes of truth 64, 66, 68, 69; as
    rhizomes 210–11; scientific 33; and
    social relations 127; socio-political
    narrative configurations of 190; teen
    pregnancy 144; and value of literacy 214;
    weight of 66, 68
discrimination: gender 140; pregnant and
    parenting students 138, 140; and
    regulatory fictions 198; against teachers
    in Australia 199
discursive activity 68
discursive connections: across/between
    texts 213; between policy and practice
    216; and rhizo-textual analysis 211
discursive formations 63–71, 184, 210
discursive maps/webs 211
discursive practices 65, 184
dispositif 66
dispositions, system of 22
dissemination of policies 178
distance, and multiplicity 225
distributive agency 117
Dreyfus, H. L. and Rabinow, P. 64, 67
Duggan, L. 197

Eagleton, T. 75, 77
economic, and the social 190, 191
economic assemblage 116–17, 118
economic capital 19
economic development, and social
    development 214
economic field, global 23
economics, liberal political 152
economy, society as 191
education: community 126; culture via 29;
    England 79; managerialist
    conceptualization of 74; misrecognition
    in 201; and nationalism 180–1; and
    nation building 180–1; neoliberal
    colonisation of 79; and policy analysis
    and culture 30; and queer theory
    195–206; and social relations 28;
    transformed into markets 153
educational activities, marginal 126
educational assumptions, anthropocentric
    163
educational authority, independent spaces
    of 126
educational effectiveness 178
educational inequalities 110, 126
educational institutions, and technologies
    of law/discipline/security 154
Educational philosophy and theory 94
educational policy *see also* policy: broader
    dimensions of 130; nature of 64; term
    39; weight of 131; what is it? 5, 6
educational practices *see* practice(s)
educational reforms *see* reforms
educational research *see* research
educational spaces 223
education assemblage 112, 118, 119
education policy *see* policy(ies)
education policy field, global 23–4
education policy studies 5–7, 48, 166–7
education system, Australia 78–80
effectiveness, educational 178
effects of policy 19
embodiment: of policy studies 134–45; and
    power 136, 143–4
emotion, and affect 102, 103, 104, 112–13
empiricism 15
emplotment 184
enactment of policies 17, 20, 21–2, 165,
    204–5
enactment studies 95, 165

epistemological scepticism 35
equality in education, pregnant/parenting
   students 137–8, 144
equality, of outcomes 58
equal rights policies 199
equal treatment, Title IX 143, 144
equity: and low Socio Economic Status
   (SES) students 190; and quality 79
erasure 56
essentialism 103, 196–7
ethical issues, and analysis 35
ethical practice 151
ethics, of affirmation 58
ethics of practice, and everyday practices 35
ethics of psychoanalysis, The 80
ethnographers, in transnational context 180
ethnography 111, 119, 157–8, 166–7, 176
everyday life: and Certeau 36;
   heterogeneity of 36, 37; official/
   unofficial realms of 29–30
everyday practices *see also* practice(s): and
   culture 28, 31; and ethics/politics of
   practice 35; and policy discourse 30
evidence-based policy solutions 131
existence, as accumulation 75

facts: matters of 96; and opinions 46;
   scientific 44
fag discourse 200
fantasy 73, 77, 78, 79
fear, Western of Southeast Asia 107
federal educational policy, US 19
feelings, and affects 103
feminism, and neoliberalism 127
feminist critique, of the public 125
feminist genealogy: as a methodology
   134–45; and power 137, 142
feminist poststructuralism 10, 135–7
feminist problematisation, of public sphere
   126–7
feminist research, on women's leadership 135
feminist socio-historical approach 130, 131
Fenwick, T. and Edwards, R. 94, 161
field(s): concept of 19, 22, 24; education
   policy as an 18–21; of gender 19, 20;
   global economic 23; global education
   policy 23–4; notion of the 180; of
   politics 20; of power 19, 20; social 19, 24
formalist approach, discourse analysis 210
formulation processes of policies 68–9

fortunes of feminism, The 127
Foucault beyond Foucault 164
Foucault, M. 8, 63–71, 88, 110, 136–7,
   147–58, 183, 198–200, 210
Fraser, N. 9–10, 122, 123–4, 125, 126–7,
   128, 131
frictional methodology 107
Frosh, S. 73
Frow, J. 31
function of the lived 47
Fuss, D. 196

gap policy 57, 58
Gardner, P. 212
Gay, Lesbian, Straight Education Networks
   205
gaze: historical 69; researcher 52
gender: field of 19, 20; as performative 197;
   theorisation of 195
gender discrimination 140
gender norms 197
*Gender trouble: Feminism and the subversion of
   identity* 197
genealogy 130, 136–7
genetic theory 22
geography, and power 222
German Ordo-liberalism 152
Gillborn, D. and Youdell, D. 198
global economic field 23
global education policy 19, 23–4
global education policy texts 20
globalization: and critical policy analysis
   188; of education policy 23; and
   education reform 178; and global
   education policy field 23–4; and
   mobility 172–3; and national
   competitiveness 152–3; neo-liberal 20; in
   policy talk 20
global media, and circulation of policy
   ideas 178
global mobility 10, 171, 173 *see also*
   mobility
global policies 23–4
good life 75
Gormley, A. 116
Gough, M. 138, 139–40, 141, 144
governance: contemporary 115; educational
   178; political 147, 150, 151; and
   psychoanalytic theory 74; state 126;
   'turn' 24

governance mechanisms, policies as 122
governing at a distance 65, 151
governing by numbers 105
government: exercise of 151; of
    populations/nations/organizations
    155–6; technologies of 191, 193
governmental assemblage 114
governmentality 10, 110, 147–58, 183–4
governmental power 152, 153
governmental rationalities, of discipline/
    security 154
governmental technologies 65, 153–4
government of self 154–5, 156
Gowlett, C. 202–3, 204
Gramsci, A. 127
gray science 157
Grosz, E. 136, 137, 209–10, 212
Gupta, A. and Ferguson, J. 180

Habermas, J. 123–4, 129
habitus 22–3
Hacking, I. 158
Hagood, M. C. 212
Halperin, D. 196
Haraway, D. 163
health education, school based 114–15
heterogeneity: and Certeau 35; of everyday
    life 36, 37; of policies 187
heterogeneous practices 32
heteronormativity 197
Hickey-Moody, A. and Malins, P. 113
hierarchy of opposition 54
Higher Education agenda, of Australia
    188–90
Highmore, B. 28, 36, 37
Hillier, J. 116, 118
historical process, governmentality as
    150–2
History of sexuality, Vol. 1 198
history-writing, as a social practice 34
homonationalism 197
homonormativity 197
housing, Bourdieu 17
Hughes, T. 88
human capital theory 152
humanities, affective turn in 100, 101
human relations, complexities of 176
humans, and things 164
human sciences, and philosophy 45
human, what it means to be/do 163

ideas: material entanglement of 164–5;
    moving across national borders 172
identification, self 76
identity categories, constituting subjects
    199–200
identity(ies): construction of 73; instability
    of 197; and narratives 186; and power 74;
    of young parents 143
ideologies, moving across national borders
    172
ideoscapes 178
imaginary register of the psyche 75–7
implementation infidelities, Bourdieuian
    approach to 17
implementation of policies 21–2, 70
indeterminacy 163
indeterminate affectivity 107
indicators 105
Indigenous students 57, 58
inequalities 57, 80, 110, 126, 192–3
information infrastructures, and control
    societies 39–40
injustice, in education 129
innovations, as 'big things'/matters of fact
    96
instability: of identities 197; of policies 187
institutional racism, in schools 129
institutional strategies, and power 30–1
institutions, disciplinary technologies of 65
intelligibilities, cultural 204, 205–6
intelligibility, rules of 202
intelligible, disruptions to 203
intensity, production of 106
interaction 164
interactional, space as 226
inter-actions, to intra-actions 166
interactivity 164
interconnectivity/relationality of policies
    188
interest, and desire 104
intergovernmental organizations (IGOs)
    177–8
international assessments 46
International Association for the Evaluation
    of Educational Achievement's (IEA) 24
international comparisons 107
international organisations, policy
    developed within 18
international students 173
interpretive complicity 33

interrelations, and relational space 222–4
interview data 54
interview transcripts, analysis of 52, 53
intra-action, notion of 164
intra-actions, inter-actions to 166
intraactivity 164
invisibility, of policies 21
Islamic schools, Australia 225

Jackson, A.Y. 53
Jackson, A.Y. and Mazzei, L. 54–5, 59
journalistic field 20
journalistic habitus 23

knowing capitalism 39, 48
knowledge: policy 165; as a product 43;
    professional and reforms 157; as
    rhizomatic 208; subjects of 74–5
knowledge economy 74, 190
knowledge/power relations 66, 69
knowledge production, practices of 149
Koyama, J. 94
Kuhn, T. 88

labour markets, equitable 192
Lacan and the political 73
Lacan, J. 9, 73–80
lack, sense of 77
Laclau, E. 73
Ladwig, J. 18–19
language: ontological effect of 204; of
    policy documents 17, 106; power of 160;
    symbolic register of 76
Lather, P. 162, 164, 167
Latour, B. 87, 88, 89, 90, 91, 92, 94, 160
law, as technology of power 153, 156
Law, J. 87–8, 89, 91, 92
*Leaders in gender and education: Intellectual
    self-portraits* 195
Leahy, D. 114–15, 118
Leander et al. 212
Leander, K. M. and Rowe, D. W. 212
learning: organizational/continuous 154; as
    a process 43
left hand, of the state 20
Letter to a Japanese friend 52
liberalism, and population management 152
liberal political economics 152
lifestyle agreements 199
line, notion of 112

lines of flight 115, 120, 210, 211, 212, 213,
    216
linguistic turn 101
liquid modernity 176
literacy, teaching of 214, 215
litigation efforts, truth regimes in 144
litigation, Title IX 140
logic, of the classroom 21
logics of practice 21–2
logocentrism 54–5
looping effects 158
loss, alienating 76–7, 80
low Socio Economic Status (SES) students,
    Australia 188–90
Luke, C. 124

MacLure, M. 56, 59
madness 63
management: and politics 74; population
    152
managerialist conceptualization, of
    education 74
mapping: of discourses 214, 215; and
    rhizomatic cartography 214
Marcus, G. 176
marginal educational activity 125–6
marginal social activity, and social change
    131
market-based competition, and social
    cohesion 78–9
market economy, globalised and education
    79–80
market logic, as meta-policy 191
markets, education transformed into 153
market, society governed for the 152
Masny, D. 212–13
Massey, D. 186, 219, 222, 224, 225, 226,
    227
Massive Online Open Courses (MOOCs)
    173
Massumi, B. 99, 102
material entanglement, of ideas 164–5
materialist studies 165
material semiotics 88
material turn, in research 160–8
matters of fact, and matters of concern 96
Mazzei, L. 52
Mazzei, L. and Jackson, A.Y. 100
McGimpsey, I. 113–14, 118
McGowan, T. 75

meaning-making ensemble 55
meaning-making, of children 116
media, and circulation of policy ideas 178
mediation, as discursive 65
mediators 90
meritocracy 55, 58
(meta)methodology, writing/practising
    cultures 34–6
metaphysics of presence 54
methodological imagination 27
methodological nationalism 24
methodological territorialism 175
methodology: actor-network theory
    (ANT) 93–4; affective 105, 107; applying
    queer conceptual ideas as 202;
    Bourdieu's 18; for Certeau 34; diffractive
    106, 161, 163, 164; feminist genealogy as
    134–45; Foucault's 67–70; frictional 107
mimesis 185
mirror stage 75–7
misrecognition, politics of 200–2
mobile methods, research approaches
    175–7
mobility: emerging forms of 172–3; global
    10, 171, 173; and immobility 174;
    transnational 180
mobility paradigm, and policy research
    171–81
mode of thought, philosophy/science/art
    as 42
modernity 176, 186
Mol, A. 183, 185
molar level, youth service assemblages 113
molecular level, youth service assemblages
    113–14
morality, Christian 155
moral panics, childhood sexuality 115
moral principles, of Western society 155
movement, and power 224–5
multimodal texts 209
multiplicity: and cultural/political practices
    226; and relational space 224–6
Murdoch, J. 223

narrative approach 10, 183–93
narratives: alternative 192–3; common
    sense 187; counter-narratives 203; and
    discourses 184; and identities 186; as
    mimetic relation 185; policies as 10, 185,
    188, 193; as political technologies 187;

problem-solution 187; as socio-political
    technologies 187; stability/authority of
    187
National Assessment Program in Numeracy
    and Literacy (NAPLAN), Australia 203
national assessments 46
national capital 23
National Coalition for Women and Girls in
    Education (NCWGE) 134
national comparisons, political reactions to
    105
national competitiveness, discourse 152–3
National Honor Society (NHS) 140
nationalism 24, 180–1, 197
National Partnership Agreement for Low
    Socio-Economic Status Schools
    Communities, Australia 66
National Partnerships programme, Australia
    66
National Women's Law Center (NWLC)
    137
nation-building 180–1, 190
nation(s): competitiveness of 190; cultural
    policy of 29; government of 155–6; and
    shame 106
neoliberal capitalism 128, 131
neoliberal colonisation, of education 79
neo-liberal globalisation 20
neoliberalism: and capitalism 114; and
    feminism 127; German Ordo-liberalsm/
    American 152; and governmentality 110;
    influence/reach of 192; spatio-temporal
    technologies of 191; take up of 129
neoliberal policy 80, 128
neoliberal state 110
Nespor, J. 96, 180
new materialism 167
New Public Management 151–2
new schooling accountability policies 202–3
new technologies, and teaching of literacy
    215
New York City (NYC) school district 141,
    142
Nobus, D. and Quinn, M. 80
No child left behind 19
nomadic philosophy 88
non-discursive 64–5, 103
non-institutional approach 156
norms: about student performance 203;
    gender 197; and regulatory practices 184

numbers, policies as 39, 46
Nyberg, D. 166

Obama, Barack 19
OECD: PISA 19, 24, 45–6, 172; reports
106
Of grammatology 51, 56, 59, 60
Ong, A. 174
ontological dimensions, of scientific
practice 162–3
ontological effect, of language 204
ontological politics 183, 187, 188
ontological research 166
ontology of policy 227
ontology, rhizomatic 11, 208
open letter approach 51
openness, and relational space 226–7
opinions: and facts 46; and philosophy/
science 42, 47
organisational ethnography 166
organizational learning 154
organizations, government of 155–6
other, and self 76
outcomes based education 177
outcomes, equality of 58

P-10 Queensland English Syllabus 214
Papoulias, C. and Callard, F. 103
Parables for the virtual 102
Pascoe, C. J. 200
pastoral power 149, 151
patterning, of everyday life 177
pedagogic assemblage 114–15, 118
performance: comparative data on 24;
global space of 104–5; national 105
performance management, governmentality
perspective 156
performative, sex/gender/sexuality as 197
performativity: and actor-network theory
(ANT) 95; and queer theory 197; and
speech act theory 198
personal, and the political 136
philosophy: creating concepts 42–3; of
Deleuze and Guattari 40–1; and human
sciences 45; as mode of thought 42; and
opinions 47; and policy studies 39; and
science 41–5, 47; and social theory 46
PISA 19, 24, 45–6, 172
PISA shock 46, 99, 105
place polygamy 174

plane of immanence 43
plane of organization 112
polemological analysis, of culture 33, 36
policy actors, as assemblages 161
policy analysis: cultural approaches to
27–34; historical contextualisation of
130; narrative approach to 183–93; and
neoliberalism 114; psychoanalytic
approach to 73–80; and relational space
219–28; theoretically informed 47–8
policy documents *see* policy texts
policy field, global education 23–4
policy knowledge 165
policy narratives, as technologies of
government 193
policy-product analysis 69–70
policy production 17, 65–7, 123, 129, 178
policy reform 126, 128–9, 131
policy research: challenges of 179–81;
feminist socio-historical approach to
131; material turn in 10; methodological
implications of theoretical frameworks
1–2; and mobility paradigm 171–81;
re-thinking 177–9; and subaltern
counterpublics 125–7
policy sociology 23, 110–20
policy studies 5–7, 48, 166–7; and actor-
network theory (ANT) 94–6;
embodying of 134–45; and philosophy
39
policy subjects, constitution of as problems
190–1
policy texts: and discourse analysis 211–13;
global education 20; language of 17, 106;
product analysis of 69; production of 21;
and rhizo-textual analysis 211–13, 216
political: meaning of 161; and the personal
136
political action, counter-narratives as 203
political contestation, of policy 127
political economics, liberal 152
political elites 123
political governance 147, 150, 151
political identity, independent spaces of 126
political philosophy of Judith Butler, The 200
political positioning, strategic and policy 78
political power, and numerical data 39
political practices 151, 226
political radicalism 129
political rationalities 157

political reactions, to national comparisons 105

political regulation, and civil society 152–3

political responsibility, and assemblage theory 118

political sovereignty 150

political technologies, narratives as 187

political theories, negative 74

politics: of actor-network theory (ANT) 93; and assemblage theory 118; of authorisation 186; biopolitics 149, 152, 184; of the body 136; counter-politics 203; and culture/education 29; field of 20; and management 74; of method 40, 45–8; of misrecognition 200–2; ontological 183, 187, 188; of policy 227; of practice and everyday practices 35; of recognition 200–1; of things 161

population, as a complex reality 147

population management, and liberalism 152

populations, government of 155–6

population (the), and political calculation/ regulation 150

positionality, researcher 18

postcolonial theory 125

post-constructionism 100

post-humanistic approach, actor-network theory (ANT) 88

post-national deterritorialization 175–6

post-qualitative turn 167

poststructuralism 10, 52–3, 88, 100, 135–7

poststructural thought, anti-Oedipal tradition 67, 70

power: and actor-network theory (ANT) 87, 91–3; ascending analysis of 69; bio-power 137; cartographies of 222; disciplinary 198–9, 200, 205; and embodiment 136, 143–4; and feminist genealogy 137, 142; field of 19, 20; and geography 222; governmental 152, 153; and identities/practices 74; and institutional strategies 30–1; of language 160; meticulous rituals of 69; and modulation of behaviour 39; and movement 224–5; multiple configurations of 153; of non-human actants 161; and numerical data 39; pastoral 149, 151; and policy 65–6, 144, 220; and practice 74; social relations of

131; and stabilisation of actor-networks 91–3; state 21, 147; symbolic 17; technologies of 65–6, 153–4, 156

power blackouts, Canada/USA 117–18

power-geometries 222, 224–5

power/knowledge relations 64, 66, 69

power relations: Foucauldian understanding of 210–11; and policies 66; and policy production 123; in public sphere 124; and space 222; and stabilisation 224; and state/activities on the margins 125; subjects of 69

practice(s): challenges to 129; competing logics of 21–2; and culture 27–8; discursive 65, 184; dispositional accounts of 22; ethical/political 151; ethics of 35; of everyday life 28; for young parents 141; and habitus 22; heterogeneous 32; logics of 21–2; outside policy directives 126; political 151, 226; and power 74; social/political contestation of 127; and social relations 127

practices of government, and practices of the self 155

practices of thought, in policy processes 48

precarity, notion of 201

pre-discursive 64–5

pregnancy: and character 140; and Title IX 137–41

pregnancy test for schools, A 138

pregnant and parenting students 135, 137–9, 140, 144

pregnant bodies 136

prejudice, in education 129

presence 54, 55–6

Preston, N. and Symes, C. 28

problems, identifying/analysing 192–3

problems in themselves, low Socio Economic Status (SES) students as 190–1

Probyn, E. 104, 106

professional knowledge, and educational reforms 157

professionals, and governmental power 152

Programme for International Student Assessment (PISA) *see* PISA

Progress in International Reading Literacy Study (PIRLS) 24

provisional linkages 213
provisional spatial ordering, policies as 224
proximity, and multiplicity 225
psyche, three registers of 75–6
psychoanalytic approach, to policy analysis 73–80
psychoanalytic theory 74, 77–8
Puar, J. 197
public of citizens 124
publics: alternative 125; gender-blind conceptualisation of 129; multiplicity of 127
public sphere: feminist critiques of 130; feminist problematisation of 126–7; multiplicity of publics in 127; power relations in 124; theory of 123

quality, and equity 79
Quality education: The case for an education revolution in our schools 78
quality improvements, reforms for 156
queer research 195–6
queer theory: and Butler 197–8; and discourse 198; and education 195–206; and Foucault 198–200; as mode of inquiry 202; and policy 11, 195–206; what is it? 196–7
queer(y)ing, and education policy 202–5
questions, of why/when/how/what 67–8

racialisation, of subjects in education 198
racialised urban problem, young mothers as 138
racism, institutional in schools 129
Radaelli, C. M. 187
Rancière, J. 161
Rasmussen, M. 205
realism, agential 160, 164
reality 78, 184
Real register of the psyche 75–7
Real, the 81n.2
realtight 76
Reay, D. and Mirza, H. 125
Reay, D. 23
recognition, politics of 200–1
reference societies 24
reforms: educational and professional knowledge 157; and globalization 178; and governing at a distance 151; and

professional knowledge 157; for quality improvements 156; and social relations 127
regimes of truth 64, 66, 135, 144; and discourses 64, 66, 68, 69
regulation: of bodies 136; political 152–3; state 126; truth regimes in 144
regulatory fictions 198, 200
regulatory practices: justifications for 187; and norms 184
regulatory technology of government, policy as 185
relational space: idea of 221–2; and policy 11; and policy analysis 219–28
relations of power *see* power relations
relative space 221
relativity of truth 44
reports, shock creating ability of 105–6 *see also* PISA shock
research: actor-network theory (ANT) 94; approaches/mobile methods 175–7; feminist on women's leadership 135; material turn in 10, 160–8, 165–7; and mobility paradigm 171–81; ontological 166; policy *see* policy research; process/writing dimension of 56; purposes of educational 179; social and mobility 171, 175–7
researcher gaze 52
researcher positionality 18
researcher reflexivity 35
Researching education through actor-network theory 94
responsibility, political 118
rhizoanalysis, as an assemblage 213
rhizomatic cartography, and mapping 214
rhizomatic framing 115
rhizomatic ontology 11, 208
rhizomatic thinking 208–16
rhizomes 112, 119–20, 209–11
rhizo-textual analysis 209, 211–13, 216
Ricoeur, P. 184, 185
right hand, of the state 20
rights: of girls to attend schools 201; of pregnant and parenting students 135, 140; U.S. civil rights law 134
risk/safety assemblages 116–17, 118
Rizvi, F. and Lingard, B. 18, 188
Rose, N. and Miller, P. 157
Rose, N. S. 114, 216

Rowan, L. and Bigum, C. 96
Royle, N. 51

Savage, M. and Burrows, R. 40
scepticism, epistemological 35
Schippers, B. 200
scholarship, as cultural writing 35
school field 21
science: and chaos 43; gray 157; as mode of thought 42; and philosophy 41–5, 47
scientific discourses 33
scientific facts 44
scientific practice, ontological dimensions of 162–3
scientific thought, and commensuration 43
security: and discipline 154; as technology of power 153–4, 156
sedentarist assumptions, in social sciences 175
Sedgwick, E. and Frank, A. 102, 103
self: government of 154–5; and other 76; technologies of 155
self-alienation 77
self-care, and self-renunciation 155
self-government 154–5, 156
self-identification 76
self-reflection, national 107
self-renunciation, and self-care 155
self-technologies 155
Senior Education and Training (SET) plans, Australia 203
sense making 4, 63
sense of agency 53
sensibility, actor-network theory (ANT) as 89
Serres, M. 88
sex, as performative 197
sexual agency, of children 116
sexuality, as performative 197
sexualization of children assemblage 115–16, 118
shame 104–7
Shame and its sisters 102
Sheller, M. and Urry, J. 176
Shields, R. 220, 221, 222
shock 99–100
signified, and the signifiers 54, 56, 208
signifiers, subjection to the 75
Simmel, G. 175
Simons et al. 5

simultaneous coexistence 224
Smith, N. 219
social, and the economic 190, 191
social change, and marginal social activity 131
social cohesion, and market-based competition 78–9
social conditions, transnational 178–9
social constructions, and policy 142
social constructivism 44, 47
social contestation, of policy 127
social data 40, 48
social development, and economic development 214
social fields 19, 24
social formations: and assemblage theory 118; deterritorialization/reterritorialization of 114
social inequalities, Australian education system 80
social interaction, across national borders 174
Socialist Sunday Schools 126
social justice 57, 58, 190
social order, queer(y)ing unsettling 204
social outcomes, of students 66
social phenomena, as networks of relations between actors 90
social practice, history-writing as 34
social processes, transnationalization of 179
social relations: and education 28; and policy discourses 127; and policy production 123; of power 131; and space 221, 223
social research, and mobility 171, 175–7
social sciences: affective turn in 100, 101; sedentarist assumptions in 175; spatial turn in 175
social spaces 32, 221
social structures of the economy, The 17
social, the 88, 95
social theory 1, 46, 48, 220
social world, and social fields 19
societies of control 39–40
society: construction of 73; disciplinary 153; as economy 191; governed for the market 152
socioanalysis, for Bourdieu 18
socio-economic background, of students 66
socio-historical approach, feminist 130, 131

socio-historical dimensions, of policy production 129
sociological imagination 15
sociology: and actor-network theory (ANT) 88, 94; beyond societies 172; of Bourdieu 25; need to re-imagine 171; policy 23, 110–20
socio-material practices 90, 92–3
socio-political narrative configurations, of discourses 190
socio-political technologies, narratives as 187
socio-spatiality 221
sous rapture 56
South Africa, education in 177
sovereign rule 150, 151
sovereignty, political 150
space(s): educational 223; independent of educational authority 126; as interactional 226; and power relations 222; as relational/in process 186; as situational/contingent outcome 223; social 32, 221; and social relations 221, 223; and time 186, 219, 220–1, 226–7; transnational 179, 180
spatial analyses 221
spatialisation, of contemporary life 220
spatialising policies 191–2
spatiality 186
spatial ordering 223, 227
spatial turn: in social sciences 175; in social theory 220
speech act theory, and performativity 198
speech, and writing 54
Spinoza, B. 102
Spinuzzi, C. 87
Spivak, G. 56, 59, 125
spoken word, and written word 54
state: and activities on the margins 125; advent of the modern 150; and capital 21; decentring of 147–8; feminist theories of 136; governance/regulation 126; and legitimate violence 17; neoliberal 110; and policy content 178; power 21, 147; right/left hand of 20
states of emergency, and policy 128
statistical systems, national 24
Stavrakakis, Y. 73
Stengers, I. 41, 42, 44, 45, 47, 48, 167–8
Stone, D. 187

stories of influence 186
story 186
St. Pierre, E. 52, 135, 161, 167, 211
strategies, and tactics 30–1
Stronach, I. and MacLure, M. 59
structuralist approach, discourse analysis 210
structuralist constructivism 23
student performance, norms about 203
students, deficit-based understandings of 203–4
subaltern counterpublics 123–7, 131
subjectivity, human 76
subjects/citizens: constitution of 199–200; as economic agents 191; and normative narratives 185; precarious 201
Swartz, D. 21
symbolic power 17
symbolic register of the psyche 75–7
symbolic, the 76

tactics: and ethics/politics of practice 35; and strategies 30–1
taken-for-granted, and actor-network theory (ANT) 96
Talburt, S. and Rasmussen, M. 195
TALIS, affective shocks/shame in 104–7
Tamboukou, M. 115, 118
teacher compliance 216
teachers: accountability of 129; agency of 216; and policy 216
teaching, of literacy 214, 215
technologies: of government 191, 193; of governmentality 183–4; of law/discipline/security 154; of power 65–6, 153–4, 156
technologies of self 155
technology of economisation 191
technology of power, policies as 65–6
teen pregnancy 137, 138, 141, 144
teen pregnant bodies 136
temporalising policies 191–2
testing data 105
texts, as rhizomes 209–10
theories, as specific material configurations 164
theory(ies): of Bourdieu 16–17; as inevitable 1; material turn in 10; and policy 2; of thought 48; what is it? 3–4
things: agency of 223; capacity/politics of 161; and humans 164; relational constructedness of 186

thinking through theory 100

thinking tools, of Bourdieu 17, 24–5

Thinking with theory in qualitative research 59

thousand plateaus, A 208, 209

Thrift, N. 39, 221, 222

time, and space 186, 219, 220–1, 226–7

Title IX 10, 134–5, 137–41, 143, 144

Title IX at 40 137

Tomkins, S. 102, 104

toolkit, analytical of actor-network theory (ANT) 89

tool, notion of 70–1

topological approach 153

Touraine, A. 192

trace 55

Transforming Australia's Higher Education System 2009 188, 189

transgressive data 52

translation, and actor-network theory (ANT) 90–1

transnational connectivities, spaces of 179

transnational corporations, and national governments 172

transnationalism, and educational policy 181

transnational space 179, 180

Trends in International Mathematics and Science Study (TIMSS) 24

truth effect, coming out as 198–9

truths: establishing 184; and interview data 54; production of 64; regimes of 64, 66, 135, 144; of the relative 44; universal 56

twilight of equality, The 197

under erasure 56–8

Undoing gender 200

unintentional effects, of policy 53

United States: American neoliberalism 152; civil rights law 134; federal educational policy 19; New York City (NYC) school district 141, 142; power blackouts 117–18

universal truths 56

university pre-requisites, as disciplinary technique 206

Urry, J. 171, 172, 173, 175, 176–7, 180, 181

utterances 53–4

Verran, H. 40

Vibrant matter: The political ecology of things 117, 161

Victorian Early Years Literacy Program, Australia 214

violence: creative 43; legitimate state 17

vitality 161

vital materialist perspective 118

Wacquant, L. 16, 22

'ways of operating', and culture 28, 30

Weaver-Hightower, M. B. and Skelton, C. 195

Webb, T. P. and Gulson, K. N. 216

Weeks, K. 130

weight of the world, The 17

welfare institutions: and dialogue technologies 156; and pastoral power 149

Western society, moral principles of 155

What is Philosophy? 39, 40, 41, 47, 48

Wittel, A. 180

women's leadership, feminist research on 135

working-class education, Britain 126

Wounds and reinscriptions: Schools, sexualities and performative subjects 199

writing, and speech 54

writing dimension, of research process 56

written word, and spoken word 54

Youdell, D. 199, 200, 203

young parents: education policy/practice for 141; identities of 143; as racialised urban problem 138; truth regimes/discourses about 144

young people, global mobility of 173

youth service assemblage 113–14, 118

CPSIA information can be obtained
at www.ICGtesting.com
Printed in the USA
BVHW04s1714280818
525771BV00001B/1/P

9 780415 736565